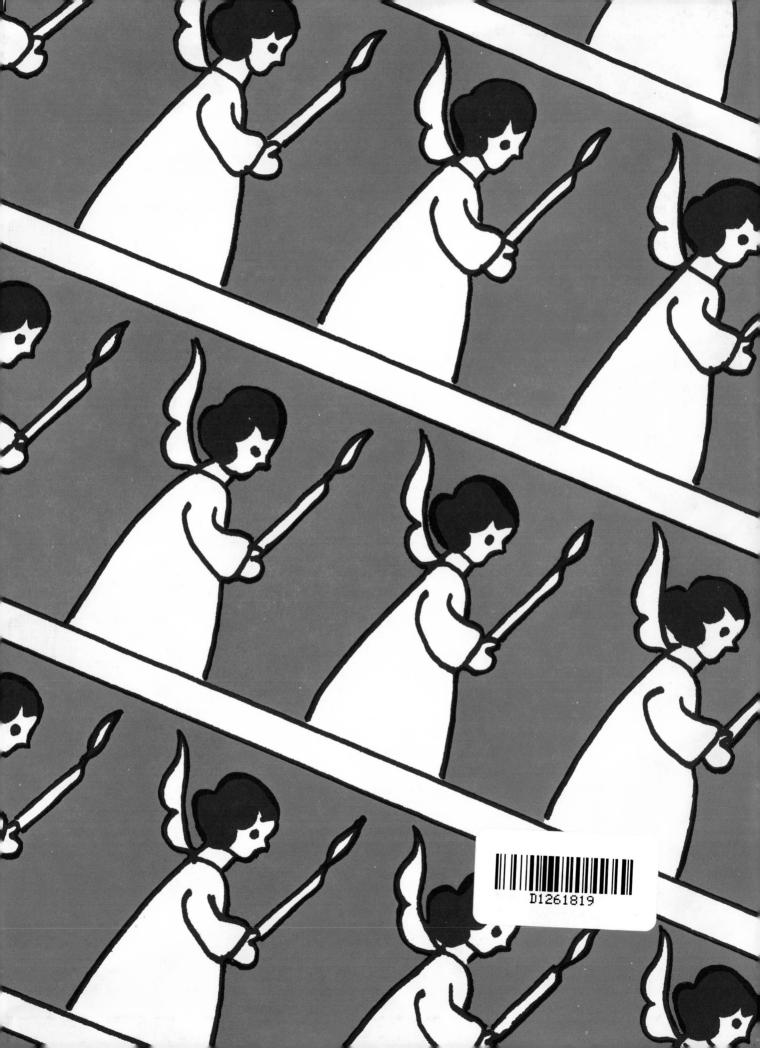

In times like these when there is so much to be done and so little is achieved in proportion to the needs of our age, it is gratifying that the POLANIE have made yet another contribution toward a better understanding of the Poles who have come to these shores with their rich cultural heritage.

Others should take heart from this handful of women who call themselves PO-LANIE (people of earth-succoring fields and meadows) who look to neither power nor wealth nor great numbers to achieve their goal. To paraphrase John F. Kennedy's famous quotation, they ask not what others can do for their cause, but do what they can to preserve the traditions of a people whose reservoir of gifts this nation has not even begun to tap.

I salute the POLANIE!

HARRIET PAWLOWSKA
Author of "Merrily We Sing"

TREASURED

POLISH CHRISTMAS

CUSTOMS

AND

TRADITIONS

First Printing — 1972
Second Printing — 1973
Third Printing — 1974
Fourth Printing — 1977
Fifth Printing — 1980
Sixth Printing — 1984

Library of Congress number
72-83746

Other POLANIE Publications

TREASURED POLISH RECIPES FOR AMERICANS

TREASURED POLISH SONGS

IF THE BRANCH BLOSSOMS

FAVORITE SONGS

ART SONGS AND BALLADS

PIOTRUSZEK — How Little Peter Got Into Heaven

PRIZE WINNING SHORT STORIES

HYMN TO POLAND — Solo

OCTAVO — 4 Part Arrangement with Piano

CHRISTMAS CAROLS

EIGHT LULLABIES

POLANIE PUBLISHING COMPANY
643 Madison St. N.E.
Minneapolis, Minn. 55413

TREASURED
POLISH CHRISTMAS
CUSTOMS
AND
TRADITIONS

CAROLS
DECORATIONS
AND A
CHRISTMAS PLAY

POLANIE PUBLISHING CO.

Minneapolis, Minn.

POLANIE EDITORIAL STAFF

Rose Polski Anderson

Josepha Contoski, *chairman*

Cecily Kowalewska Helgesen

Lucille Jasinski

Eleanor Julkowski

Harriett Zocharski Multaler

Harriette Sadowski

Falyce Sadowski Sentyrz

Individual Contributions

THE STORY OF A POLISH CHRISTMAS —
Cecily Kowalewska Helgesen

THE KULIG — Harriett Zocharski Multaler

RECIPES — Eleanor Julkowski, *coordinator*

JASELKA, THE NATIVITY PLAY —
Josepha Contoski

JASELKA MUSIC AND CHRISTMAS CAROLS —
edited by Rose Polski Anderson

CHRISTMAS CRAFTS, ART —
Harriett Zocharski Multaler

CHRISTMAS CRAFTS, ART, AND STRYJENSKA
ADAPTATIONS —
Falyce Sadowski Sentyrz

COPY — Lucille Jasinski

PUBLICATIONS COMMITTEE SECRETARY —
Lucille Jasinski

PUBLICATIONS COMMITTEE CORRESPONDING
SECRETARY — Harriett Z. Multaler

PUBLICATIONS COMMITTEE CHAIRMEN —
Rose P. Anderson, 1970; Josepha Contoski, 1971;
Cecily Kowalewska Helgesen, 1972

LAYOUT — Harriett Z. Multaler

Other Active Polanie Members:

Eleanor Auvinen
Marion Beamish
Mary Bullis
Helen Busyn
Virginia Fitzsimons
Mary Jane Gustafson

Irene Jasinski
Carrie Puzak
Agnes Laska
Julie Leaon
Cecilia Lynch
Evelyn Nahurski
Stella Welch

DEDICATION

We dedicate this book

To the memory of our parents and Polish ancestors,

who gave us the gift of their heritage;

To the Polish people who had to leave

their native land and are scattered all over the

world today;

To the youth of Polish descent, and to all others who are

interested in research in the areas of folklore and other

ethnic studies.

WESOŁYCH ŚWIĄT

ACKNOWLEDGMENTS

We are thankful to the many Polish people in America as well as in Poland, who contributed directly or indirectly to the "TREASURED POLISH CHRISTMAS CUSTOMS AND TRADITIONS" by sharing with us their experiences of a Polish Christmas season. We are grateful to the late Marja Sokolowska, a Polanie charter member, for her inspiration and to MARYA GINALSKA for permission to use her very informative book "POLSKIE BOZE NARODZENIE," published by B. Swiderski, London 1961, as a reference and source material for our book.

Pictures of Polanie members at the Vilia Supper first appeared in color in the Christmas Edition of The Minneapolis Tribune, on Sunday, December 26, 1971. The Editors of this book express their appreciation to Mr. Bower Hawthorne, Editor of The Minneapolis Tribune, for permission to use these staff photos by Mr. Arthur Hager who captured with great artistry the spirit of the Vilia Supper.

Pictures of the Vilia Supper, Copyrighted, Minneapolis Star and Tribune Company, 1972.

Songs in this collection have been edited with permission of the composers and publishers, where known. If omissions have occurred, such information will be included in future editions.

— EDITORS

FOREWORD

Drawn from all the corners of what was once the vast Polish-Lithuanian Commonwealth and from the various people who dwelled therein, Polish Christmas traditions are among the richest and most colorful in the world. Yet despite this, and despite the fact that Poles have played so significant a part in the development of our country, these traditions are still little known in the United States.

It was largely to correct this situation and to enable their fellow Americans to share in the beauty and warmth of a Polish Christmas that the remarkable group of women known as the Polanie Club undertook to prepare and to publish this work. It was a difficult task. How to choose that which is specifically Polish when so much of the enchantment of Eastern Europe is shared by many people? How to choose that which is typically Polish when the traditions of every province and often of every village have a distinctiveness all their own? Difficult, indeed. Yet the authors succeeded in capturing the essence of a Polish Christmas.

In the pages which follow one will find not merely a description of Polish Christmas traditions but also a guide for a do-it-yourself Polish Christmas: recipes for Christmas meals, the words and music for some of the more representative Polish carols, and even detailed directions for making typically Polish Christmas decorations. Followed, this guide will bring happiness and enrichment to many at Christmastide. Hopefully, it will encourage some to dig more deeply into the traditions of a remarkable people and to expand upon this first significant attempt to bring the story of a Polish Christmas to the attention of the American public.

EUGENE KUSIELEWICZ, *President*
The Kosciuszko Foundation
New York, May 18, 1971

PREFACE

The Treasured Polish Christmas Customs and Traditions tells the Christmas story of the Polish people in the Polish countryside of long ago. It is a collection of religious and folk customs and traditions together with some of the early superstitions. It describes in detail the pleasurable times and tasks of the *Prządki*, the baked goose on St. Martin's, the excited children on St. Nicolas Day (December 6) and the countless preparations for the Christmas holiday season with its joyous events and celebrations. The star carriers *Gwiazdorze*, the romancing on St. Sylvester's Eve, the comical *Turon*, the popular *Koleda*, and the nativity plays and puppet shows are all a part of this Christmas story.

So is the *Kulig*, the grand sleigh ride with its fanfare, its masqueraders and its fun filled progression of parties. It was one of the great social events of the Christmas and carnival season. Omitted during Poland's times of stress, its wars, and its occupation by Russia, Prussia and Austria, it always returned, but never quite with the earlier glamour.

This book also contains recipes for the traditional Christmas foods and menus. The *piernik*, one of the Christmas pastries has a story of its own; as do the *plecionka* and *strudel*.

The *Jaselka*, the nativity play was especially popular in the middle ages. It was to many folk their first introduction to theatrical entertainment. It can be produced in one, two, or three acts. This *Jasełka* is in three acts, and contains songs and Christmas carols. The research material for this play came from many small books and brochures, purchased from the *Antykwariaty* in Poland. One play is over two hundred years old. Some pamphlets were ready to be discarded. They had no covers, no authors, no data and pages were missing.

The collection of Christmas carols with accompaniment includes many of the well known favorites. Some have new arrangements. *W Żłobie Leży* melody is hundreds of years old. Poland has many beautiful carols.

The chapter on Christmas decoration is included, because we felt there was a need for it. Polanie members have been repeatedly requested to decorate Christmas trees the Polish way, in Art Institutes, various auditoriums, schools, banks, large department stores and in the rotunda of the Minnesota State Capitol. A reproduction of one of the Polanie trimmed Christmas trees was featured in a national magazine and is reproduced on the cover of Treasured Polish Christmas Customs and Traditions.

This book is the Christmas section of a book currently being written by Polanie members, on other treasured customs, traditions and Holidays. We are fortunate to have the permission of the Polish artist Zofia Stryjenska to use her art work for our entire book.

The Polanie Club is a group of women of Polish descent interested in the study of Polish culture and in sharing this information with others. Treasured Polish Christmas Customs and Traditions is our ninth publication.

JOSEPHA CONTOSKI

SZOPKA

TABLE OF CONTENTS

ORIGINAL ILLUSTRATIONS
By
ZOFIA STRYJENSKA

KEY TO PRONUNCIATION

Unlike the English, the Polish vowels have only one sound each.

Polish vowels:

a . . . like "a" in the English word "Mars."
ą . . . nasal like "on" in French "mon."
é . . . like "e" in "met."
ę . . . nasal like "in" in French "fin."
i . . . like "ee" in "see."
o . . . like "o" in "horse."
ó . . . like "oo" in "book."
u . . . like "u" in "true."

Polish accent falls as a rule on the last syllable but one.

Consonants:

c . . . . like "ts."
ć–ci–cz . . . like "ch" in "church."
ch . . . like "h."
dż . . . nearest to "dj."
j . . . like the English "y."
ś–si–sz . . . like "sh" in "sheep."
ł . . . like "l" in English pronounced like "w" in won.
w . . . at the beginning of a word, like "v," but at the end of a word and before or after a voiceless consonant like "f."
y . . . like "i" in "it."
ż–zi–rz . . . nearest to "z" in "azure."

THE POLISH CHRISTMAS STORY

ust as flowers enhance spring and summer, so the Christmas holidays become the adornment for winter living in Poland. Customs and traditions connected with these holidays, and the preparation for them are brought about by conditions of environment, generations of living together and the harmonious blending of ancient folk lore and Christian beliefs.

Come to the countryside of the Poland of long ago for the Christmas holidays. Here you will be warmly enfolded by the wings of faith expressed in the Pole's tender love for the Christ Child. Here the irresistible spirit of *Gody** love for all of God's creatures will be brought to you with Poland's treasured traditions preserved through the ages.

PREPARATION

Advent (detailed in a following chapter) was the religious preparation for the holidays. It was heralded by a very old custom, that of eating goose with its complements on St. Martin's day, November twelfth. It originated when Advent lasted for forty days instead of for four weeks. Wild and domestic geese said to be most succulent now were roasted this day. People sat long at the table feasting, since with the strict rules of the Church, meat would be scarce for some time to come, in fact until Christmas day. Bones were scrutinized carefully. The winter weather could be forecast by their color. White bones indicated much snow and sunshine, while mottled bones would bring storms and blizzards. Usually the first snow of the year fell on this day inspiring the old saying that St. Martin came to Poland on his white horse.

Proverbs calling on the saints were used to admonish and instruct for almost every occasion a Pole could think of. They could be long or short, had a point to make, were witty, sometimes ungrammati-

cal, rhymed, and always seemed to sing a little tune. Diminutive endings make translation inadequate. Here is one of them. "From St. Martin's day, winter is on its way." *Od Swiętego Marcina, zima się poczyna.*

When Advent was shortened to four weeks instead of forty days, the time between St. Catherine's (November 25th) and St. Andrew's (November 30th) became a festive period of frivolity for young people. "St. Catherine lost her keys this day; St. Andrew found them and locked the fiddle away." *Święta Katarzyna klucze zgubiła. Swiety Andrzej znalazł. Zamknął skrzypki zaraz.* Soon there would be no gay music! "Catherine gaily jumps and skips. St. Andrew frowningly forbids." *Katarzyna rada podskakuje; Święty Andrzej zakazuje.* Only five more days of dancing!

Boys played games on the eve of St. Catherine's, but not nearly as many as the girls played on the eve of St. Andrew's called *Andrzejki,** games filled with romantic prophesies and fortune telling. A young girl ran to the orchard on this cold November day, to break a twig off the old cherry tree. She placed it in water in a jug on the window sill, where she cared for it tenderly, and examined it often. Boys too, broke a branch off the cherry tree, (but on the Eve of St. Catherine's) to tend, until Christmas or New Years. If the branch blossomed by that time, the young man was sure to find the sweatheart of his choice, within the following year. If the branch blossomed for the young lady, she would have a marriage proposal. Several buds might mean several proposals. Whom and when she would marry, occupied many of her thoughts and dreams, since being a good housewife was the only career for which she had been trained. The geraniums on the window sill must be in excellent bloom, and the curtains above them, crisp and snowy white. The walk before the cottage must always be thoroughly swept, so that a passerby,

---

* *Gody — days of harmony and good will.*

* *Pronounced — on jaý kēē*

1

Preparing the Wilia Supper

at least one special one, could see what a good home-maker she would become.

It is the vigil of St. Andrews, *Andrzejki*. It is late at night, almost midnight. A fire burns in the stove in a Polish cottage and a young girl is bustling about. Others in the family are asleep. Only she keeps watch, preparing everything for this night of magic. First the wax, then the water from the well. The church bell can be heard in the distance striking the hour of twelve. It is midnight, the first rooster has begun to crow, but inside the cottage, everything is quiet. The fire from the stove is throwing rays of light against the wall. The young lady pours the melting wax into a bowl of water. Carefully the tender young fingers grasp and break off a piece of the wax in the water, raising it high in mid-air. The melting wax gives out a sweet fragrance reminiscent of church and of summer time. A mysterious ritual seems to be taking place as she gazes intently upon the wall. Nothing of importance seems to be happening! *Retv! Rany!* She waited a 'whole year for this moment. Then suddenly a shadow seems to emerge on the wall. What will it be? Will a young girl's dreams come true? Whatever shows up on this night of *Andrzejki* will tell her everything. Will that one come to court her about whom she secretly dreams? Will her looks please him? Will he desire her for his wife? Will anybody fall in love with her and send match-makers to her parents? What is to be her fate? With trembling hand she keeps pouring the wax into the water. On the white wall, designs and figures of some sort begin to appear. If one is lucky, sometime it is a masculine figure, slender handsome. Then a wreath of myrtle might show up. Every girl knows it is meant for a bridal wreath — And these several shapes of girls? They must be bridesmaids. Oh *rety* everything is at it should be, a wedding in the cottage and in the heart. But these shadows do not always appear so smoothly on the wall. Sometimes it is long after twelve, and the first rooster has crowed long ago, and on the wall, nothing worth noticing appears. One can only cry and bemoan one's luck. There will be no wedding, no marriage, no nothing. The magic of St. Andrew's is not for her this year. It is unfruitful and

2

unfavorable. Maybe next year it will not be so indisposed toward her, but what a sorrow to again have to wait a whole year. But, one must keep on pouring the wax upon the water. This is the night of St. Andrews, so one must. This is what her ancestors did for ages. She would be unwise not to follow their footsteps. These shadows on the wall always foretold for them what it was necessary to know. So be it. If a Polish maiden paid no heed, St. Andrew might really get angry, and tell her nothing next year. Better to pour the wax.

If nothing meaningful comes up, all is not yet lost. The long autumn November night is not yet over. One could dream something that had meaning. Anyway the results can be no worse than was the pouring of the wax. So, better kneel, say one's prayers, get into bed and try to fall asleep, and then to remember what one dreamed, because dreams on this night are sure to come true especially in matters of love. So, to sleep. Please St. Andrew, a sweet dream, dear and gratifying. You know best, what kind.

So next morning no dreams? Well, one must try one's luck some other way. She can take her slipper and measure from the wall to the opposite threshold with it, first pointing the toe, then measuring over again, this time pointing with heel. If the toe happens to come closer to the threshold than does the heel, she is likely to have a proposal this year. If this plan falls through, here is another. She is to leave the cottage early in the morning for the village. The first unmarried young man she meets, is likely to be her intended. What if he should be the man of her dreams? It will not hurt to try. Sometimes one can have better luck if one tosses one's fate in with that of several girls, all with the same purpose in mind. Take for instance the favorite pastime of pouring wax into the water with several pair of shining eyes gazing with rapt concentration at the outline made against the wall. Even if it seems like nothing at first, one girl is very likely to exclaim "A wreath! Look everybody, very plainly a wreath! This year you'll be wed!" Girlish phantasies can always spin out what they wish to have happen, so the shadow becomes a wreath.

One does not only work at night. While it is still light, a group of young girls run arm in arm to the fields. There beginning at random, each counts to the fourteenth post of a fence, to see what her future husband is to look like. Will he be thick like this post, or thin, like that one? Short? Tall? Gnarled or old? If not to a girl's liking, the post is refused emphatically, amid much hilarity.

Again the girls might be standing in a circle leaning over a bowl with water without the wax but floating a small walnut shell, containing a tiny lighted candle. Each girl pastes a slip of paper with the name of a favored youth on the inside edge of the bowl, above the water. Whichever name the lighted candle sailed to and burned, prophesied a marriage proposal from him, to its owner. A crown of blond and brunette heads are bent low, each with her young girlish breath trying to steer the little boat toward her property. If several of them suspected they had the name of the same man, the game could cause a great deal of furor. One girl blowing toward the nut shell might easily accomplish what she was after, but too often all of them blowing, only kept the little shell in the center, not sailing anywhere, until the flame of the candle died.

In another game at *Andrzejki*, a kerchief, a ribbon and a rosary could be placed separately under three plates. The girl eager to learn her fate, was obliged to turn around three times with her eyes blindfolded, while the girls re-arranged the plates. If she drew the kerchief, this meant a speedy marriage; if a ribbon, she would be single yet for another year; if she drew the rosary, she was to become a spinster or a nun. All the young girls might each make a dumpling, arrange them in a yard and bring in a hungry dog. Whosoever's dumpling he ate first, this girl would also be the one to marry first.

Such were the customs which took place in a Polish village long ago, on the eve, the night and the very day of St. Andrews.

"The eyes of the girls were big, bright
Bronisia felt it had to come out right,
Each wondered what fortune had hidden for her,
In that dark unpredictable future.
Anyway, this melting wax can solve the matter.
Just drop a spoonful upon the water.
An awesome moment. What magic will unfold?
Let's hope the image of a youth, handsome and
   bold.
But what is this odd shape we see?
Oh no! Wax, no! No fatty for me!
All the girls laughed at this plump jolly prospect
Teasing, they said 'give him love and respect.'
She cried 'never! never! no! never!
I could never love him, ever!'
Is it possible that this innocent girlish heart
   under cover
Has already been solen by *Franek, Tomek*
   or another?"*

---

* Translated from Władysław Sobowski (1837–1888) by C.K.H.

PRZĄDKI *

The rainy November days brought a most delightful activity called prządki,* meaning to spin, but used for any kind of work which was made easier and more pleasant when in good company. Now during Advent, prządki would be used primarily to get ready for Christmas holidays. Every one old and young, felt useful and contented seated in a large room called a świetlica, family room, fragrant from the scent of pine and juniper and lighted with the glow of the fire burning in the hearth. Each woman had her distaff. When the spinning wheel began to hum and whirr, long white silky looking strands emerged. They would be used for the making of the altar cloth, the snowy white Wilia tablecloth, for embroidered blouses, petticoats, pillow cases and for new attire for Christmas day. Just as the yearly customs mirror a nation's character, so too the different regions have their individual style. Thus the women of Kurpie used predominantly two colors, namely red and black when they designed the decorative trim, while the Krakow and Szlask women edged theirs in the white laces for which they were famous. The Kaszubki used green, blue and red, while the Łowicz ladies made one almost giddy with their warm colors like the ripened grains in the fields. The Rzeszowki also used multiple colors, while those in Podlesie wove austere patterns of black and white, with a sapphire colored border.

Kolberg in 1885 tells of the prządki being held in the Lubelski region, where both men and women gathered. Usually the home of a widow was chosen. Men tied and mended fishnets, twisted straw for binding sheaths of grain, whittled and carved wood, and brought kindling wood and resin for the fires for that evening. The girls brought small amounts of oats, flour, potatoes and salt with some well flavored sauce, while occasionally one of the men produced a piece of venison. All the work done on the last three nights was given to the hostess in payment for her hospitality.

Marya Malewska tells of the prządki in Warmia in the nineteenth century. In the fall, when evenings grew long, a large room was selected. Each housewife had several distaffs with as many reels and bunches of flax and a card for combing the flax. Only the hostess did no spinning since she prepared the evening repast. When a large wooden spoon was beaten loudly against a frying pan, notice was being given that it was time to assemble. Boys and girls snatched their distaffs and ran quickly, while the elders came at a more leisurely pace. All sat in two rows the length of the room. By the dim light of resin chips, and later by kerosene lamps, the wheels began

Baking the Pierogi

to whirl so swiftly they stirred up a breeze in the room. Although the night outside was dark and the frost kept painting flowers on the window panes, the inside of the cottage was warm and comfortable.

Until nine o'clock, each had his or her share to spin. One of the girls would begin to hum a folk song. The drawn out lightly bewitching notes of the Warmian folk song filled the room with its charm. Later came the time for the telling of legends.

The hostess meanwhile, baked potatoes in the hot ashes of the stove, dropped them hurriedly on the table, then brought bowls with sauerkraut from the pantry along with plates of oil and salt. Blowing to cool them, all ate the delicious potatoes dipping them in oil and salt.

After the repast everyone hurried home. All that could be heard on the frozen road, was the clatter of wooden shoes. Kolberg comments on the custom of prządki, saying he was sure the villagers had much better times at these gatherings, than did the city dwellers at the kawiarnie, coffee houses.

Prządki were not only confined to cottages in villages. Here is an excerpt from Sienkiewicz's "Deluge"*in which he describes such gatherings as taking place in manors:

The year is 1655. "There was in Jmud a powerful family, the Billeviches. . . . Panna Alexandra with her relative Panna Kuboyets, sat in the center, and the girls sat around on benches; all were spinning. In a great chimney with sloping sides, pine logs were burning, now dying down, now flaming freshly with a great bright blaze, or with sparks, as the youth standing near the chimney threw on small pieces of birch or pitch-pine. When the flame shot upward brightly, the dark wooden walls of the great hall were to be seen, with an unusually low ceiling resting on cross-beams. Many colored stars made of wafers, trembling in the warm air, hung from the beams on threads. Behind from both sides of the beams, were bunches of combed flax, looking like captured Turkish horse-tail standards. Almost the whole ceiling was covered with them. On the dark walls, tin plates, large and small standing straight, or leaning on long oaken shelves, glittered like stars.

"In the distance, near the door a shaggy haired man of Jmud was making a great noise with a hand-mill, and muttering a song with nasal monotone. Panna Alexandra slipped her beads through her fingers in silence; the spinners spun on, saying nothing, the one to the other.

"The light of the flame fell on their youthful ruddy faces. Then with both hands raised, with the left feeding the soft flax, with the right turning the wheel, they spun eagerly as if vying with one another, urged on by the stern glances of Panna Kuboyets. Sometimes too, they looked at one another with quick eye, and sometimes at Panna Alexandra, as if in expectation that she would tell the man to stop grinding, and would begin the hymn. They spun and spun on; the threads were winding, the wheel was buzzing; the distaff played in the hand of Panna Kuboyets, the shaggy-haired man of Jmud rattled on with his mill."

Prządki were most closely bound with early folk lore. As fascinating as flowers in a green meadow were the ancient fables hinting at witchcraft, whispered in awesome tones. Dreams were discussed and people's future foretold. Songs that were sung, some wistful, some with happy refrains, all added anticipation and entertainment to work done on long Advent evenings in a beloved village in Poland.

Usually some one in the village considered a good entertainer was invited to join the group. Occasionally a wandering story teller or roving songster travelled from village to village. Such a guest was welcomed to *prządki* for he was considered learned in the ways of life. To those of the long ago who could not read, who had never been outside their own village, he opened up a new world. He had news to bring from neighboring villages, legends to tell, new

songs to sing, Poland's wars to recount and her heroes to praise. By dipping into his treasury of memories he helped to weave the chain from which history is made. At sewing and spinning, he led the group in singing, made them laugh at his humorous, sometimes personal remarks, and frightened them with his awesome ghost stories.

A favorite *Prządki* was the stripping of goose feathers to make soft new *pierzyny* (feather ticks) for the holidays. Mothers made the light fluffy pillows which were usually a part of their daughter's dowries out of the soft down (*puch*) from under the wing of the goose. Friends, neighbors, relatives got together. All activity centered at a long wide table around which women and young girls were snugly seated, and here, on the table and around the table all of this white feathery plumage was concentrated. A mound of white goose feathers rose high upon the center of the table, with the hostess adding more to this tower as needed.

The entertainer's task is a special one at feather stripping. The feathers must not be disturbed. He must tell his tale so well, no questions are asked. He must not put the group in the mood for singing for there is always the risk of clapping hands, stamping feet and exertion over reaching a high note. Above all, he must not be so witty that the feather strippers laugh uproariously, or tell such a sad tale that they cry. Any one of these responses could make the high tower of fluff scatter. Plucked feathers could get mixed with the unplucked and fall like clean white souls into the ample laps of the feather strippers, tickle their noses and mouths or leave a tracery on the hand carved clock. The entertainer must make the mood something like a *pierzyna*, comforting and very dear.

At least once each season, his precautions come to no avail. Everything is as it should be, peaceful and quiet, all is serene, when suddenly the doors are opened wide from the two opposite ends by two young male culprits, and feathers fly wildly in all directions. Although the feather strippers know this prank is bound to take place, they are never ready for it when it happens. Amid laughter and scolding the mischief makers are driven out by older matrons with the aid of brooms, but not before laughing eyes bestow a caress on some young girl demurely plucking goose feathers.

ST. NICHOLAS DAY

December *Grudzien* (taken from the word *grudy* — clods of hardened frozen mud) made travelling on narrow Polish country roads virtually impossible. With the snow fluttering down to the ground in its milkiness for days and nights, the earth was now covered with a soft white blanket to get ready for Jesus' birth, just as the mother prepares the crib of her new born babe, in snowy white linen.

The impassable roads brought little neighborly visiting, but the cottage did not lack for guests as the dogs, cats and sometimes the pet stork begged to be allowed near the warm hearth. Young geese, ducks and chickens were often brought into the entry of the cottage for the night, not only because of the cold, but because the wolf or fox in his quest for food, was edging nearer and nearer the cottages.

December sixth, St. Nicholas day *dzien Świętego Mikołaja* brought a slight reprieve to gray monotonous days, especially for the children, who felt that the Christmas *Gwiazdka* (Star) would never come. St. Nicholas was revered because of his compassion and love for orphans whom he often visited and comforted with little gifts. His name's day is celebrated more in some countries than is Christmas day itself. The one selected to represent St. Nicholas was usually driven in a sleigh to the homes in a Polish village. He was dressed in a long white robe, wearing a tall head piece much like a bishop's mitre, a long white flowing beard, and in his hand he held the shepherd's staff. The sound of snow bells and horses' hoofs could be heard on the cobblestone pavement, while eager young faces with their noses pressed to the window panes shouted "He has come! he has come!" *Już idzie! Już idzie!* . . . Because he always asked "Have you been a good child?" there would be a hurried frenzied examination of conscience while the "Już idzie!" was being called out. "Have I been greedy? Did I block *Józia's* path once or twice so she fell? Was I lazy? How many lies did I tell?" While the owner of all of these "dreadful" childish sins shuddered and shivered, St. Nicholas entered, filling the room with not only his big presence, but with his smile, the twinkle in his eye and his teasing booming voice. He rebuked the mischievous, praised the obedient, and passed around heart shaped *pierniki*, honey cookies, holy pictures and big red apples, which he produced magically from under his cloak.

He left with the children's shining eyes following him, the brightest, on the littlest one hiding behind mother's apron.

PIERNIK, HONEY SPICE CAKE

Early December was the time to bake the honey cake *piernik* for Christmas, since its flavor increased with age. Formerly the *piernik* was made without milk or butter out of deference to the cattle, who not only were present with Jesus in the stable, but warmed him with their breath. Instead, oil and lager beer were frequently used. The recipe kept in families for generations, was a well guarded secret given to a young bride as part of her dowry. Bread was often baked in the oven first to provide the correct temperature. There is an old Polish saying: Vodka from Gdansk, the *piernik* from Torun, a young miss from Krakow, a dainty slipper from Warsaw, these are Poland's best. *Gdanska gorzałka, Torunski Piernik, Krakowska panna, Warszawski trzewik, najlepsze rzeczy w Polsce.*

The Torun *Piernik* is known the world over. As early as the fourteenth century, Torun became one of the first cities in Europe to add spices to the old time honey cake. Situated on the Vistula, and having a direct trading route on the Baltic with both the Orient and northern Europe, it was one of the first cities to receive the spices brought back from the Orient by the crusaders. Its lands were rich with grains, and honey was plentiful. Soon factories were established for the making of the fragrant *piernik*. In time, nuns in convents began making this tasteful pastry. St. Catherine's order of nuns in Torun attained such fame, their cakes became known as *Katarzynki*, little Catherines.

It was not only necessary for the *piernik* to be tasty; the hard wood mold in which it was slowly baked, had to have artistic shape as well. The mark of distinction was indicated by how many *klaceks* (forms or molds) a *piernik* artisan owned. They were hung on the walls of the kitchen, and the apprentice's duty was to keep them in good condition. In time competition and experience both, provided for much increased artistry in the making of the *klaceks*.

Pierniki were so popular, that they were kept with herbs and fruits in containers for medicinal purposes in the homes of the aristocracy. Having this exotic well-liked delicacy among the other spices, vegetables and roots gave the entire cellar storeroom a refreshing aroma. It was even said to contain magical powers. Mothers were told that if a child ate several *pierniki*, he or she would learn to read more fluently. Sweethearts tendered each other *piernik* hearts, and people returning from pilgrimages bought *pierniki* with the images of saints upon them, and hung them between the holy pictures on the walls of their homes.

Pierniki Honey Spice Cookies

Many homemakers sprinkled the crumbs of the *piernik* in the pans in which all other Christmas delicacies were baked.

As craftsmen became more and more skilled in the making of the *piernik*, it began appearing in edible and inedible forms (the inedible, a hard dough without the use of rising compounds.) In the middle ages the *klaceks* were frequently shaped in the images of saints, with St. Nicholas appearing most often. During the renaissance and up to the eighteenth century, manor life with knights and their ladies, was often depicted as well as their favorite animals which included the horse, deer, bear, the running hare and the cow. The rooster *piernik* always symbolizing success and fertility was usually sent to someone for whom one wished well, and was accompanied by verses. Sometimes entire scenes were depicted, such as "The Flight to Egypt." *Pierniki* in edible and ornamental inedible forms began appearing at the palaces of kings. The *piernik* of Poland had its individual symbol, and this in very old folk tradition, indicated circles or wheels. As an example, the *Katarzynki* were six circles, placed parallel in two rows.

The wooden blocks or molds which still remain in *Muzeum Etnograficzny* in Krakow are but a very small portion of those which had been made throughout the ages. After the last world war, many were lost, particularly those with the likenesses of the Polish Kings for which the Torun factories had been famous.

At present, the factories, Kopernik in Torun, and

Wawel in Krakow, still carry on the honorable tradition of the Polish *pierniki*, and export them to many parts of the world. Some are frosted. Others are in the shapes of hearts, St. Nicholas, Santa Claus, reindeer, in fact in any shapes suitable for hanging as ornaments on the Christmas tree.

Should you wish to make your own *piernik* for *Wilia* supper, and your own cutouts for the Christmas tree, here is the guarded recipe given to our bride:

JANINA'S PIERNIK

5 cups flour	1 teaspoon baking soda
2 cups sugar	¼ teaspoon cream of tartar
1 cup honey	½ teaspoon cloves
½ cup butter	¼ teaspoon cinnamon
2 eggs	¼ teaspoon nutmeg

Melt one tablespoon sugar in large skillet and allow to carmelize. Pour in one fourth cup water, allow to boil. Add rest of sugar. When sugar has dissolved, add honey and spices. Allow to come to boil. Let cool. Sift flour. Put aside one cup with which to flour the board. Add to the carmelized sugar, butter, the eggs, flour, baking soda and cream of tartar. Knead very well, adding more flour to make elastic dough. Refrigerate dough for thirty minutes. Roll out on floured board and make favorite cut outs. Bake at 350 degress for fifteen minutes

Imagine baking this *piernik* on a day when fasting and abstinence was the order of the day just as it had been for many days before, and for more to come. The tantalizing aroma of its baking was so tempting that it was indeed a punishment not even to be able to lick the spoon or the bowl! Grandmother was there! She sat fingering her rosary watching every move one might make.

ADVENT

Loud noises were hushed
The last spark of gayety was dimmed.
Advent had begun.

The liturgical year, in its song, tradition and every day living, began with Advent. This was when the winter season began, and this was when the spiritual cleansing for these holidays took place. There would be no weddings, parties or dances, but there would be meatless days, fasting, frequent church attendance, prayer and meditation within the home.

Advent, from the Latin word *adventus*, means to come (coming of the Christ Child). The formal religious service in church was called *Roraty* derived from the Latin hymn sung at the mass, *Rorate Coeli*. According to Zygmund Gloger, *Roraty* originated in

Rome and was initiated in Poland early in the seventeenth century during the reign of *Boleslaw Wstydliwy*, Boleslaw, the Shy. It became a part of the Advent church ritual in every part of Poland, always on Sunday, and in many localities, every day at dawn. In the *Mazowsze* region, entire families attended this daily service. The *ligawki*, rustic fifes of the shepherds, reminiscent of those played by the shepherds greeting Jesus at his birth, were much in evidence. They were played by young men at the church entrance before the service began. Then again, from the church loft, while the 'host' was elevated. At still other times they were played outdoors at dusk. The tones of the *ligawki*, made sweeter by being immersed in icy troughs, could be heard on quiet crisp evenings, in far off villages.

In Krakow, the early sun lying across the garth of the Cathedral on Wawel Hill reflected the stained glass windows, in red, blue and gold. The choir began the *Rorate Coeli*, "Drop down dew, heavens from above and let the clouds rain the Just one." These were the words of Isaiah pleading with God. This was the voice of ancient Israel awaiting the coming Messiah. This was the song of a young mother waiting for the child who was to be the Savior of the world. This was the supplication of the worshippers, to so live that they might be ready for Judgment Day. Its haunting melody filled the church.

In an impressive ceremony, at Roraty, distinctly Polish in character, a representative of each of the seven economic and social ranks prevalent at that time, walked to the altar, and lit a candle on a seven armed candelabra. The king, as head of the nation, lit the first and highest candle. He was followed by the Archbishop, as head of the Church, by the legal adviser, the nobleman, the soldier, the merchant and farmer, until all seven candles shimmered their soft lights on the nave below. Wladyslaw Syrokomla wrote a poem expressing the entreaty of these seven. In the flowery language of the times each when lighting the candle asked God's help to do his work well. The king whose crown like Jesus' was also thorned, begged for help so that it would never be tarnished. In the last prayer, the farmer makes the plea that the growing grains be saved from fire and flood; that goodness and love flow from the heart; that harmony exist within the cottage and that there be bread for all of the nation. Each one's plea ended with "only then, will I be ready for Judgment Day." And all the while the *Hejnal* (bugle call) was played daily, on the hour, from the *Maryacki* church tower signifying that all is as it should be.

HEYNAL

CHRISTMAS DECORATIONS

hen the high snow-drifts became a formidable foe to the farmer as he struggled to get to the barn to feed the domestic animals, then life began to center within the home in preparation for the holidays. The walls were white-washed, particularly where the smoke from the hearth had darkened them. The daughters washed and ironed the linens until they lay in starched attention, and holiday china and tea glasses were polished to a glitter. Father repaired the chair which would be needed, should an uninvited guest come for the *Wilia* Christmas Eve supper. He mended the shoes which must be sturdy for that walk to the *Pasterka* midnight mass. He sharpened knives and scissors, as well as the axes which would be used when the *choinka*, Christmas tree was brought in from the forest. In the *swietlica*, children made *wycinanki*, paper cutouts with which they decorated the scrubbed shelves of the larder. Here the fragrance of the honey cake still lingered. Sacks of dried mushrooms, dried fruits, nuts and poppy seed hung on special hooks along the wall. Kegs of sauerkraut and pickles, and bins with sugar, flour and salt stood on the clean cement flour. Soon all the shelves would be filled with Christmas foods.

Now mother took out the box with its hidden treasures. There were the egg shells, empty and whole, blown out as early as spring when eggs were most plentiful. Peas, beans and corn were strung on wires in the summer when they were still fresh. Now painted and lacquered, they would look like tiny corals between paper or straw chains of flowers or stars. Metallic silver and gold wrappers from candies, fancy paper, broken necklaces, beads, fringes and silk threads from vests, shawls and other decorative fabric, colored and white tissue paper, wires, tin foil, feathers, straw, dried moss, nut shells, weeds from the fields, and colored yarn all became a part in the magic of hand made Christmas ornaments, one of the most pleasing of folk arts.

PAJĄKI

Before the appearance of the Christmas tree, handmade mobiles and chandeliers called *pajaki*, spiders, were hung at the ceiling in the Polish cottage at Christmas time. They are still in use in some localities in addition to the Christmas tree. The ingenuity in their making can be traced directly to the villager who got his inspiration from the chandeliers in church. Skillfully made, *pajaki* are a delight to the eye and not only an embellishment to the ceiling, but also to the entire room as well. Although called *pajaki*, their ornaments and designs are more like that of an intricate spider web.

At first, the materials from the *Dożynki** wreaths were used. Having been made of the best grains of last year's harvest, they were a visible sign of the earth's generous outpouring of its bounty and the link for its future continuation. Dressed with apples, nuts, and little worlds, *światy*, (made of thin unleavened dough wafers) the wreath hung from the center of the ceiling, or directly above the *Wilia* table. Later the wreaths were enlarged with the use of clay, feathers and colored tissue in many different shapes and forms, with each region having its own distinctive style. Chains made of straw were also added, symbolizing in part, during certain periods of the nation's history, Poland chained under foreign rule. The clay center was the axis from which all decorations stemmed, and was hung to the ceiling by wire or a strong thread. Straws of uneven length were attached to the ball. When colored tissue paper became available, different sized stars, crosses or flowers, were cut out of the tissue and glued to the open ends of the straws, so that each became the background for the one preceding it. When blended together, the many colored tiny cutouts formed an effect of immeasurable beauty, reminiscent of a garden from which tiny fresh flowers radiated in every direction.

Stars

Stars were used in Poland more frequently than any other type of ornament. Christmas day itself is known in Poland as *Gwiazdka*,† the little star. Those made in the oldest tradition were of straw, duck or goose feathers, glued together with clay or candle wax. Others, skillfully made out of wooden chips and shavings, were hung above the altar in church.

Egg Shells

Egg shells have always seemed appropriate as Christmas decorations, since the egg symbolizes the miracle of birth. Their use as ornaments is so attractive, one cannot have too many, especially of the white duck or goose eggs. One of the most popular egg shell ornaments is the little pitcher, decorated with a base, spout and handle of stiff paper, bordered with a folk art edging. A two handled pitcher becomes an urn, a half shell cut vertically becomes a flower pot for colored tisue paper flowers.‡ The surface of the egg shell can be used as the face of a Polish historical personage, or an angel or clown, with the characteristic features painted upon it. Silk threads are used for the wings and hair of the angel, and bits of material, lace and jewelry are used for the headdress.

---

* *Celebration at the end of the harvest.*
† *Pronounced gvyahzd′ kah.*
‡ *See illustration, page 176*

Birds are frequently made with the egg shell for the body. The white dove symbolizing peace was sometimes made, but the most popular bird was the rooster,. typifying health, fertility and good luck. His feet, cockscomb, wings, wattle, eyes and brightly feathered tail, were made of stiff colored paper, attached appropriately to the blown egg. With his head cocked proudly,* he made a gay figure perched on the limb of the Christmas tree.

OPLATEK

Much mention is made of the lacy ornaments fashioned of the *Oplatek* (Christmas wafer) which is shared symbolically with every one in the household on *Wilia†* day. Although it is no longer used as an ornament, it is distinctly Polish in character. Mentioned frequently in Polish literature, it is a vital part of the Christmas festivities and has an interesting history.

Oplatek is taken from the Latin word *Oblatum*, meaning sacred bread. In the tenth century directions for its use in church ceremonies included selecting the largest and choicest wheat grains. The stones for grinding and the screens were especially cleaned for this occasion. Workers wore liturgical garments and sang special hymns during the process. By the middle century, the organists, nuns and aristocracy were given this privilege, performed with ceremonial rites.

At about this time, the custom appeared in Southern Europe of sending nonliturgical wafers, made like the sacred wafers, with accompanying tributes to the homes of the faithful as a sign of harmony. Both types were made of the finest wheat flour, to which water or milk was added. A spoonful of this unleavened dough was placed between two iron plates, much like our waffle iron, and allowed to bake for three minutes. The liturgical wafer was always white, with a religious motif engraved on one side. The non-liturgical wafer formerly colored, is now also white and has designs on both sides.

The iron plates of the *Oplatek* were originally of foreign origin, but Poland is the one country in which the village craftsman dignified them by his artistic engraving, improving and transforming them into a new and original work of graphic art. Immortalized within the designs of the discs holding the *Oplatek*, was much of the loveliness of Polish folk lore. Displayed were visions of striking phantasy as well as actual reality, always retaining the traditional Christmas theme, while finding beauty in everyday village life. These opposite themes displayed on one *Oplatek* could be so different and yet could harmonize in so unusual a way. One side of the *Oplatek* would have the stable in Bethlehem with the Holy Family en-

* *See illustration in chapter on decorations.*
† *Pronounced veele'ya.*

Breaking the Oplatek

graved upon it. The other side would picture chickens or geese in a Polish farm yard. At first the contrast seemed incongruous, but it blended as one saw the stable in Bethlehem similar to that on a Polish farm. Another *Oplatek* might have familiar birds on the limb of a tree, while the other side portrayed the Three Kings paying homage to Jesus. Everything was envisioned which came into the village artist's experience as something beautiful gleaned largely from church scenes, the pastorals, canticles and Christmas plays.

Often many *Oplatki* remained after *Wilia*. The Poles had a profound respect for this paper thin holy bread, and a desire to make it more lasting. The custom of making flat miniature stars, cradles, churches and steeples, arose first in the cities as did the innovation of the Christmas tree. Once it was accepted in the countryside, the same phenomena occurred with the *Oplatek* as with the iron molds. The rich phantasy of these anonymous folk artists came to full expression, and there seemed to be little which they could not create out of this white fragile substance.

As their skill increased, the world *świat* was developed. It was made of circles, half circles and quarter circles of the Christmas wafer, so interlaced with each other as to make wings, crosses, stars, finally becoming the three dimensional sphere, the "world." Sometimes an opening was left in the center, into which a

Lighting the Candles for the Wilia Supper

small ball made entirely of quarter circles, was inserted. Often a tiny figure of Jesus holding the cross was placed on this inner circle, signifying His rule over the universe.

Frequently the *świat* or star made of the *Opłatek* was carefully hung to the ceiling by a thread. There, with each movement of air, it swayed gently and people prophesied the coming weather from the direction in which this lacy ball moved. The very quality which made the *świat* so attractive, its delicacy, was also its liability, since it was perishable, particularly during damp weather. Much patience was required. It was patched again and again, but when completed, it was the finest of all the handmade ornaments with its light lacy texture, and was proudly displayed at the very top of the *choinka*. There are still a few original *światy* in the Museum Etnograficzny in Krakow.

Kazimierz W. Wojcicki wrote of his own childhood (in the beginning of the 19th century) explaining that the church organist visited the various homes with colored *Opłatki* during the four weeks before Christmas. He and the other children cut stars out of them which were hung above the *Wilia* Christmas Eve supper table.

In 1835 Juliusz Słowacki wrote in the play *Horsztynski*, "Blind, and yet I found the *Opłatek*. Who led my hand? I can feel its trembling fragile substance in my hand. How I loved Christmas! In this very room, I cut out many hued suns and cradles which I made of the *Opłatek*. Then what blessedness and happiness filled my heart!"

Adam Plug writes "When father glued together a fine star enclosing a tiny cradle, he hung it to the ceiling by a thread. I knew for certain this was the same star which shone down upon Jesus in the manger. I rocked the little cradle on the thread with my childish breath, and really felt I was rocking the real little Baby Jesus to sleep, singing him a *kolenda* (carol).

CHRISTMAS TREE CHOINKA*

The *choinka* is a beautiful spruce,
On one of its branches, stands a golden goose,
On another, a pussy cat in scarlet boots;
Nearby a little boy made of *piernik* dough.
He is quite brown from head to toe.

* By L. Krzemieniecka.
Translated by C. K. Helgesen.

11

In the cottage, the precious *choinka*, beckons
Come visit me, dear little ones,
Do hurry! Come here by the window!
See my pretty Krakow ribbon tied in a bow,
And the saucy gnome, made of nuts, you know.
    The *choinka*, with its lighted candles aglow —
    Glistens like sunshine, after heavy snow.
    Come children, stand all about me,
    I want to hear the beautiful *kolendy*.

The first known notation of decorating a tree in the Polish home, was in 1720 when Father Anthony Zapcinski wrote about the green branch decorated with candles and toys, called "maiden branch" *panna rózga*, appearing in Warsaw and other Polish cities. Gilded confections, walnuts, apples, miniature dolls, animals, slippers and colored candies decorated the branch. The villagers were the last to accept this innovation. Their handmade chandeliers and ornaments hanging from threads were steeped in symbolism. It was believed that on the day of *Wilia*, they would become filled with the magical strength of fertility insuring good crops for the following year. Anticipation and pleasure both, went into the making of the chandeliers which filled the ceiling with stars, reflecting the heavens and dressing the entire room. It was not easy to discard this.

Green trees however, were always an attractive sight, when other vegetation was dormant and barren, so that in time they were brought into the homes of the villagers. Of all the green trees, the fir is the favorite in Poland. According to ancient Christian belief, the cross Jesus carried in Golgotha was made of fir. Since then, it is said, the branches springing from its trunk form crosses with each other, and the tree is said to have become an evergreen from the time Jesus' blood was spilled upon it.

Marya Gerson Dąbrowska who lived during the time of the first World War, disapproved of the artificially made confections, miniature fruits and gilded objects other than walnut shells. They were expensive and often unattainable and it was her strong conviction, that they were not nearly as attractive as the handmade ornaments of the villager, which were enveloped in tradition. She wrote "Choinka Polska" "The Polish Christmas Tree" published in 1922 and it was due to her influence that the Poles in the cities began to take pride in returning to the early folk art for the making of Christmas decorations.

On the day the *choinka* was brought in from the forest, this adage came to the farmer's mind as he hitched the horses to the sleigh, "He who is earliest to arrive in the woods, is sure to have his grains ripen first." *Kto bowiem pierwszy do lasu przyjedzie, temu najpierw zboze dojrzeje.* If you wish to relive a Polish country scene of the past, choose a stately fir, with many branches. Bring it into the house, and place it in *Boży Róg*, God's corner, where the two freshly scrubbed benches meet. Here the favorite holy pictures are hung, and facing it, is where the worthiest guest is privileged to sit. Gather all of the branches of the fir which remain from shaping the tree. Hold them closely in your arms. Each branch, each needle is precious. Let the strength of this legendary tree flow through your veins as you bless the room with them. Then hang them behind pictures and above the windows. Make a tiny cross out of the little branches and place it above the door. From these parts of the room, they will exude their fragrance and goodness upon you, until long after the feast of the Three Kings. When you go out to feed the cattle, take the rest of the branches and place them crossed above the barn, to help keep pestilence away from the cattle.

PODLAŻNIK

In the southern part of Poland, the custom had arisen among the villagers to cut only the top of the fir, and to hang it inverted from the ceiling. Dressed with candy, apples and nuts, it was called *podlaźnik*. It made such a pleasant sight in the cottages of the Krakow area, that the custom spread to the homes of the gentry. If the room was small, it could be seen, and still kept out of the way when guests and carolers arrived. If the time ever comes when this little top of the *choinka* is no longer seen, hanging from the ceiling, it will always be kept alive in Polish literature, as in S. Wyśpianski's writings. He writes "It swings and swings — from the ceiling — but alas — there is a reason for this. Already all morning I have been creeping about the salon, with my head up, my face way back toward the ceiling, and my mouth open, waiting to see if something off that tree might not fall into my mouth. All day long I waited for evening because then the tree would be lowered on the rope. . . . This little tree taught me something; first, I had better behave ever so politely to my sisters during this entire holiday season, or that tree will not be lowered; second, that during this same time, the days dragged on and on. It seemed as if evening would never come, and each day my longing was greater. Sisters who are girls, can have those dolls but for me it is the soldiers I want that are hanging up there so near the ceiling.*

---

* Translated by C.K.H.

12

WILIA (Wigilia)

igilia or *Wilia* from the Latin word *vigilare*, to watch — *czuwać* is reverently close to the heart of the Pole. It is greeted with such anticipation, such careful planning, and such mystical symbolism, that it is considered by many to be a greater holiday than Christmas itself. The very word *Wilia* which in Poland was formerly known as the day before a feast day is now used only as the day before Jesus' birth. The *Wilia* supper is so special there is no other like it throughout the year. The day itself had significance many centuries before Jesus' birth. Since it followed the longest night and the shortest day it was considered the last day of the year and the mystical symbolism associated with it was closely tied to the solar system. At that time, there was celebrating on this day, honoring the god Saturn for what was believed to be his victory over night. Because Saturn was the god of fairness and justice to all, the feasting began with forgiveness and sharing, resulting in Poland's *gody*, days of harmony and good will. The severe cold weather and deep snows made families hold their festivities near the hearth within family groups. This day became known for generations to come as the holiday which strengthened family ties.

Another custom arising from the past, was the belief that the spirits pervaded the home on this (as it was considered then) the last day of the old year.

Everything was to be made as comfortable as possible for them. Cottages were to be kept warm, water was to be left for their cleansing, and non-perishable foods like peas, beans, apples and nuts were set out to appease their hunger. Sharp utensils, pins, knives and scissors were not to be brandished in the air, or left carelessly on chairs, for fear of hurting the wandering souls. It was hoped that once refreshed and made to feel welcome, the spirits would no longer envy the living but would concentrate instead on blessing the cottages and their inmates.

Another superstition believed in, was that this last day of the year would prophesy everything that was to happen in the coming new year. These rites were adhered to traditionally as would be the painting and engraving of a wooden chest. When questioned, for instance, about leaving foods for the spirits, a housewife would simply say, "My grandmother did this as did her grandmother before her. This is how I have been taught." The Church wisely did not prohibit these traditions, when people incorporated some of them into Christian beliefs. Christ's humble birth appealed to all, but particularly to the man who labored in the fields, who had little opportunity to improve his lot. Christ the King of all creation who could choose the most splendid castle, chose instead, to be born under the poorest conditions. This elevated a

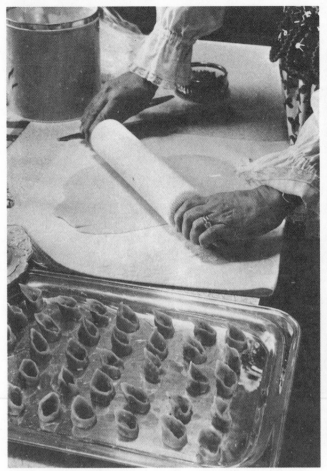

Rolling Out the Dough for Uszki

Serving the Barszcz

poor man's status, giving him a feeling of worth. To him it was the greatest of all miracles, so that on this very awe inspiring *Wilia* day, he believed that the greatest phenomena took place. At midnight, the exact hour designated for Jesus' birth, it was said the earth opened to show its treasures. Water in wells changed to wine, stones moved, the smallest pebble, the tiniest insect, each blade of grass was aware of what was happening. Animals became almost human and the cattle privileged to be present at His birth, could speak with human tongue at this magic hour, but only those pure in heart could see and hear these wonders.

"Glory to God in the Highest and on earth, peace to men of good will — *Chwała Bogu na wysokości, a na ziemi pokój ludziom dobrej woli.*"

In the countryside at the dawn of *Wilia*, the homes, people, and the very air seemed to awaken as if from a stupor of the past weeks. This was a day like no other and must be treated with great respect, for it honors, bewitches, and gives something special to all five senses of man; snow in its shimmering brilliance, flowers etched upon the window pane, chimneys smoking, the ringing of sleighbells, winter birds

chirping, happy voices of children, a neighbor's greeting, the warmth from the glowing hearth, the Christmas tree in all of its beauty, an old man's hand upon a child's head, the bundle of fresh spruce in one's arms, the mingling fragrances of ginger, orange peel, burning logs and baking bread, all of these bring particular rewards to man on this day. Indeed this is no ordinary day.

Fishermen had been up since dawn, not only to catch as many varieties of fish as possible for the all important *Wilia* supper, but also so that fishing would be good in the new year. People rose quickly from under the sweet smelling feather ticks, *pierzyny*, fluffed to twice their size to behave well over the holidays. No one wanted to sleep late that day, which prophesied whether one would be alert or lazy next year. A dry crust of bread and a coin were placed in the basin with cold water in which hands were washed briskly; the crust so that there would be plenty of this staff of life, and the coin for one to be as strong as was the metal on the coin.

Cooking and baking had begun at a very early hour. There were many foods to be prepared for this day, and also for Christmas day, which was deemed so great a holiday that all menial work was eliminated. If a young man wanted to tease a young lady, he would whitewash a window of the cottage where she lived, on *Wilia* evening, He knew she would be very chagrined to see one unclean window in a spotless house on the following day.

There would be little to eat all day of Wilia until the first star appeared in the heavens. The fragrances coming from the kitchen were almost more than one could bear. Children cracked nuts, pounded poppy seed using the pestle and mortar and brought in wood from the outside, coaxing the fires to burn in the kitchen stove and in the hearths or tile stoves of rooms unused for months. They obeyed mothers' orders without being told twice. Soon they would be banished from the kitchen, while the *babkas** and all the important *strucel†* for Christmas day were baked in the oven: for then there must be no disturbances, no opening of a door, no heavy footstep, no kettle dropped, no talking above a whisper, not even a sneeze. The *babka* must come out golden, shining and high.

Thankfully the housewife had made plenty of vinegar for the salads and herring. It was well know that to make good vinegar, one needed to be in a dour mood. What a calamity to run short of vinegar, to have to make more on this day, and to be left with a sour disposition until the next *Wilia* supper!

The master of the house wisely kept himself busy with outside chores. Thanks to the teachings of St. Francis, who believed that animals had souls, though not like those of humans, a worthy consideration was given to them on this special day. The horses had an extra portion of hay for breakfast, and good grooming. The well fed dogs were aware that there was something unusual about this day. They ran in every which direction in crazy abandon, and guided grandfather, whose step seemed less faltering than usual. He was on his way to the apiary to inform the bees that the anniversary of Jesus' birth would soon take place. They should be the first to know, for they made the wax for the candles which glowed, reflecting the tenderness in Mary's eyes, as she looked down upon her newly born Son in the *szopka‡* in church.

Sheaves of the best of last year's harvest grains, were arrayed in the corners of the room, poetically described by Mickiewicz as 'the gold of the wheat, mingling with the silver of the rye.' Sweet smelling hay was placed under the snowy linen of the *Wilia* table. This custom most probably originated with the pagan festivities rejoicing at the rebirth of nature. Now it was used to remind the Christians of Jesus' birth in a manger in Nazareth.

* *Yeast coffee cake.*
† *Fancy pastry — see recipes pages 22 and 23*
‡ *Szopka — the manger scene.*

WILIA SUPPER

The menu for *Wilia* supper was traditional, unchanging, and so carefully planned that it contained all of nature's elements that produce foods except the fat and meat of animals which were to be considered like humans on this day. From the forest came the mushrooms, the nuts, honey and wild berries; the fields yielded grains, cereals and vegetables from which oil was derived; orchards produced the fruits, and from gardens came the stored vegetables. Here is an excerpt from Wladyslaw Reymont's "Chlopy" at Christmas time,

"In the cottage there was a happy bustle. *Juzka* hummed quietly, cutting paper into interesting mysterious cutouts, which she would paste to the ceiling or to the frames of pictures. They were painted in such lively colors, they played wih one's eyes. *Jagna*, with her sleeves rolled above her elbows, stirred the yeast dough hurriedly. It was already rising and overflowing and needed to be made into loaves. She glanced approvingly at *Juzka's* work as she ran to peek at the coffee cake with cheese and honey which was warming under the feather tick *pierzyna* and was ready to be baked. Then she ran to the other side of the kitchen, where a strong fire roared in the stove, to peer at the oven . . ."

Everything for the *Wilia* supper was to be in readiness, the moment the first star appeared in the sky. When a child, its face pressed to the window for what seemed like hours, finally exclaimed "It is here! It is here!" every one knew what was meant.

An even number of guests were to be seated at the *Wilia* table. The number thirteen was to be especially avoided. An odd number seated, signified the death during the ensuing year of one of those present, and every effort was made to invite someone to share the supper. An orphan, stranger or wanderer was made to feel most welcome, true to the age old proverb of Polish hospitality, that "A guest in the home is God in the home." *Gość w domu, Bóg w domu.*

The first star in the heavens brought family, servants and guests to the *Wilia* table. The host and hostess graciously served all. Grandfather seated next to the youngest, whom he helped with gentle hands, became for the moment imbued with the child's enthusiasm, and faded colors became bright for him again. Married daughters and sons, some coming from distant parts, were happy once again under the parental roof where they had shared the springtime of their lives. Little or no food had been eaten during the day. All waited for the most significant moment of the entire *Wilia* supper, the breaking and sharing of the *Oplatek*. The host and hostess enacted the ancient rite of the *Oplatek*, facing one another each holding an *Opłatek*, each breaking and sharing a part of the other's. They embraced warmly and expressed their love by wishing for each other, a fulfillment of their deepest yearnings. Then they broke and shared the *opłatek* with each one present, with messages of love (sometimes in rhyme) of good health, happiness, and an untroubled life, for one to be as sweet as the springtime and to live *do dosiego roku*, to live as long as "Dosia" lived. She was reputed to be many years over a hundred when she died, jolly and alert to the end, but no one could be found who knew her. The hostess performed a special task when she shared her *opłatek* with all those present. Besides the good wishes and love, she expressed without words that she would share her bread with those present here, should they be in need, just as she herself would be willing to take from them, should her position be reversed.

The *opłatek*, frail, perishable, has for all Poles a mystical meaning which cannot be explained logically. At Christmas time it is sent to absent members and close friends in strange lands, who in their loneliness, partake of it, as of communion with their loved ones at home.

The *opłatek*, of little monetary value, is the treasured link that brings warm memories of Poland to her children settled in different parts of the world. Losing reality for the moment, they once again dream that they are seated with the family at the *Wilia* table, enjoying the blessing, forgiveness and warmth of those under the parental roof. At the time of this writing, it can be obtained from the nuns in the convents of those parishes in America where a large number are of Polish ancestry.

In this atmosphere, with the home, the meal and the hospitality at their loveliest, *gody*, days of good will begin in Poland to last until the Epiphany, the Feast of the Three Kings. They are days of harmony, when what is to be forgiven, is forgiven; what is to be forgotten, is forgotten, and when the sharing of the *opłatek* signifies that every one in the universe is one's brother.

With this good feeling, the members of the family partake of the *Wilia* supper. Usually a soup was served first. Most commonly the soup was *barszcz* a clear beet soup, often with tiny dumplings filled with mushrooms, called *uszki*, little ears. The landed gentry, customarily served a light and dark soup. The light, would be a creamed fish, creamed mushroom, or an almond soup cooked with milk, honey, raisins and rice. The dark, would be the *barszcz*. The soup was usually followed by pickled herring served with boiled potatoes. Fish was considered one of the *Wilia* supper's most important courses. Sometimes as many as twelve different fish were prepared for the supper at the tables of the nobility, and much ingenuity and

skill was used in their preparation. Herring was dipped in flour and fried. Carp, *karp*, or trout *pstrąg*, would be steamed in vinegar to provide a silverish color. The well loved Polish saffron, *szafran*, the pit of the hilly crocus, was used to shade the pike, *szczupak*, a golden yellow. Tench, *lin*, might be baked and served with a tasty horseradish sauce. Perch, *okónek*, was smothered in an egg and olive sauce; eel, *węgorz*, pickled and jellied; fresh salmon, *łosos*, sauteed in oil. Other fish to be made more tasty would be cooked in red cabbage, or would be ground, seasoned with bread crumbs, apple, potato and eggs. If the ground fish were that of the herring, or salmon, it was sometimes restored to its original shape, tastefully decorated; or with the addition of beaten egg whites, it might be baked into a souffle. The variety of preparation was great, and the cooks in the wealthy homes guarded their methods. To complement the fish, a meatless bigos was cooked, consisting usually of sauerkraut, mushrooms, and yellow peas. Cauliflower was baked with a sauteed bread crumb topping, and mushrooms tasty and plentiful in Poland, were used in more than one of the foods prepared, such as with peas or beans. A variety of pastries could accompany the meal. They could be *blinczyki* little individual cakes, fried in oil, noodles with poppy seed; *pasteciki*, baked tarts of French pastry with a meatless filling; or *pierózki*, little dumplings, perhaps the most popular of all the pastries, made of noodle dough, boiled and sauteed with different kinds of fillings: sauerkraut and sauteed mushrooms, onions and sweet cabbage, or cheese and fruit filling, particularly prune or cherry.

In the literature of Poland there is a frequent mention of a pressed ruddy colored dough, steamed with boiling browned honey and mixed with spices and southern fruits. These were called *fluczence* and were pressed between two iron molds like the *opłatek*.

Kutia or *Kucya* was a mealy dish served particularly in areas nearest the Russian and Ukrainian borders. It was one of the grains, rye, wheat or barley, shed of its skin, cooked in as little water as possible, sweetened with poppy seed and honey, and baked in the oven to complete its taste. Since spices have come to Poland from the Orient, the *piernik* or ginger cake has begun to take the place of *kucya*, although the grains in their original form are still sold in cities. Some do wish to retain the old tradition, since each of the ingredients used, had a symbolic meaning; peeled grain as a reminder of the time when there were no mills, poppy seed for peaceful dreaming and restful sleep, and honey, the sweetening or easing of daily toil.

The dessert could be the unsurpassed ginger cake, with a fruit compote of apples, pears, peaches, plums

Eggs with Horseradish Sauce

Traditional Poppy Seed Cake

and cherries; *bakalie*, oriental sweets and fruits, like raisins, dates and figs with orange and lemon peel, poppy seed coffee cake, candies and nuts, sometimes to the warming accompaniment of *krupnik*, a holiday drink, a brandy made of honey, spices and alcohol.

After the supper, crumbs were gathered for the birds, chickens, and other small domestic animals. The *gospodarz*, host, tied the sheaves of grain from the room to the trees in the orchard, even speaking to the fruit trees in the hope they will bear plentiful fruit. The wife mixed parts of the *opłatek* to the food which she fed to the cattle, since they had warmed the baby Jesus with their breath in the stable.

In the home the violin was tuned, kolendy were sung and candles were lit on the tree. Girls pulled a straw of hay from under the table cloth to foretell what manner of man they were to marry. A young green wisp meant a young strong lad; a wrinkled one, old, not in the best of health. So that the magical strength of the sheaves of grain in the corners of the room might provide plenty of bread, nuts, and also many children in the home, sometimes bread, apples,

nuts and one or two children would be bound with the braided straw. The binding was then cut with the glance of a knife, and everything which had been imprisoned, children, apples, nuts, loaf of bread fell to the floor with laughter, cries and thuds.

Another excerpt from Reymont's Chlopy illustrates the faith with which Jesus' birth was greeted on *Wilia* day.

"*Witek* in the meantime, deeply touched by the words that during the night, cattle speak with human tongue, whispered to *Juzka*, and both crept quietly out to the barn. Tightly holding hands, trembling with fright, repeatedly making the sign of the cross, they crawled in close to the cattle. They knelt by the largest, as if by the mother of them all. They began to lack breath; their hearts beat tremulously; tears came to their eyes and a holy awe enveloped them, the kind they had in church at Consecration time; but they did have sincere trust and faith. Witek leaned to the cow's very ear, and whispered shakily, 'Grey one! Grey one.' She did not even answer with one word. She only grunted a little, chewed her cud and occasionally licked her mouth with her tongue.

17

'Something happened that she does not answer, — maybe as a punishment.' They knelt by the second one, and again Witek whispered, practically crying by this time 'Spotted one! Spotted one!' Both leaned their ears to her mouth, listening with bated breath. They heard not a sound — not a word — nothing. 'We are sinners, that's why we cannot hear them. They only answer those without sin, and we are sinners.' 'You are right, Jużka, we are . . . Dear Jesus, I took the master's halter and . . . and . . . that old leather sling and . . . and . . ." he could speak no further. Sobbing and filled with sorrow and remorse, he could hardly control himself. Jużka, too, seconded his laments. Both wept and could find no comfort until they had confessed to each other every sin they could remember."

Soon it was time for *Pasterka*, the midnight Shepherds' Mass.

Katarzyna Swiątek Balalowa, in her memoirs, tells of Wilia in her home at Mędrzechowie.

"The Christmas holidays were like a sheaf of golden rays spilling down to our cottage, because we had dreamed about them through the long everlasting Advent, and had fasted so severely that even our gruel had to be eaten dry without the sour milk.

"At last came the longed for day, *Wilia*. The treadmill of our cottage life stood still. The daily hum and rattle ceased. Everything changed, became lovely and kept improving by the minute. In my poor childish heart I felt with firm belief, even a kind of certainty that the Bethlehem stable in which *Jezusek* would be born this night, is surely not far beyond the forest. I could wear my warm boots and coat and I would walk and walk and then Oh *Jezusicku, Jezusicku*, I will give you that delicious red apple father will surely give me right after the *Wilia* supper.

"From dawn there was feverish activity. We had to be very careful with our every act, or it would have to be repeated day after day. Worse than anything would be to quarrel, for these daily quarrels would be a certainty and there would be as many as there are Amens in our prayers.

"Quietly like mosquitos we spun around with tongues hanging down our chins. When the red sun, big like a loaf of bread, finally began to sink, we, utterly spent by this time, brought hay and straw from the barn, saying as we entered "Praised be Jesus Christ. The Savior was born today. Hej *kolenda*!" *Niech bedzie pochwalony Jesus Chrystus. Narodził sie dziś Zbawiciel. Hej kolenda!*

"With noses pressed to the window, we kept watching for the first star, and when it winked at us with its golden eye, we began buzzing like bees, *jest! jest! jest!* is! is! is! Then we knelt with father to pray. Later he shared the *opłatek*, first with mother, then with us. Kissing our parents' hands we wished each other health, happiness and of course, good fortune.

After an all day fast, we sat down to the *Wilia* supper. Smacking our lips, we began the delicious meatless courses sauteed in oil. Soup with mushrooms, noodles with poppyseed, cabbage with mushrooms, *kucya** and a pudding filled with prunes. Heaven forbid that we should eat potatoes this day! Then we really would get boils on our chins! Invigorated, with our stomachs bulging we still ate the apples and the tiny forest nuts. Father called *Bukiet* our dog and nuzzling him, gave him a piece of *opłatek* so he would not go mad. Mother cut up the *opłatek* with vegetables and gave this to the cattle, so their milk would not spoil, and so that there would be plenty of it. The horses didn't get any, because they were too lazy to go to the stable to greet the *Babe Jesus*. Father walked around all of the buildings with the *opłatek* in his hand so that God would protect them from fire and lightning, while we children ran after him jumping and skipping happily, foolishly. Then we returned to the cottage, sat on the hay spread on the floor, and sang *Wsród Nocnej Ciszy*, "In the Stillness of the Night." My oldest brother Szczepus opened a great big hymn book, and he and my father sang several *kolendy*, carols, and we *gapy*, gapers listened. We did not attend the *Pasterka*, midnight mass, because the church was a long distance away."

---

* *Kucya — millet with pearl barley.*

PASTERKA

A t midnight, it was time for the *Pasterka* or Shepherd's Mass. The entire village was lit. Then fires were extinguished in hearths, lights in cottages blinked, shone briefly, then went dark. The bells of the church could be heard calling the worshippers out into the cold brisk moon-lit air. People, the very old, the very young, the sprightly, and the feeble, came out of cottages in throngs on foot, and in sleighs. It seemed as if surely there were no inhabitants left in cottages, yet part of the family or domestic staff remained to watch over the sleeping infants or the very infirm. Young lads carried lighted rosin, and in later times, kerosene lanterns to lead folk out of the snow drifted paths. All the while, the bells kept ringing, guiding parishioners to the church's open doors, its lights and its blessed warmth.

Oscar Kolberg writes (in 1875) that in some provinces, like in the *Poznan* area, young men made stars out of strong colored paper, which they attached to their caps as they went to the *Pasterka*, for soon it would be *Gwiazdka*, Christmas. Householders took bundles of straw to the services to be blessed. Upon their return from church, young girls and boys intercepted them pulling a straw out of the bundle. If the straw drew with it another straw, this meant the youth or maid would be married that year. Again, the shape of the straw indicated the prospect's appearance. Householders tied the nut trees in the orchards with the blessed straw to insure a good harvest.

In some villages the organists trained the youth, who at a designated moment in the *Pasterka*, made sounds imitative of the birds and animals said to be present at Jesus' birth.

Bystron in his *Dzieje i Obyczaje Polskie* reports that early in the eighteenth century, this midnight service was crowded, merry and noisy. It was then the custom for the priest to verbally bestow gifts upon his parishioners. With facetious artfulness, his presentation was at times amusing, touching, even noble, and at other times crude. He would mention a new lock for this one's door, a baby crib for another, or a stable and a pair of horses for Mr. Adamyk, who always came late to church. People accepted this attention with embarrassed enjoyment and good humor, happy to be singled out. Many were sorry when this type of sermon became outmoded in the last half of the eighteenth century.

Oscar Kolberg tells of other instances in which the youth released from the restrictions of advent, still playing the game that what happened today would be happening the rest of the year, tried to be witty by playing mischievous tricks at the *Pasterka*. They tied together the shoe laces of two individuals standing or kneeling next to each other, or they might sew together the skirts of two women. Students in larger cities sometimes poured ink into the holy water in

19

the font at the entrance of the church, and then watched gleefully when the parishioners crossed themselves with the inked water. There were isolated cases however, since to most, after weeks of fasting, abstinence and prayer, the *Pasterka* was a reverent joyous occasion. Happy at being re-united with absent members, with family ties strengthened, with the fragrance of green pine all around them, with the beloved *złóbek* again present at the side altar, they jointly partook of the holy communion while the lights from the ornate candelabra reflected on the golden tracery of the priest's vestments and on the chalice in his hand. After the sermon, *kolendy*, Christmas carols were sung by the entire congregation. They were sung by women in colorful kerchiefs, in white lace embroidered caps, or in black shawls. Some men wore clean white *kapoty*, long coats with brilliantly colored trimmings, some wore patched grey *kapoty*. Small dark wiry men of one province, as well as tall flaxen haired men of another, all joined in singing *Wsród Nocnej Ciszy* — In the Stillness Of The Night. Some sang softly, piously, hopefully. Most sang with confidence, joyously. This was one of the rare occasions of the year in the long ago, when the villagers were as one with the aristocracy.

Kolberg tells in his visits to the provinces, of talking with professional musicians who had come from the cities to hear the villagers sing *kolendy* to the accompaniment of their violins. Amazed at the nuance, the tone and rhythm, the musician would ask "Who taught you to play like this?" and the answer was invariably, "No one. I taught myself." When asked for the source of the melodious carols, young girls would say, "My mother taught me this *kolenda*, and her mother taught her." These natural gifts of inborn music and poetry were well expressed in their singing and playing of the *kolendy* and *pastoralki*.

After the service, men visited friends, neighbors, relatives or the parents of one's betrothed. Sometimes a young man visited the home of a young maiden whom he liked. Playfully he snatched an apple off the Christmas tree. If the young lady allowed him to keep the apple, he could begin his courting in earnest.

The hosts had appetizers *zakąski*, prepared in advance for their guests, including two very important essentials, vodka with honey called *krupnik* and hot tea to warm the visitors who came in from the cold and soon would go out again.

Jan Wiktor writes: "not too much time had elapsed since the *Pasterka*, maybe only two or three hours and dawn seemed far away. It was warm and snuggly under the *pierzyna* after the biting cold of the outside. Some one was knocking at the door. It was the same every year. Mother rose quickly, hunting around for a match to light the lamp. All three of us

children ran to the center of the kitchen like three mice peeking out from between the straws of a broom. We were excited because if a man was the first to visit us after the *Pasterka* it meant success for us. It was just what we expected. It was Micheal Kowalik, beginning to sing one of the verses he memorized or made up to suit the occasion. Father appeared suddenly and broke the *Opłatek* with our first guest as was customary. Then father brought out our prized crystal decanter which we were told was used by Stanislaw Poniatowski, God bless his name, and was brought from a Warsaw castle by a bricklayer to our village. Mr. Kowalik drank the honeyed *krupnik* from it in one gulp and joked that the tiny glass which held it should be tied to a string or he will swallow that too. Then in detail he wished us, the house, every corner of the rooms, every lump of sod outside, much success, changing his voice occasionally.

Soon noises and whispers of newcomers were heard in the entry. "You first! Why me? I'm too shy. Wait until I stop my giggling." Then sounds as if a cap were being stuffed in one's mouth. "Sing real loud. Jezusek will be pleased." When father bade them enter, a little one barely up from the ground, was pushed to the foreground. He seemed to gather his breath together and started a solo off key in his childish treble, not even beginning at the start of the verse but somewhere in the middle which the chorus immediately corrected. We had heard these verses wishing us success many times but father listened gravely, then distributed the *grosze* pennies carefully, since they had been earned laboriously through the harvest. Some one would get five *grosze*. Which one? Then mother gave them all *placki* and cheese and we were sent off to bed."

20

CHRISTMAS DAY

By Papal approval, three masses could be said by one priest, on this very special holiday, and people attended one, or all of them. They were called *Pasterka* or midnight mass, Angel's Mass, and the mass of the Three Kings. After the masses, with their beloved *kolendy* still running through their minds and on their lips, the worshippers thronged to the side altar to marvel at the beauty of the *szopka*,* and at the new creations which the monks of the church might have added that year. Some of the wealthier people had scenes of the nativity within their homes, among the most famous being that of the Zamojskis of Warsaw, and of Stanislaw Wyspianski of Krakow.

This day was considered so important a holiday, that menial work of any kind was not to be thought of. Oscar Kolberg in his visits to the provinces, quoted from newspapers, diaries and letters in which this is frequently mentioned. The home owner would always caution his domestic staff to complete any work which had to be done for Christmas, on *Wilia* Eve. One such from the Poznan area, a *Pan Wach*

was quoted in 1863, as saying, "God forbid that any of you should scrub even a small portion of the entry, tomorrow on *Gwiazdka* (Christmas) or dare to bring in wood or a bucket of water."

This day was spent in comparative quiet, within the intimate family group. Visiting friends and relatives would not begin until the following day, the day of St. Stephens.

Christmas day had its traditional menu, just as had *Wilia*, but there was no special number of courses. Meat was the main feature in the planning. Ham was very popular, since pork had always been eaten at the time of these festivities, dating from Pagan days, when the pig was the sacrificial offering of the Saturnal ceremonies of Christmas, then known as the New Year. Polish sausage was always on the fare. Both Polish hams and Polish sausage have become universally known, and along with Polish dried mushrooms, can be purchased in many markets in the larger cities of the United States. The writer has memories of a tantalizingly appetizing Polish sausage which her mother, a Polish immigrant had made for the Christmas holidays. The fresh

*(Jaselka *and* szopki *are discussed fully in a following chaper.)*

meats and spices she had learned to use in the old country, went through the meat grinder, larger than those we see now for domestic use. After having been stuffed into casings, the sausages were sent to the butcher for smoking. She also made a tasty breakfast sausage called *okrasa*, a ground mixture of pork, goose and seasonings. It must have been a family secret like the *piernik*, since the writer has found no recipes with that combination and that title in the Polish cookbooks she has perused. The meat and its juices were sopped up with home made rye bread for breakfast and never lasted through the period of *Gody* as they should.

There is much in the old Polish literature to testify that *bigos*, hunter's stew was often used as the principal menu of Christmas day. This is understandable since with no menial work done on this reverent day, a housewife could prepare the *bigos* in advance, which with all of its vegetables and meats, could be a complete meal in itself. When wild animals were plentiful in the Polish forests, some of the meats of these animals, like that of the boar, were used in the succulent stew. *Bigos*, hunter's stew, as the name implies, was made outdoors, in big pot bellied kettles, after hunting. Mickiewicz describes bigos in his Pan Tadeusz as being so good, so full of flavor, that only one used to country life, healthy at that, could fully appreciate its flavor. He mentioned that it must have the best of meats, and the best of vegetables, the principal of which was sauerkraut. Sauerkraut could find its own way into one's mouth. In bigos, the sauerkraut sought out all of the best juices, covering the meats, snugly, so that the tantalizing fragrance escaped only from the steam as the *bigos* simmered. A large kettle of the *bigos* would be cooked two or three days before Christmas. Krystyna Skrowaczewski, wife of the noted composer and director, at present music director of the Minnesota Orchestra, gives her modern recipe for *bigos*.

HUNTER'S STEW – BIGOS

1 large white cabbage (about 2 lbs.)
2 lbs. sauerkraut
2 medium white onions, finely chopped
1 medium can beef bouillon
1 small can tomato paste
2 lbs. pork roast baked with 1 Tbsp. caraway seed
   and 1 large onion sliced
1 lb. Polish sausage coarsely chopped
4 oz. dried mushrooms
½ lb. baked ham, coarsely chopped
1 crushed bay leaf
12 coarsely ground peppercorns
¼ lb. dried prunes pitted
1 large apple coarsely chopped
1 cup dry white wine
Left overs of venison roast or boar ham (optional)

Slice the cabbage and squeeze the sauerkraut almost dry. In a large pan, simmer the cabbage and sauerkraut in two cups of water, adding the chopped onion, beef bouillon and tomato paste.

After twenty minutes, add gradually the coarsely chopped pork roast with its gravy and onions, chopped sausage, ham, mushrooms (boiled for 2 minutes in a cup of water), mushroom juice, bay leaf, peppercorns, prunes and apples. Stir in the wine.

Simmer for one hour, mixing and turning the entire time. Refrigerate overnight. The next day, simmer again for an hour, mixing constantly. Serves eight to ten. Home made rye bread usually accompanies the *bigos*. Here is a recipe for rye bread:

RYE BREAD

1 c. boiling water	1 tsp. soda
2 tbsp. molasses	2 c. rye flour
2 tbsp. shortening	1 yeast cake
1 tsp. salt	¼ c. warm water
¼ c. brown sugar	4 c. white flour
1 c. buttermilk	

Mix together boiling water, molasses, shortening, salt and brown sugar. Boil for a couple of minutes. Add buttermilk and soda. Cool.

Add rye flour, yeast cake (softened in the warm water) and white flour, Kneed. Let rise in greased bowl until double in bulk.

Shape into two loaves, place in greased bread tins and let rise again. Bake about 45 minutes in a moderate oven. (350 degrees). Makes two loaves.

The bread must not be cracked when it leaves the oven, but should instead be so smooth as to look lacquered. When tapped at the bottom with the closed hand, it must respond with a hollow sound. The horse radish leaves which were often placed underneath the loaf in the pan, formed a lovely pattern when baked. Blessed is this black rye bread. It must not be dropped carelessly, nor be placed on the table, bottom up. The housewife had for centuries past made the sign of the cross over it before cutting the first slice. With all of this goodness centered upon this daily, never tiring food, it is fitting, that it, along with an offering of salt, contain all of Polish good wishes, friendship and hospitality, when tendered to new neighbors, or to friends in new homes.

Just as *babka* in the form of a plump lady is baked for Easter, so the two Christmas coffee cakes *plecionka*, braided bread, and *strucel* have had a place of honor for hundreds of years at the Polish Christmas table. Here is the recipe for *plecionka*:

PLECIONKA – HOLIDAY STRUCEL – STRUCEL ŚWIĄTECZNY

8 c. flour	1 t. grated orange rind
2 c. milk	1 t. grated lemon rind
4 yeast cakes	1 c. melted butter
8 egg yolks	4 egg whites beaten
2 c. sugar	1 t. salt

Dissolve yeast in ½ cup of the milk. Make thin sponge by mixing yeast with rest of milk and 1 cup of flour. Mix thoroughly, sprinkle top lightly with flour and set aside to rise. Add salt to egg yolks, beat until thick and lemon-colored. Add sugar, rinds and mix with sponge. Add two cups of flour, alternating with the milk. Using spoon or electric beaters mix thoroughly. Carefully fold in the beaten egg whites. Add remaining flour and butter and knead until the dough comes away from the hand. Set in warm place to rise until double in bulk. Separate dough into 4 parts, roll into long strips and braid into loaf. Brush top with lightly beaten egg yolk and sprinkle with poppy seed. Let rise. Bake in 375 degree oven for 40 minutes.

The second, the *strucel* or *strudel* is more difficult to master but when freshly baked, or reheated, it is most delicious, and a real work of art.

STRUDEL

Filling (to be put aside, then strewn alternately over the surface of the dough).
Mix:

1 tbsp. cinnamon

with:

4 to 6 tbsp. browned bread crumbs
1 tbsp. lemon rind

grated into:

1 c. sugar
¾ c. raisins
¾ c. currants
½ c. shredded blanched almonds
6 to 8 c. finely chopped tart apples
Have small pitcher with melted butter ready.

Preheat oven to 400 degrees. Have a cloth ready on a large table-height surface, around which you will be able to walk. Work flour lightly into the cloth; Sift into a bowl.

1½ c. all-purpose flour
¼ tsp. salt
1 egg beaten with:
⅓ to ½ c. tepid water or milk
2 tsp. vinegar

Depending on your flour, you may have to add a few tablespoons more of tepid water. Combine the ingredients quickly with your fingers and kneed them on a board until the dough no longer sticks to it. You may brush the surface with melted butter. Cover the ball of dough with a warm bowl and let it rest for 20 to 30 minutes. Roll it out on the board as thin as possible. Move dough to the table. Begin to stretch the dough gently from the center out, trying not to tear it, as patching is difficult. If you are skillful, this should stretch to about a 2 yard square. A heavier edge of dough or a border will develop as you work and whatever remains of this must be cut off with a knife before the filling is spread or the pastry rolled up. Use this excess dough for making patches. Before filling, brush the dough with some of the melted butter. Sprinkle over the surface the bread crumbs, sugar and lemon rind, currants, raisins, almonds and apples. Dust with cinnamon.

Then comes the forming of the roll. Using both hands, pick up one side of the cloth, and while never actually touching the dough itself, tilt and nudge the cloth and the sheet this way and that until the dough rolls over on itself — jelly-roll fashion — completely enclosing the filling. Finally, slide the long cylinder onto a greased baking sheet and curve it into a horseshoe. Form the roll not too tightly, as the dough will expand. Brush the surface of the roll with some of the melted butter and sprinkle it lightly with water. Bake for 20 minutes at 400 degrees, then lower the heat to 350 degrees, brush the strudel again with the remaining butter, and bake about 10 minutes longer, until brown. Remove from oven and dust with confectioner's sugar. Cut in wide diagonal slices and serve.

Sometimes this *strucel* was baked to an enormous size. During the baroque period, namely in the seventeenth century, a Warsaw bakery baked a *strucel* so large that four bakers dressed in white, carried it along the street, followed by an ever increasing crowd, to the home of the burmeister, where it was requested that the burmeister's wife uncover the *strucel's* separate top crust. Out jumped the little son of one of the bakers who after bowing in all directions, sang a *kolenda*. Many came to observe the *strucel* which was later placed in a glass case at the hospital of *Świętego Ducha*, the Holy Spirit.

In 1608, Jozef Smolinski, King Jan Sobieski's baker, baked this feast cake, with a topping of raisins, nuts and other fruits, so arranged as to portray the exact image of Queen Marysienka. The cake looked like a beautiful Florentine mosaic painting. Jan Sobieski was so pleased, he tendered his baker a huge sum of money as a reward, which, it is said, Smolinski immediately turned over for the poor of the district.

ST. STEPHEN'S DAY

his day is also called the second Christmas in Poland. In some districts, this is the day reserved for sharing *opłatek* and *kucya* (sometimes made with buckwheat dumplings), with domestic fowl, birds and animals. The *gospodarz* gave this food to the animals by hand, speaking to them. For the horses he had an especially tender message. They shared with him his daily toil, and so should also share the *Opłatek*. Horses were of special concern. They seemed to be ailing at this time. When it finally became known that their ailment was no more than their sudden complete inactivity over the holidays, St. Stephen's became the day on which they were harnessed to sleighs, and taken out for exercise, a custom, which later developed into the all important Polish *Kulig*.

The sacraments of baptism and matrimony were not celebrated during Advent, so that many christenings and weddings were performed in church on this day of leisure, St. Stephen's.

People attended mass, taking with them various amounts of oats and peas, which could be more than a bushel, or as little as a handful. The larger amounts they presented as gifts to the priest after mass. They threw the smaller handfuls at either the priest as he departed for the sacristy, or at themselves, in commemoration of St. Stephen who was stoned to death. (This practice has not been in existence for many years.)

On this important day, domestic help was hired or re-hired for the coming year, and was absolved of all work. *Na Święty Szczepan, każdy sobie pan.* On St. Stephen's, everyone is his own master. The men seeking new employment, as well as those who needed help, visited the local tavern in the morning, to begin negotiations. In the meantime the *gospodyni*, housewife, prepared an excellent meal for her domestic staff, graciously serving those accustomed to waiting on her. When one left the table, and did not eat, he indicated he was leaving for employment elsewhere. If the hired help did partake of the meal, a new contract had just been sealed for the following year. In Kolberg's writings (in 1850) according to custom, both men and women received a special award of money and clothing, with the women being given one half the amount the men received.

In contrast to the quiet of Christmas Day, St. Stephen's was spent in visiting friends and relatives, sometimes driving long distances.

Szopki and *Jasełka* began appearing in villages, in cities and in homes. *Kolendnicy*, carolers began their rounds and doors of manors as well as of cottages were opened to them invitingly. Fiddles were tuned. *Kolenda* had begun.

Each of the twelve days between *Wilia* and the Epiphany were to prophesy by their weather, what the climate would be for each of the following months; cold, stormy, sunny, mild, etc. The evenings were called Holy Evenings, when no menial work, spinning or working with sharp utensils was done. This time was spent in extending hospitality to acquaintances, relatives, and to wandering carolers, as well as in visiting old friends and neighbors. At Christmas time Polish hospitality is in its best form. Food dainties, the *piernik* and *strucel* were sampled. The violin was tuned, kolendy were sung, and the candles on the tree were lit to better show its treasures.

The Poles have a great fondness for candles on a Christmas tree. Many have continued to use them even after electricity became available. In Poland a candle is lit during man's most ceremonious occasions; at his baptism, his subsequent birthdays; when a bride and groom are pledging their troth; and again when one is in his last moments on earth. It seems fitting that candles should be lit to welcome Jesus' birth.

The flames from the candles make not only an effective picture, giving warmth and light of themselves, but as a remnant of Pagan beliefs, belong to the custom of lighting fires for the departed souls, at a time when Christmas as the beginning of the new year, was also a day set aside for the departed souls. Fire containing hidden forces, according to primitive logic, had the magic strength to avert evil, drive away unclean spirits and the power to spread fertility and good will.

Knowing full well the danger of fire, especially in a small cottage, the wicks of the candles are trimmed evenly, the candle is set straight into its holder away from the branches, and then the tree is watched carefully during the entire time the candles are burning. Electric Christmas light bulbs might be easier to light but they have no fragrance, do not sizzle, nor do they drip a nice warm pink petal-like deposit of wax on the tree's green branches.

TURON

During the twelve nights between Christmas and Epiphany, the village was alive with unusual characters. First came the *Gwiazdorze*, star carriers, young lads carrying the illuminated star on a long pole. They carried it proudly, for it possessed magic. By one pull of the string it began twirling rapidly. The lighted candle encased in its center, made the colors of the many hued iridescent paper, come alive. People in cottages could see the *Gwiazdorze* coming from a distance, with the twinkling shimmering star, high up in the air. Some groups sang *Kolendy*, and recited verses in rhyme, most of which were cajoling, humorous or complimentary to the *gospodarz* or *gospodyni*, host or hostess of the home. They would be amply rewarded with gifts of food and money. One of their verses might go something like this:

May the dear Lord give you
Success and plenty of health,
And in the pantry and barn much wealth.
Dear Lord, give them everywhere
In the sack, in the field, here, there,
In every corner a tiny tot,
And near the stove, three more to add to the lot.
For these good wishes, we would like some cheese,
Pastry, ham or *kielbasy*, please
May the good Lord bless you for it.

27

Some *Kolendnicy* put on the puppet shows, *Szopki*. Others enacted the nativity plays *Herody*. After the *Gwiazdorze*, the older group came, in which one of them was dressed as a bison, a goat, or a combination of several animals.

This practice of being seen dressed as an animal, stemmed from pagan days during the period of *Gody*, when there was so much rejoicing because of the sun's victory over night. It was felt then, that peace must be made if possible, with those animals harmful to man, like the *turon* bison, *wilk* wolf, and *niedzwiedz* bear, who seemed superior to him, since they found food and shelter with no effort, while man labored for his existence. Some primitive people dressed in animal skins to acquire these same advantages.

For years, even to this day, a group would choose a nimble man or lad with a talent for tricks and a sense of humor to be the *Turon*. He usually wore an overcoat with the fur lining on the outside, covering as much of his body as possible, including his head. A wooden head, which consisted of several animal parts, was tied to his head, while his own was concealed in the folds of the overcoat leaving a small slit for him to see through. The wooden head might have ears like those of a donkey, horns like those of a goat and a very large wide mouth with movable clappers and a long red tongue. He wore ram's skin on his hands and feet and had a horse's tail attached appropriately to the coat. This comical creature was called the *Turon*. He was led by a chain. He walked on all fours, sometimes hunched on two feet. Usually the leader carrying the illuminated star would ask for permission in rhyme or verse to enter the home. He was eagerly welcomed, since he provided excitement, hilarity and entertainment for all.

In Reymont's *Chłopy*, Peasants, the leader upon entering the cottage, told of coming from a far away country beyond the sea; from a huge forest where people walked upside down, where fences were made of sausages, and cooled with fire; where pigs swam in the water, and where vodka dropped freely from the sky like rain.

"Show us what you can do, and there will be something from the pantry for you," his hosts responded. "We will show you at once. Hej, piper play! Dance bear, dance!" The leader might then countermand his order, giving the *Turon* a couple of kicks, who in turn, on the leader's command, would crow like a rooster, whinny like a horse, cry like a bear, jump on all four legs, move his ears, lick his tongue, make loud noises with his clappers, and run after the girls. He ransacked the entire cottage, jumped on the table, overturned furniture, opened drawers and cupboards as if searching for something, and pretended to butt older people with his horns. Sometimes he was tricky enough to get some whiskey or an apple through the big clappers, into his own mouth underneath. He made such a tumult that little children and dogs alike hid under benches. When the *Turon* saw them he would run toward them so that they hid even deeper, still peeking out, so as not to miss the fun. It was not always known who he was since he never spoke. The *Turon* could be somewhat brazen upon his departure, pinching the ladies as well as the young girls.

JASEŁKA

hrough the centuries, each nation has built up a store of traditions centering around the appealing festivity of Christmas. One of the interesting expressions of Polish feeling, is the *jaselko* taken from the word *jasto* which is synonymous with *złobek* or manger. In its simplest form *jaselko* is a tableau of the Nativity.

St. Jerome, living in the fourth century, was the first person known, to initiate this scene in a grotto in Bethlehem.

In the twelfth century, St. Francis of Assisi (1182-1226) having received permission from the Pope, recreated the scene of the Nativity in a grotto in Italy. The locale was hilly and the background was filled with forests. In this cavern, surrounded by a wreath of warming torch lights, St. Francis solemnized the first Christmas midnight mass, with the aid of the Franciscan monks. The night was brilliant and the forest rang with the sound of the monks' choral singing. Imbued with the solemnity and majesty of the moment, worshippers old and young, town people and villagers, as well as shepherds with bagpipes, sank to their knees on the ground under the open sky.

Greeted with much enthusiasm, this custom was brought into other countries by the monks. This was an era of darkness, of primitivism, in which the art of writing was unknown to many, even to kings. It was the monks who in their travels, made the *Jaselka* so popular and widespread.

A letter from Pope Innocent the Third dated May first 1207, has been preserved in the Krakow museum. It was written to Archbishop H. Kietlicz, suggesting that nativity scenes be displayed in the Polish churches.

The *Jaselko* which first began to appear in churches in Poland, was three sided with the entire front open. It was supported by four pillars, was transportable, and had a thatched roof. It was usually placed at a side nave. The figures in it were made of wax, clay or wood. They were displayed from Christmas, December twenty fifth, to Candlemas Day, February second. The scenes shown might be Mary and Joseph seeking a lodging, the Nativity, the adoration of the shepherds, and on the Feast of Epiphany, the visit of the three Kings. The figure of the Christ Child at the time of this last feast, might be seen sitting, to receive the homage of the Kings, rather than lying prone. On Candlemas Day, the *Jaselko* was dismantled to the accompaniment of the singing of carols, *kolendy*.

In time, monks undertook the roles of the Angel, Mary, Joseph, the shepherds, and the Three Kings, while the Infant Jesus and the animals remained unchanged. Soon dialogue began to take place. Upon finishing the Mass, the priest might ask "Shepherds, whom have you seen?" and those dressed as shepherds might answer, "We have seen the Infant Jesus etc." This was a pleasant innovation and an introduction to the theatrical form of art for many. For a long time St. Francis in his effort to increase the fervor of the simple folk, had been urging them to take part in the *Jaselka*. Folk lore possesses so much charm and individuality, it brightens any creation it is a part of. So it was with the *Jaselka*. When students and village folk assumed roles in it, the folkiness in their dialogue injecting Polish folklore and Polish locale, soon supplanted the Latin text and the Bethlehem locale previously used. They added new scenes called inter-

ludes, as well as additional characters consisting of Herod, the devil and death. Herod, especially, was created to be scoffed at, being the symbol of the feudal system, and his death, the penalty for being a cruel tyrant.

In some churches skillfully made small figurines became the attraction of the *Jasetka*. New characters were constantly being added. By the eighteenth century, the entire scene, with its innumerable characters, became the picture of Polish life as it was lived then. The following is a description of a *Jasetko* of this period, reported upon by the author F. Wadowski:

Szopka in the 18th century

"The inanimate figure of Jesus made of chamois, tissue or buckram could be seen in the *złobek* lined with a blue pillow. The oxen and donkey made of the same material, were kneeling near him as if warming him with their breath. The figurines of Mary and Joseph stood leaning over him with looks of awe and tenderness. An angel with spread wings, appeared on the thatched roof and seemed to be singing. In the foreground, shepherds, kneeling, were offering their gifts to the Babe; this one a lamb, another a jar of butter, and still another, a piece of cheese. Some were tending their flocks, others appeared to be sleeping. Interspersed among them were people in many walks of life; nobles, fancifully dressed, riding in carriages; gentry and villagers alike in Polish dress, hurrying to the stable; farmers with wagons filled with grains, leading their oxen, stopping on their way to market; others tilling the soil; women milking cows; bakers baking bread and Jewish merchants selling their wares. On the Feast of Epiphany, The three Kings were added with their armies, including cav-

alry and infantry of white, African and Asian races; grooms, mounted on elaborately dressed horses, camels and elephants; pitched tents; the Polish guard, as well as the guard of many different countries, each carrying the flag of their nation . . ."

The introduction of the puppet theatre in churches

The religious order of Bernadines, Capuchins, Franciscan Reformers and Franciscan monks, in an effort to attract the populace to their churches, added action to the figurines, modelling them after the Italian and French marionette theatres. The puppets were manipulated on strings. Rustic humor made its appearance and worldliness began to creep into the religious theme. A Jewish merchant might shake out a fur coat, showing it on the inside and out, to a prospective purchaser. Another might steal it. There would be a hassle and the instigator and his soldiers would come running to the rescue. *Małgorzata* would be dancing with the hussar. Death and the devil would be seen dancing together, then fighting. Much mischief making, humorous gesturing, would be shown to the delight of children and adults both. The church became filled with people, pushing to the front, often standing on pews and climbing the altar to see better. At this unbecoming behavior, some servant of the Church, often one of the manipulators of the puppets, would rush out from behind the curtain and with the aid of a cane, would forcibly try to eject the violators. They in an effort to escape the blows rained upon them, would push, scream and tumble over each other in their haste to get away causing almost as much merriment to the audience as the *Jasetko* itself. It was inevitable that the Catholic Hierarchy should strenuously object to this. In the last

30

Offering Sweets to the Carolers

A Tray of Mazurek

half of the eighteenth century, not only in Poland, but in other countries as well, movable puppets were forbidden in the church, and only immovable, strictly religious characters were to be displayed. Having been expelled from the Church, in the height of its flourish the *Szopka* as the *Jaselko* was now called in both of its forms, the moving puppets as well as the live actors, easily passed into the hands of the lay people, to whom it had already become a tradition. Setting up the *Szopka* became the task of the poor, the students, tradesmen and the servants of the Church. With the live actors the *Szopka* usually consisted of three scenes. The first showing the Shepherds being awakened by the Angel, the second, Herod ordering the execution of all infants, and the third, people worshipping at the stable.

The live performance

Marya Konopnicka writes of her experience in witnessing a *Szopka*, in which actors had come visiting to her home:

"Came the vigil of the Three Kings. The evening was fair but cold. *Szopka* was being shown around town. Not the painted one with the oxen, donkey and *Małgorzata* dancing with the *Hussar*, but a real theatre with live actors among whom Death, the Angel and the Devil would be shown. When the parlor maid ran up the stairs with the cry 'they are coming' my heart palpitated so that I could not find voice. This was to be the first theatre I had ever seen in my life.

"It was necessary to wait quite some time because the performance was played first at our landlords, downstairs. I thought they would never come up. At last there were sounds of heavy footsteps on the stairs. There was a clank of chains and the actors entered our apartment, headed by a dreadfully black devil with his red cloth tongue hanging down to his chest, saying in a devilish low voice 'Praised be . . .'

"I clutched the maid by her jacket, the soul within me began to die with fright. Following the Devil, King Herod's ambassador entered with light short footsteps. He wore pantaloons encased tightly to the knees, a blue cape made of an old petticoat flung over his arm and a beret with a lovely white feather made of fine English tissue paper. He bowed graciously, and taking a chair from the side wall, set it in the center of the room. Bowing low, he opened the door before his majesty. King Herod entered with cloudy mein with his head bowed as if in deep thought. He had a long cloak evidently improvised from some kind of bedding, a gilded paper sceptre in his hand, and a crown on his head. It seemed to me,

31

his face looked familiar. The figure of unearthly white Death crept in covered with a sheet from which his black boots protruded. With a scythe in his hand, he stood menacingly behind His Majesty's throne. Seemingly unaware of Death's dastardly thoughts, Herod sat with his cloak (upon which a few feathers still lingered) spread out on the arms of the chair. He began his bloody dialogue, and had barely uttered his first words, when a loud clapping of hands and a shriek could be heard from the outside hall, 'Jasiek! My Jasiek! My King! My golden King! Before Herod could recover his mother *Urbanowa* entered and threw herself on the ground, weeping hysterically and kissing his hands and cloak. The monarch wanting to stay steadfast in his role, tried to continue his monologue, but his voice broke, his lips trembled, and tears began to trickle down his ashen face.

"Bedlam arose, The ambassador cleared his throat loudly. Death recommended that the scene be repeated from the beginning again. Through it all, the squeaky voice of the angel from behind the stove, could be heard at even intervals with its 'Gloria in Excelsis Deo.' The devil on the other hand, did not lose his composure for a moment. Standing before King Herod he kept clinking his chains and thumping the floor with a long black stick, condemning and cursing the trembling king. This thundering effect caused the monarch to return to his sensibilities. *Jozka*, our parlor maid, and her younger sister, who worked in the downstairs apartment, led *Urbanowa* to the side, and the performance ended successfully on the final note when the king's crowned head having been slain by Death's scythe, was lowered onto his arms, while the devil, nudging him with his pitchfork, shouted:

> *Królu Herodzie, za twe zbytki*
> *Pojdz do piekła, boś ty brzydki.*
> King Herod for your offence,
> Come with me, you brute to hell."

The transportable Szopka

The transportable *Szopka* brought into the homes, with its movable puppets was built much the same as the former *Jasełka* in church only in smaller form and was carried around on four poles. The manipulators spoke the dialogue for the puppets, and there was a front curtain which was raised and lowered on the different scenes. This type of *Szopka* with its many puppets, was more convenient than the one with live characters since it took much less space in a small cottage, or room. The puppets now became marionettes and included *Krakowiacy*, *Gorale*, *Mazury* and *Cygany*, all in native costume. Sometimes the three visiting Kings were figures from Polish history, like *Sobieski*, *Władysław Łokietek*, *Piast*, *Mieszko* and *Bolesław Chrobry*. The shepherds were Polish being named *Wojtek*, *Bartek*, and *Kuba*. *Jasełka* were shown in cities, in villages and in certain prominent homes and palaces.

Every province had some original and ethnographic differences in the creation of its *Szopka*. Primarily it was Warsaw which displayed the *Szopka*, generation after generation. It lacked however, the individual style which might identify it as the Warsaw *Szopka*. The Krakow *Szopka* developed in text and architecture such grandeur in so unique a fashion, it has no precedent in the world. Already in the last half of the nineteenth century the structure had become two storied and the primitive thatched roof was changed into a handsome cupola, with high winged towers adorned with clocks. Small artifices were annexed in front of them, enlarging the proscenium area, and the towers became gradually more and more similar to that of the *Maryacki* church in Kraków. The original dome later contained two staircases with more towers, arcades, columns and galleries so that in time there were three stories to the *Szopka* and different scenes could be displayed in different parts of it, reminiscent of the three horizontal levels of the theatre of the middle ages, representing heaven, earth and hell.

In about 1900, Karl Estreicher who wrote the book "*Nie od razu Kraków zbudowano*" (Krakow was not built in an instant) introduces the reader to the three personages who had most to do with the development of the *Kraków Szopka*. One was Lucien Rydel, the author of "*Bethlehem Polskie*" the Polish Bethlehem, a Nativity play, the other Ludwig Solski, famous actor of the times who undertook principal roles in the performances related to the *szopka* and the third, Michael Ezenekier, the most famous of all *szopka* creators in Poland. The author tells of all three being at his home, when he was a child. Mr. Rydel was saying that it was important for the actors to learn from the people. They must never cease to draw on the exuberant fertile imagination of the simple folk, which converts a stray little tune into song, which has just the right gesture, a little touch of irony or humor and yet gives the feeling of great sincerity.

Mr. Estreicher also discussed Mr. Ezenkier's genius, explaining that his golden hands could masterfully build a huge mansion in the warm season, and those same hands never idle, took to creating a small *szopka* in the winter time.

Of his own experience, Karl Estreicher writes:

"The snow fell in great flakes. By the light of the lantern, I could see through the window, that the *szopka* protected by an oil cloth, was arriving by sleigh and being carried into the dining room, while we waited in the adjoining salon. Suddenly, the lights went out, and everything became quiet.

We could see a ray of light, emanating from the dining room. Then the wide doors began slowly to open, until suddenly there was the spectacle of the *szopka*, in all of its beauty, filling the framework of the portico. First it was the colors that enthralled one; red, green, violet, azure, yellow, black, bronze, silver and gold, like a live fire, drawing us ever nearer. The *Mariacki* Church towers appeared before us, only more richly ornamented. Between them stood a golden cupola, reminiscent of the Jagielonian dynasty. All of the fairy land of the East, stood reflected before our phantasy, kingdoms and palaces both below and above the sea.

"Over the *Szopka*, above the dome, a luminous star began turning to give the sign that the puppets were about to enact a great drama. As the star began turning more rapidly, losing its points, it changed into a whirring circle of rainbows. Behind the *Szopka* disturbed whispers could be heard, 'Where you rascal are you meddling around with your paws? Look you tore the petticoat of the queen. Now how is she to make her appearance?'

'Silence' came the voice of the stage manager. 'Start the carols.'

"Harmony struck. The base viol, the fiddle, the harmonica and six male voices began *Wsród Nocnej Ciszy*. The curtain arose. The puppets Bartek and Simek were carrying a calf, a goat and a little ram, as gifts to the Babe. Only the merchant would not believe. Bartek threatened him with a stick. The merchant screamed. A fat constable entered and arrested Bartek for causing confusion. Every scene with the comical merchant puppet created laughter, especially among the children. *Pan Twardowski* was another popular puppet. He entered in a nobleman's overcoat with split sleeves, and sang boasting that he was merry day and night, although never quite sober; but when the devils appeared, up came his sword while he pulled his cap to one side, and splash! Quickly he made two crosses with his sword. The devils disappeared! Out sprang the *Krakowiacy* with much grace, clanging and jingling, for their belts were studded with nail heads and fastened with buckles. Then came a pause. Just knowing what was to follow brought fear and trembling into our childish hearts.

"The curtain arose with Herod making the horrible proclamation of infanticide. . . . After Herod's dreadful death came the climax. Slowly the floor of the little palace began to open up, then drop, while a multicolored fire burst into flame from below. In the midst of heavy thunder and smoke, death, the devil and the king's body, all disappeared, while we cowered in our seat and did not recover until the favorite of the children, the

Bowl of Fruit Compote

dziadek the little old man with a bag at the end of a stick came in begging for donations, to get a pint of whiskey and a shave of his whiskers. He looked right at us promising that those who gave would be rewarded; those who did not, would be put in jail. We all had our pennies ready for him. This was more fun than the collection box in church, for he would address us directly, displaying many of his tricks. The curtain was lowered. We sighed . . . The singing of the *kolendy* began again."

Mystery plays on a country road

Jan Bujak wrote an article in the Poland magazine for December 1967, entitled "Mystery Plays on a Country Road" and we quote:

"The Wladyslaw Orkan Musieum of Krakow decided to organize a festival competition of Folk Christmas puppet shows (Jaselka) a challenging undertaking in view of the fact that the last published information about Christmas puppet ensembles in this region, comes from 1888.* The only argument for the organization of this event was the vague information obtained as part of the

---

* *Its decline was noted at the close of the nineteenth century, contingent on the changes in the rural civilization, society and customs. It survived in the Rabka region.*

ethnographic field study, conducted on other subjects, and the accounts of chance tourists who happened to spend their Christmas holidays in the villages, near Rabka. They reported that they had seen Christmas puppet shows put on in the winter nights in several of the local cottages. The group of ethnographers who were sent out to investigate these reports, turned up much exciting material. They learned that there are six puppet ensembles active in the region. These are composed of adults, and often of older people. It was discovered that they also have their own village bands. . . . The jury which sat in on the Rabka competition awarded the first prize to the Jan Bielski ensemble of puppeteers, representing the old tradition. The prize was awarded in recognition of the high artistic level of the setting, as well as for the wide variety of puppet characters which included figures of whom all memory had vanished elsewhere. Notable are the picture peddler, the travelling medicine man, the nobles, the Hungarian hussar, the gypsy with a bear and a whole gamut of rural characters. The old dialogues were spoken with dignity, while the carols and folk ballads added color to the performance.

"Equally interesting was the *Stoszek* brothers' ensemble, whose director is an accomplished sculptor. The setting of the two storied *złobek* was richly embellished with regional motifs. The puppets were simply facinating, each a small masterpiece in itself. Even the expression on their faces reflected their characters. All the figures were painted and dressed in folk costumes, uniforms, church and royal robes. Although the dialogue centered on the traditional subject, it was nevertheless permeated with a sharp satire against the many undesirable manifestations of contemporary life. Some of the remarks were witty, some rather pungent. A beautiful rendition of Christmas carols added a fine finishing touch to the performance.

"Encouraged by this good beginning, the Museum of Rabka is now making plans for a mammoth festival of Christmas puppet theatres and carol singers which was to be open to the public."

This modest little *szopka* with poor and primitive beginnings strides triumphantly through the ages, giving inspiration to actors, artists and poets. It is always dear, whether diminished to microscopic measurements, and hung on the branch of the Christmas tree, or whether it is so large, it takes up the stage of a theatre and uses live actors. It seems to be immortal, like its sister the *kolenda*.

KOLENDA*

he *Jasełka* and the Polish Christmas carols or *Kolendy* are so interwoven, it is difficult to tell where one ended and the other began. It is evident that the moving puppet shows, the Christmas plays and tableauxs with live actors, were the inspiration for many *Kolendy*; while the *Kolendy*, especially those sung in the homes rather than in church, with their rustic humor, were responsible for creating new scenes in puppet shows and plays.

The word *kolenda* is taken from the Latin word *colendae*, meaning the first day of the month, but celebrated particularly on the first day of the new year, which as we learned previously, was celebrated ages ago, at around Christmas, rather than on the first of January. Great feasts including singing, greetings and good wishes took place on this day. With the advent of Christianity, the singing theme became Jesus' birth.

The seventeenth and eighteenth centuries produced the golden age of the Polish carol. Up until then, many had been literal translations from the Latin. Now they began to radiate their own richness and individuality.

Unfortunately, the greatest number of early carols was handwritten unaccompanied by melodies. Schoolmasters, organists and the cloistered tried earnestly to preserve the works of their predecessors for posterity, but found the task difficult especially if there was a note accompanying the words, "to be sung to the tune of the skylark," and that particular tune unavaliable. Rev. M. Mioduszewski deserves much credit for collecting the melodies of the *Kolendy*. His *Pastoralki i Kolendy z Melodiami*, Pastorals and carols with Melodies, edited in 1838-1853, was one of the first complete collections, from which others were to follow.

The *kolenda* may be divided into three categories; the legendary or apocryphal, the religious and the pastoral (*pastoralki*).

The lengendary, based on the books of the Apocrypha used only parts of the gospel relating to Jesus' birth, enlarging and enriching upon the content, so that they became in part religious, and in part, fictional. These carols were found to be entertaining and harmless, but were not sung at church service, since they did not contain strict historical truth. This fact however, did not make them less popular and they continued to spread more and more. The people loved to sing of the many wonders, of the talking birds and animals. As an example here is a *kolenda* about the wolf, the shepherd's greatest foe.

Idzie wilk z płaczem do Pana
Niosąc na sobie barana.
Prosi o pokutę.

The wolf comes crying to the Lord,
carrying a lamb on his back.
He begs for penance.

Examples of the sixteenth, seventeenth and eighteenth century *kolendy* which have permanence, beauty and depth that cannot be erased through the centuries are: *Anioł Pasterzom Mowił,* (The Angel Spoke to the Shepherds) from the sixteenth century; *W Żłobie Leży,* (In a Manger He Lay), seventeenth century; and *Bóg Się Rodzi,* (God is Born) in the eighteenth century. All three are in the religious classification of *kolendy*, and each represents a different style.

Anioł Pasterzom Mowił, written anonymously belongs to the oldest group and has its popularity through generations as evidence of its beauty. It is dignified, earnest, even plain and yet, like bread, most vital, and most often requested.

W Żłobie Leży preserved the Polonez which had been played at the coronation of Wladyslaw the Fourth (Ladislaus the Fourth, 1632-1648). It indicates the author's full knowledge of the bible. In contrast to *Anioł Pasterzom Mowił,* it deals more with earthly matters than with the Heavens. In spite of its learned tones and theological references, it is easy to see why it is so beloved. It not only has the well known rhythm of the Polonez, but has scenes which sound as if they were taken from the pastorals, ringing with the beat and life in a Polish village. No other *kolenda* creates such an impression as does this one. It is like a mosaic, in which everyone finds what he is searching for. We understand the mystery of its immense power, when we learn that its composer is Peter Skarga (1536-1612) one of the greatest evangelists of Poland as well as a great political reformer.

Bóg Się Rodzi (God is Born) another polonez, has a haunting majestic melody that is hummed for hours after it is sung. It came out in the age which followed the golden period of literature, in a period with less enthusiasm and spirit, following the partitions of Poland. The creation of *Bóg Się Rodzi* in this era is a happy exception due to the exquisite poetry of an exceptional poet Franciszek Karpinski who was called the soul of Polish poetry. Although all of the words may not immediately have been understood by the country folk, they soon learned them because of their lyrical quality.

* The correct spelling of Kolenda is Kolęda...

The religious, among the most beautiful and profound in feeling of all Polish hymns, owe their origin to a great extent to monks in cloisters.

The *pastoratka* or shepherd's song, has an essentially folk song character, which makes it specifically Polish. It introduces local color, pastoral scenes and familiar melodies. It rings with rhythm and pulsates with life. Melodies are gay, sad, tender and humorous. There is a native unconscious poetry about them. The theme of the Infant Jesus, poor and homeless, born in a stable among familiar domestic animals, appeals to the heart and imagination of the entire nation, but particularly to the poor villager or mountaineer to whom the idea that the shepherds were Jesus' first visitors, was of great comfort and solace. *Pastoratki* contain customary Polish scenes, are sung in the cleanest dialect and people described in them have Polish names, bring Polish favorite foods to Jesus, and wear Polish dress. Their writers, many of them anonymous, were not concerned with the language or customs which existed in the Holy Land, nor were they concerned with building a verse of rhymes or literary style. Yet, one feels in them the archaic goodness of the psalms, the sincerity of a praying child and the wisdom of a patriarch.

Dzisiaj w Betlejem (Today in Bethlehem), *Przylecieli Aniołkowie* (Little Angels Came) and *Ach Ubogi w Żłobie* (Ach Poor in a Manger) have immortalized the *Mazur*. The *Krakowiak* is represented in *Hej Bracia, Czy Wy Śpicie*? (Hej Brothers, are you Sleeping?)

For Mickiewicz, Słowacki and Chopin the *kolenda* was a synonym for childhood happiness, spent with those dearest to them. The memory of its fascination had a bearing on their works, particularly while living in exile for the rest of their lives. Whether the *kolenda* was vigorous, swash-buckling, spilling over with exuberance, or wistful, sensitive and endearing, it appealed to the simple man in his rustic coat, to the nobleman in his grand attire, and to the praying religious as well as to the loving mother singing to her child.

This then is the Polish *kolenda*, composed by famous literary poets as well as by simple folk. It is charming and sincere and contains the breath of the purest Polish spirit.

NEW YEAR'S EVE OR ST. SYLVESTERS

In Poland, as well as in other European countries, New Year's Eve is known as St. Sylvesters. As legend would have it, Pope Sylvester the First, imprisoned the dragon Leviathan in the year 317. The belief grew that Leviathan was to escape in the year 1000, devour the land and its people, and set fire to the heavens. So strongly and universally had this fear spread, that historians call it the millennium crisis. When the young Pope Gregory learned that his end was near, in 999, he rejoiced that he would not live to witness the dreadful first day of 1000. The Benedictine monk Gerbert became his successor as Pope. He was thought to be a sorcerer because he studied Arabian works and spent his free time in his cell building machinery. When to make matters worse, he took the name of Sylvester the second, then it seemed doubly certain that Sylvester the first had imprisoned Leviathan and Sylvester the second would release him.

At midnight of December 31, 999, all the bells began ringing in Rome. There was no sign of the dragon. The rejoicing and the release of tension when it was learned that the world was not at an end, was as strong as had been the previous apprehension, especially, when it was learned that Pope Sylvester the second, had been using his spare moments to build a clock which perfected with time, became the one we use today.

Few spent this day alone. Entire families gathered together; there were visits from friends and the youth collected in unison to finish the old year on a happy note. This day, being the last day of the calendar year, was comparable in tradition to *Wilia* the Eve of Christmas, the last day of the church year. People again reached into their rich treasury of superstitious beliefs and fortune telling, prophesying on what the New Year would bring, while the youth repeated many of the customs belonging to the November *Andrzejki*, only this time with more spirit, and perhaps a few more tricks.

Kolberg tells of young mischief makers near Tykocin who took logs to block the doors of a cottage, or pulled a wheelbarrow up the roof near the chimney, where they pretended to build a stork's nest in it. Girls made a thin paste of clay mixed with ashes, daubing this on the outside of cottages in which young men lived. They also entered these cottages, quickly snatched some piece of apparel belonging to the young man, and ran off with it. On the following day they gathered at the home of one of the girls, with their assorted articles. Each man who lost something had to pay a forfeit to regain it. The collection was usually enough for a festive party. Both young girls and lads dressed as gypsies; some brought children, begging for alms for their supposedly starving youngsters, others emitted sounds of different animals. Sometimes upon being invited into a cottage, young men gave recitations during which time the girls in the group would throw flax seed upon the hot stove which would burst with a crackling noise. A few seeds of oats were sometimes thrown by the carolers on the host as he opened the door, or were placed on the corner of a table by them, signifying their wish for a plentiful crop on his land.

In some villages women baked special little cakes, to which they added some of the grain of the wheat sheaves which had stood in the corners of the room during the *Wilia* supper. These were called *nowolatki*, little summers, idiomatically meaning, little New Years.

In *Nasza Ojczyzna** there is an article relating to the little cakes made in the Kurpie Region. Here the women still make a good dough out of which they sculpture animals of the forest, domestic animals, tiny people, sometimes even scenes of village life,

---

* *"Our Nation" magazine for January 1964.*

called *Nowe Latka*, symbols of the New Year. Baked especially for St. Sylvesters, they symbolized a future production of wealthy game in the forest as well as prevention of hunger and pestilence. Now that their power is no longer believed in, the little cakes have become mostly playthings for children. Their simple charm however, has not lost its appeal.

Photographs shown in the magazine were of a Marianna Konopka, a woman of about sixty with a white kerchief over her head, and a large white homespun apron protecting her clothes. She was forming dough on a bread board and several little shapes already made, lay on a bench nearby. Singly illustrated in the magazine they were entitled, A Deer, Man with a Flail, New Year (a shepherd holding many newborn lambs), and another called Cradle, on which the Babe lay covered with a blanket, while his mother knelt near. All were not more than two or three inches in height.

NEW YEAR'S DAY

n spite of the revelry of St. Sylvesters, the New Year began surprisingly early for some. (Countess) Maria Smorczewska Bullis, one of the Polanie members, tells about the farm lads and stable boys, standing beneath her bedroom window, soon after dawn of this day with cries and invitations for her to come out. Although their urging appeared to be spontaneous, both she and they were prepared for this tradition which was believed to bring health and fertility to both animals in the stables and crops in the fields.

Maria Bullis, hastily donned in riding attire, came out of the home, and was immediately helped onto her horse which was bedecked with garlands of flowers, grains and fruits. A young lad led her on the horse in a promenade around the courtyard, to the rhythmic stomping, cheering and singing of the rest of the group. This was followed by treats and hot drinks with honey, with which the lads toasted the health of their mistress and her favorite stallion.

In many churches the service was elaborate. In some districts, the girls wore the cherry blossoms which had blossomed on *Wilia* day, tucked in their hair, under colorful scarfs. Young men wore cherry blossoms tucked in their belts. All were aware that the coming months before Lent, when there was little farm work to be done, were most propitious for *zaręczyny*, engagements, and weddings. Girls had to guess whether the branches the men wore were snatched from the young maidens of their choice or whether they had used the branches strategically while they explored the field.

The pastor's sermon included good wishes for his parishioners, admonitions against believing in *zabobony*, superstitions, and the announcement of his approaching visits to the families of certain villages for census taking.

Villagers began to make special plans when they knew the Priest was coming to their village that week. His visit was also called the *kolęda*. There was planning on which problems should be discussed. There was the customary reminder to the aged invalid to get ready for his semi-annual confession and Holy Communion. Foods were put aside; a chicken or two, eggs, butter, sausages and perhaps a slab of bacon which would surreptitiously find its way into the pastor's deep wagon. There was the thorough dusting of the top inner frame of the kitchen door, upon which the Priest lettered with chalk, the first initials of the Three Kings from the East, and the date of his visit, between the letters. This would not be erased, until the pastor's next visit. The Priest was usually accompanied by the organist and students. They announced the Priest's entrance by ringing bells and singing *kolędy*. Daughters of marriageable age, placed chairs which they dusted and shined, in strategic positions, where they hoped the priest would sit during his visit. He was a special personage. Sitting in the chair he had just vacated, was bound to bring good luck to the one who sat in it immediately after him, and what could be better luck than the hope for a good proposal of marriage!

EPIPHANY OR
THE FEAST OF THE THREE KINGS

lthough the story of the Three Kings is taken from apocryphal literature for which strict historical truth is not assured, the love and respect held for these three wise men was so strong, so universal, that the church also paid homage to them. Wherever the initials K M B for Kaspar, Melchior and Baltazer, with a cross between them, were seen written in chalk at the top of an entrance doorway, it was evident to a wayfarer that a Catholic family lived there. In areas like the mountainous regions where the priest was not able to travel, people brought chalk to church on this day to be blessed. Upon their return, they wrote the initials of the Three Kings on the door themselves, not to be disturbed until the following year. These initials written with blessed chalk, along with the palm from Palm Sunday and the blessed candle from Candlemas Day, were together to be a force to avert disaster.

In church liturgy, this day is called Epiphany commemorating Jesus' baptism in the river Jordan. In the eastern terrain of Poland the ceremony of the orthodox Christians on this day was colorful, festive and unique. An ice hole was chopped out of a pond near the church and an altar was improvised out of the chunks of ice which had been removed. Decked with evergreens, the altar shimmered in the rays of the sun as if it were made of crystals. The procession coming from the sacristy of the church, with the leader singing in a deep bass voice, was led by the bearded priest in a golden-threaded cape. One saw men garbed in white coats with beautiful ornate belts, with their feet encased in yellow and red boots. Colorful kerchiefs on the heads of women; columns of steam rising from every pair of lips to the pale blue heavens: and occasionally a golden icon, vying with the sun itself in its brilliance; the sparkling snow, and everywhere banners *chorągwie* flying in the wind, all remindful of ancient colorful pageantry. The blessing of the water in the ice hole would hardly begin, when women commenced tittering and young girls hid their faces in their kerchiefs, peeking nevertheless. Hardly had the sign of the cross been completed when one sturdy lad, two, three — ten — one after another, took off their clothes, along with their boots and plunged into the ice hole. Each submerged his head three times, then red as a lobster, steaming like a racing horse, he donned his heavy coat on his bare skin, his boots on his feet, and *hajda*, he sped to his cottage.

His proudly contented wife or mother, picked up the rest of his apparel, ran after him and found him already lying on the warm tiles of the stove in the cottage. She treated him with a *kieliszek* of *gorzałka* — a glass of whisky. This ritual had the double purpose of commemorating Jesus' baptism as well as insuring the man's good health for another year.

Since this holiday was still a part of the *gody* a time of strengthening family ties, guests who had come to be with their relatives from great distances, were likely to be with them at the Feast of the Three Kings. When families belonging to the nobility got together, this was the day on which the almond king was chosen from among them, to rule for the following year. A large coffee cake was baked with an almond hidden in it. The hostess usually planned to choose the one who would get the piece of cake with the almond. It might be the one who was wisest, or the bravest, her beloved spouse, the dearest of her children, or her most respected friend who was almost like one of the family. The almond king had the responsibility of being the leader of social affairs, protecting the honor of the family, settling their quarrels and accepting guardianship over all.

Less serious and more romantic were the games in which almonds were hidden in cakes for both young men and women of marriageable age. From the daily newspaper of Franciszek Krasinski written by Klementina Hoffman during the Saxon reign, comes this account of the almond king festivities. "Today is the day of Three Kings and an enormous *placek*, cake is being baked in the kitchen with an almond in it. Who will get it? Oh my Lord, what if I should become queen?

"The cake was distributed at the end of the meal. *Basia* got the almond! Her face became drained of all color. Our madame seated next to her, announced it in a loud clear voice, and everyone stood up and shouted '*Wiwat!* Hail!' Mathew said with a smile '*Kto dostanie migdała, dostanie Michała*.' 'Whoever gets the almond, gets Michael.' It seems there is such a prophesy, whatever young lady gets the almond on the day of Three Kings will be married during zapusty."*

So ends the greatest group of holidays of the year. The Torun† sheds his fur coat, his wooden head and clapper; the iridescent star of the gwiazdorzy‡ caught in the wind may need some repairing, and the Herody° may very well have lost Death's sheet or the angel's wing, all of which are carefully replaced with tender loving care and regretfully put away for the next Christmas season. Finally safe in warm cottages the carolers can look over and taste their assorted bounty, tokens of good will from their many hosts for entertaining them. The page falls from the calendar. The old year and the new have already been united, and a new cycle of yearly traditions begins. *Kulig! Za pusty! Carnival time!*

---

*Zapusty — *Carnival time before Lent.*
† *Torun — page 28*
‡ *Gweizdorzy — page 28*
° *Herody — page 28*

KULIG

 ne of the colorful customs of the Poles is a festivity called *Kulig*. To the Pole, life is divided into the calendar year according to the generous sprinkling of saints days, holy days, and church festivals. The gayest and most enthusiastically participated in, is the carnival season which precedes Lent with its somber quiet days of meditation, prayers and self-denial. These are the days of penitence that lead up to the glorious festival of Easter. In the rural areas the carnival is punctuated with days of merrymaking, tricks, parades, music and folk dancing, but the most loved social event is the winter sleigh party or *Kulig*. The time for *Kulig* is anytime from Christmas to Ash Wednesday, depending mainly on the occasion when the snow is very deep. It originated with the gentry, but has been practiced to different degrees, and with variations, by most of the population.

In the past, the preparations for *Kulig* were very extensive and festive, and the celebration involved several days, depending on the geographic area and willingness of the planners. Families get together and may visit a neighbor who they mutually agree will be willing to be the first host, and treat the guests with customary Polish courtesy. If possible, the householder who has a birthday or namesday during these days is considered the obvious choice for host. Everyone in the families, young and old, becomes an actor and eagerly joins in the fun-filled days of merrymaking.

There is much to do and it is done with the most enthusiastic spirit. The visiting folk feverishly work on plans and costumes, if they have decided to wear costumes. The obviously unsuspecting host begins frantic preparations of baking *ciasta, babki, chrusti, strucle* and sausage-making. The host must load his table with foods that match a wedding feast.

The day is set, the actors are ready, and the revelry begins. It usually starts with the sleigh ride at night. If the air is crisp, the moonlight bright and the necessary snow as high as the fence, then *Kulig* has no obstacle to a round of hilarity that will sustain them through the quiet days of Lent.

In the country, horses ply the snowdrifts, sinking to their bellies in the feathery billows as they pull their happy cargo, and crisscross the farmlands, sometimes forsaking the roads and paths for a more hectic and turbulent ride through the fields to thrill

41

the passengers. Sometimes firecrackers bursting with sharp, staccato cracks, flung out by the merrymakers, rip the crisp air and excite the horses to fling their decorated manes in a picture of charged and high spirits. Even the sleighs pulling the happy cargoes become a part of the act. Some of these vehicles, filled with hay for warmth and comfort, are rustic and simple, with daubs of paint smeared on in gay abandon; while others have gracefully carved swans proudly holding up their long necks, or fierce eagles sitting atop, adding to the spirit and fun of the gay ride.

Cares are forgotten. Happiness takes over and bubbles in a medley of shouting noises, songs and music. The traditional *fujarka*, a fife or whistle carved of a willow stem, can be heard in its high pitch tooting staccato notes to add to the hilarity and confusion.

Should this caravan of revelers have a long ride, or have an unexpected breakdown before they get to the home of the host, they may choose to make a stop at the nearby inn. This is an occasion for wine and pranks, and is a beginning of the hilarity that will last until the day breaks after the last stop of the sleigh ride. Usually this is an opportunity for the ladies to put on their costumes which were carried carefully on the sleigh in order not to crush them. If the inn could not provide separate chambers, the makeshift partitions inspired the young men to much devilment. While the girls would be changing into the costumes, the bold young men would leap over the thin barriers to raise a chorus of squealing and screaming protesting the invasion of their privacy. The teasing became bolder and protests louder if the delay was long and the wine plentiful.

When the ride is resumed there is much jostling and crowding to get back onto the sled. Merriment is boundless, and conversation is flowing freely and the air is filled with laughter. This is the opportune time for holding hands and for a stolen kiss. The horses start and the air bursts with song. The most popular form of singing is a ballad of teasing and taunting by the women to the men and they have their turn to reply.

The ladies sing:

> "Felled has been the little oak tree,
> Felled and hewn away.
> Heart and hand have I betrothed,
> If wisely, who can say?"

and from the men in a mocking bass, they answer:

> "Pray tell me what the reason is,
> I've found no answer yet,
> One day I love a fair-haired maiden,
> Another day — a brunette."

Now the ladies answer gayly with this jingle:

> "Silken, fitted frocks, coats, spurs and
> embroidered gloves,
> Men today, as always, will have themselves
> a score of loves!"

While the merrymaking sleigh makes its way, numerous bells jingling on the horses' harness, and young men darting alongside carrying burning torches and shooting off firecrackers, add to the excitement. The play unfolds when a messenger is dispatched to the home that is to be visited. Dressed as a Kossack, the young man gallops into the yard of the host, signalling his arrival with outbursts of fire crackers, and flings the *awiz* into the doorway. The *awiz* is a note, sometimes written comically in verse, advising the *gospodarz* that the *Kulig* is coming. Mission accomplished, the young Kossack races back to rejoin his group.

The *Kulig* arrives with all the noise and commotion it can muster but the home of the host is dark and silent! The pretense is played out that this is all a surprise and all the actors are a serious lot! The host pretends he is asleep. When the noisy band makes its loud and raucous presence known, the host slowly emerges and sleepily asks, "Who is it?" The reply is that the merrymakers have heard that he offers generous and warm hospitality and they have come to partake of it. "Ah," says the host, "Do come in." Then with Polish humility he adds, "My house is small, my dear friends, but it would disgrace my home to have such distinguished company dancing outside in the yard; so please do come in, come in under my lowly thatched roof." The roof need not be thatched, but the lines imply the humility of the host. Once the greeting is over, the house suddenly blazes with lights, fun, and confusion reigns. All along the host has been well prepared for his dear friends and neighbors.

The revelers make their costumed appearance in the order of traditional importance and status in their community. The play begins. . . . First comes the *Starosta* and *Staroscina* (the Elder and his wife); then the Organist and his wife; the Miller and the Innkeeper. The musicians come in with the guests, still playing rhythmic dance tunes of the *Oberek*, *Krakowiak* and *Mazur*. Then follow the "Young Pair" *Panstwo Młode*. This pair of play actors is usually selected with an eye to matrimony, or if available, they are a betrothed couple, and the *Kulig* serves to spur them on to marriage. They are followed by attendants, dressed as *Górale*, mountaineers; the gypsies and the fortune tellers. There is no limit to the characters the neighbors portray, however they realistically reflect the life of the community, only this time they are all masked.

There is an animated and profuse greeting of guests, with affectionate embracing and exaggerated complimenting and kissing of hands. While the *gospodarz* (host) has signalled for the food and drink, the musicians squeezed into a tight corner of the big room, begin the festivities, or rather continue them with a spirited *Krakowiak*. The couples begin to dance, and now everyone moves from room to room, where the furniture has been removed, to make way for the dancers for there is little room for the whirling and flying colorful skirts and ribbons, ballooning lacy sleeves, the stamping of boots and clicking of heels. Over the din the host scurries from one knot of merrymakers to another encouraging them to dance saying, "There is plenty of room for everyone, dear neighbor!" and passes out endless servings of cakes and wine.

Meanwhile the table is receiving the traditional load. The ladies are setting it with food delicacies they have been preparing beforehand and kept hidden for this event. The feast begins with *zakąski*, hors-d'oeuvres, which could be a meal in itself. These are usually herring, sardines, slices of ham, cucumbers, mushrooms and other delicacies. Then comes the main part of the meal. There is smoked goose, *czarnina* or duck soup, beet soup, jellied pig's feet, homemade sausage, chicken, *kiszka* or barley sausage, head cheese (made of gelatin, pork and herbs), cooked cabbage, *babka*, a tall round yeast cake, especially delicious with wine, fried cakes, honey mead, or *miod* which is a drink made of honey; *krupnik*, a whiskey made with honey and spices, and of course, a good supply of vodka. The favorite desserts stacked high on platters are *pączki*, deep fried jam-filled yeast cakes. These are still popular and every Polish housewife has a favorite recipe. Here is one:

PĄCZKI *

1½ c. milk	1 t. vanilla
2 yeast cakes	½ t. mace or
1 t. salt	½ t. nutmeg
½ c. sugar	½ c. butter
3 eggs	4½ c. flour

Scald milk and cool to lukewarm. Break yeast into the lukewarm milk. Beat sugar and butter until fluffy, add eggs, salt and flavoring. Add flour and milk gradually, beating well. Let rise in warm place until double in bulk, about 2½ hours. Punch down, knead and let rise again. Place dough on lightly floured board, stretch toward you and fill with thick filling (do not use jelly because it is not thick enough). Rose jams, apricot or peach preserves and prune butter, are good fillings. Fold over and cut into desired size and shape like a ball, place on lightly floured surface and let rise. Fry in deep hot fat, turning only once. *Pączki* should have a very dark brown color before turning, to insure baking thoroughly. Drain on absorbent paper. Sprinkle with vanilla flavored powdered sugar or mixture of granulated sugar and cinnamon.

It is a tradition that the leader of the *Kulig* or Elder is also the master of ceremonies for the entertainment. When he manages to get himself heard, and there is a pause in the dancing and eating, this intermission is used for "playacting" a comedy. At his signal an organist appears, in costume, and with much stammering and pretending, pompously enacts the role of the official greeter. He unfurls a long, and seemingly endless scroll and begins to introduce the play actors with elaborately foolish commentary about each one. The guests jokingly interrupt, interfere, and harass, and even take the show away from him. This tomfoolery goes on, until the next player takes his turn to perform some act of foolish comedy amidst chiding and laughter. The miller and his wife might carry in a sack of flour and during their act spill the flour on those who get near them. The innkeeper spins tales, impossible legends and stories, which brings on much teasing. Then back to the dancing which, aided by the glow of wine, becomes a sport for colliding and bumping. That in turn calls for extravagant play-acted apologies. Everyone, even the oldsters, contribute to the joviality of the occasion. When the guests are weary from dancing, food, drink, laughter, and singing, they prepare to leave, and the elder delivers a carefully planned oration of extravagant thanks to the mistress of the house, and offers her a board made to resemble a make believe wheaten cake as a token of appreciation for her hospitality.

---

* Pronounced "Ponchki." From Treasured Polish Recipes For Americans

The musicians play a parting melody, and this traditional *Biały* (white) *Mazur* signals the arrival of a new crisp dawn. The din of music, singing and dancing quiets down, and the conversation now deals only with unscrambling and finding of coats and wraps. Even though everyone is very tired, the host persists that his company remain and offers more hospitality and asks they stay even a "little longer." But the masked messenger appears, swishing a birch rod over chairs, proclaims the end of the festivities at THIS home by shouting, "*Hey, Kulig, Kulig!*" Everyone scrambles into the sleighs with spirits high for the next stop and more merrymaking, almost always taking their genial host and family along with them until the last home on the list is visited.

As years passed some of the customs have changed. With growth of industry in the cities and towns, although the traditions of *Kulig* remained the same, they are carried out in a more modern and practical way. Transportation changed, but "fun" continued to be part of the celebration. Even the food, like *kiełbasa* (sausage), *bigos*, and poppyseed breads are still on the menu and good fellowship and merriment help to perpetuate the delightful *Kulig* in Poland.

Kulig has survived much Polish history and has undergone many changes to adapt to the "times." It is interesting to recount a description of Kulig dating back to 1695 during Jan Sobieski's reign. In the earliest recollections this celebration was an event primarily for royalty and for the lesser nobility to enjoy. A true historical account, taken from the sketchy notes of Clermont, secretary to Queen Marysienka, tells of the pomp and elaborate preparations, jotted down for personal record, but never meant for publication. The notes read: "The imposing retinue started in the following order. First came twenty-four tartars in the service of Prince Jacob, riding horseback . . . Then came ten sleighs, each driven by four horses and each carrying an individual orchestra. There were Jewish musicians with cymbals, Ukranians with theorbos, and still others with fifes, drums, and bells . . . All were gathered from different Polish magnates who had a musical band in their own private court . . .

"A caravan, about a fourth mile long, consisting of one hundred and seven sleighs of invited guests followed the musicians. The sleighs contained Persian, leopard, and sable fur robes for the guests, and the horses were colorfully adorned with feathers, ribbon bows, flowers, and tassels . . . Women and girls in the sleigh were accompanied by gentlemen riding horseback on either side. Toward the end of the caravan, a sleigh shaped like Pegasus, carried eight young men who scattered the rhyming greetings to the selected hosts . . . Wherever the party arrived, the gospodarz (host), gave the keys to his wine cellar to the guests, while his wife tended to the food. This is in keeping with Polish tradition indicating that the guests are to make themselves comfortable and eat and drink whatever they pleased . . . There was music, gay laughter, feasting and dancing, and then the caravan hurried on to the next stop . . .

"The last visit was to Wilanova where the King and Queen royally hosted not only the guests but also the servants accompanying them . . ."

Gołębowski wrote about the Polish Kulig as it had been observed before the Saxon reign. He writes, "The Kulig drew people together from outlying districts, and it served as a help to settle quarrels and gave the young people a chance to become acquainted. The atmosphere was always merry and pleasant, and every effort was made not to insult a lesser noble by passing up his home for that of a wealthier landowner . . . It was a gay, buoyant winter pastime, full of spirit, and it brightened the traditional early Polish life."

The history of Kulig is the history of one of the folk festivities of the Polish people, and it has survived through the ages. Though it has changed in details, it is still celebrated to the present day, as testimony to the Polish love of hospitality and friendliness.

CHRISTMAS DAY DINNER

Christmas Day was formerly spent quietly visiting relatives and friends within the family group. Little or no cooking was done on this holy day in the past. Food was reheated or served cold.

Dinner:

HAM	BABKA OR PLECIANKA
POLISH SAUSAGE	STRUCEL
BIGOS — (HUNTERS STEW)	KRUPNIK (LIQUEUR)
RYE BREAD	COFFEE, TEA, MILK

Delicacies and Confections from Wilia Supper.

SUGGESTED CHRISTMAS EVE SUPPERS AND CHRISTMAS DAY DINNER

Appetizers
Pickled herring
Chopped herring
Pickled mushrooms

Soups and Additives
Vegetable stock
Easy barshch
Fish soup
Clear mushroom soup
Ushka
Meatless filling
Egg drops
Dumplings

Pierogi
Cheese and potato filling
Cheese
Mushrooms
Sauerkraut and mushrooms
Prunes
Blueberries and cherries

Fish
Boiled northern pike with horseradish sauce
Baked pike
Trout or pike au gratin
Creamed shrimp with rice
Creamed fish
Fish in aspic
Jellied fish

Sauce
Horseradish

Salad
Herring salad
Sauerkraut, apple, carrot salad

Vegetables
Mushrooms in butter
Creamed mushrooms
Sauerkraut with dried peas
Baked sauerkraut and mushrooms
Red cabbage
Beets in orange sauce
Harvard beets
Green beans
Cauliflower

Desserts
Cottage cheese cake
Cream cheese cake
Cheese cake with sour cream topping
Christmas "Kutia"
Chopins filled cookie
Dried fruit and prune compote
Mazurek
Nut pudding
Poppy seed coffee cake
Nalesniki
Poppy seed filling
Walnut filling
Walnut torte
Polish tea cakes

Liqueur
Hot vodka with honey

Compiled from "Treasured Polish Recipes for Americans."

CHRISTMAS EVE SUPPERS

Seven Course

Herring and pickled mushrooms
Clear barszcz and mushroom *uszka*
Pike with horseradish sauce
Baked sauerkraut with yellow peas
Fried fish with lemon rings
Dried fruit compote
Pastries, coffee, nuts and candies.

Nine Course

Pickled herring and boiled potatoes
Mushroom soup
Pierogi
Baked lake trout
Baked sauerkraut with yellow peas
Fish in aspic
Rice ring with creamed shrimp
Jellied compote
Pastries, coffee, nuts and candies

Eleven Course

Appetizers:
Pickled herring, individual salads, *pierozki*
  with mushrooms and browned butter
Creamed fish soup with dumplings
Pike fillet baked with cream
Baked sauerkraut and mushrooms
Pike in aspic
Cauliflower with crumb and butter topping
Fried fresh salmon and potatoes with tomato sauce
Prune compote
Poppy seed cake
Nut pudding
Pastries, coffee, nuts and candies.

Pickled Herring

Śledzie Marynowane

3 whole salt herrings	4 peppercorns
2 large onions, sliced	4 whole allspice
1 cup vinegar	1 t sugar

Soak herrings in cold water for at least 24 hours. Change water every 8 hours or oftener. Save the milch from herrings. Skin, remove bones and cut each herring into 4 pieces. Arrange onions in a bed on a deep platter. Place herring on top of onions. Boil vinegar and cool. Rub milch through fine sieve, mix with vinegar and sugar and pour over the herring. Serve with whole boiled potatoes.

Chopped Herring

Śledzie Siekane

2 fat salt herrings	3 small onions
3 hard cooked eggs	2 T sweet butter

Do not soak herring. Remove head, tail and skin from herring. Do not remove the bones. Chop herring, eggs and onion very fine. Add butter and mix well. Serve as spread on canapes or appetizers.

Easy Pickled Mushrooms

Łatwe Grzybki Marynowane

1 8-oz. can button mushrooms
1 cup mild vinegar
2 T sugar
1 t salt
1 bay leaf
1 t pickling spices
  (in cloth bag)

Bring vinegar and spices to boiling point. Add mushrooms and liquid and boil for 3 minutes. Cool. Serve whole on toothpicks for canapes or finely chopped, spread on plain or toasted rounds of white, rye or whole wheat bread or salted crackers and serve as appetizers.

Pickled Mushrooms

Grzyby Marynowane

1 peck mushrooms
2 qts. vinegar
Olive oil
¼ cup salt
Small white onions
Whole pepper, allspice
  and bay leaf

Wash mushrooms in cold water. Cook with vinegar and salt for 20 minutes. Let stand over night. Next day, drain, wipe dry and arrange in jars. Blanch and peel onions and put a few in each jar. Cook vinegar with whole pepper, allspice and bay leaf. Cool and cover mushrooms. Add 1 tablespoon of olive oil to each jar.

SOUPS

Vegetable Stock

Postna Zupa

2 qts. cold water	1 onion
4 carrots	2 sprigs parsley
4 stalks celery	2 T butter
Salt and pepper	

Wash vegetables, cut into small pieces and saute in butter under cover until they turn yellow. Add water and simmer for half hour. Strain before serving.

Easy Barshch

Łatwy Barszcz

12 medium beets	1 medium onion, sliced
1 qt. water	Juice of 1 lemon
1 T sugar	2 cups bouillon
Salt and pepper	½ cup sour cream

Wash and peel the beets. Cook beets and onion in water until beets are tender. Add juice of lemon, sugar, salt and pepper. Let stand over night. Strain. Add bouillon (made by using 2 bouillon cubes and 2 cups of hot water). Chill thoroughly and serve in cocktail glasses. Top with sour cream.

Barshch
Barszcz

2 qts. vegetabl stock	1 cup sour cream
1 pt. beet *kwas*	2 T flour

Mix vegetable stock with beet *kwas*. Bring to boiling point and add flour blended with sour cream. Bring to boiling point again and serve with strips of cooked beets, fried croutons or boiled potatoes.

Fish Soup
Zupa z Ryby

2 qts. vegetable stock	½ cup sweet cream
1 bay leaf	Fish or fish head
2 peppercorns	Chopped parsley

If you can spare 3 or 4 sunfish or a small pike, cook it with the vegetable stock and spices for 20 minutes. Lift fish out of soup carefully; strain soup and serve with boiled potatoes. If you have a large pike that you prefer to fry or broil, clean the head thoroughly and cook with vegetable stock and spices. Add half cup of sweet cream to soup just before serving.

Clear Mushroom Soup
Zupa Grzybowa Klarowna

2 qts. vegetable stock
6 large dry mushrooms or
1 cup chopped fresh mushrooms
Chopped dill or parsley

Simmer mushrooms in vegetable stock for 1 hour. Strain. Chop parsley or dill fine and add to soup before serving. You may prefer not to strain the soup if you have used the fresh chopped mushrooms. Serve with *uszka*.

Mushroom Soup with Cream
Zupa Grzybowa

½ lb. mushrooms	1 egg yolk
2 T butter	¼ cup sweet cream
2 T flour	1 cup milk
2 cups water	Salt and pepper

Wash and chop mushrooms. Cook in the butter under cover for 10 minutes. Stir in the flour and cook slowly until the mixture bubbles. Add water and simmer 15 minutes. Beat egg yolk with cream until well blended and add milk. Pour egg mixture slowly into mushrooms. Reheat to just below the boiling point, stirring constantly. Season to taste.

Almond Soup
Zupa migdałowa

6 cups milk
½ pounds almonds
½ cup rice, cooked separately
¼ cup sugar
1 teaspoon almond extract
6 T or ½ cup seedless raisins

Blanch and peel almonds, grind and mash with a little milk. Scald remaining milk and add the other ingredients. Serve after the fish course.

Mushroom Barley Soup

6 dried mushrooms
¼ cup pearl barley
2 qts. water
2 t salt
¼ t pepper
1 large onion chopped
3 T butter
3 T flour
1 cup milk

Soak mushrooms in cold water for 20 min. Slice. Combine mushrooms with barley, water, salt and pepper in kettle, cover, simmer for 45 minutes to 1 hour. Saute onion in butter, add to soup and cook for 30 min. While stirring soup, mix flour with milk and add to soup. Cook stirring for 15 minutes.

SOUP ADDITIVES

Ushka
Uszka

1 egg
½ cup water
2 T mashed potatoes (optional)
½ t salt
2 cups flour

Mound flour on kneading board. Beat egg with water and salt slightly and carefully pour into mound of flour. Mix and add the mashed potatoes. Knead until dough becomes elastic. Cover closely with warm bowl and let stand about 10 minutes. For easier handling, divide the dough in half. Roll out very thin, cut in 2 inch squares. Place half teaspoon of filling a little to one side on each square. Moisten edge with water. Fold over and press edges together. Join the two upper corners. Drop into salted boiling water and cook until they float to top.

Meatless Filling

2 cups cooked chopped mushrooms
1 T chopped onion
3 T butter
Salt and pepper

Fry onion in butter until light brown. Add chopped mushrooms and fry very slowly for 10 minutes. Add pepper and salt. Cool.

Egg Drops
Kluski Lane

2 eggs, beaten	1 T water
¼ t salt	½ cup flour

Mix ingredients and stir until smooth. Pour slowly from end of spoon into boiling soup, and let boil 2 to 3 minutes. If poured into soup from a considerable height, shape of drops will be improved.

Dumplings for Soup

1½ cups flour ½ cup water
2 small eggs, beaten Dash of salt

Mix ingredients and stir until smooth. Drop from wet teaspoon into boiling soup or salted water. Cook uncovered until dumplings come to top.

PIEROGI

Pierogi
Basic Dough

2 cups flour
½ cup warm milk or
½ cup water
1 whole egg and 1 yolk
2 T sour cream
½ t salt
1 t butter for richer dough (optional)

Mix ingredients and knead into soft pliable dough. Let rest for 10 minutes covered with a warm bowl. Divide dough in halves and roll thin. Cut circles with large biscuit cutter. Place a small spoonful of filling a little to one side. Moisten edge with water, fold over and press edges together firmly. Be sure they are well sealed to prevent the filling from running out. Drop pierogi into salted boiling water. Cook gently for 5 minutes. Lift out of water carefully with perforated spoon and serve with melted butter.

Fillings for Pierogi

Cheese and Potatoes

1 heaping cup mashed potatoes
1 small cup dry cottage cheese
Salt and pepper to taste
Few chives or onions, cut fine

Mix thoroughly but lightly and fill. Serve with melted butter and crumbs.

Cheese

1 cup cottage cheese 3 T sugar
1 t melted butter 3 T currants
1 egg beaten 1 t lemon juice

Cream cheese with melted butter. Add other ingredients and mix well. Fill pierogi. Serve with melted butter and sour cream.

Mushrooms

1 cup chopped mushrooms 2 egg yolks
1 onion, chopped fine Butter
Salt and pepper

Saute onion in butter. Add mushrooms. Season. Remove from heat and add egg yolks and stir well. Cool and fill pierogi. Serve with melted butter.

Sauerkraut and Mushrooms

2 cups of sauerkraut
1 cup mushrooms
1 small onion, chopped fine
Butter, salt and pepper

Cook sauerkraut for 10 minutes. Drain and chop fine. Fry onion and chopped mushrooms in butter, add kraut and fry until flavors are blended. Cool and fill circles.

Prunes

1 cup cooked prunes
1 T sugar
1 t lemon juice

Soak prunes in water over nite. Cook with sugar and lemon juice. When cool, remove stones and fill pierogi. Serve with bread crumbs browned in melted butter or with whipped cream.

Fruit: Blueberries or Cherries

1 qt. of blueberries or 2 lbs. of pitted cherries
Mix the fruit with 2 T bread crumbs. Spoon and fill each circle, fold, seal the edges and cook. Serve with melted butter and sweetened sour cream.

FISH

Boiled Northern Pike with Horseradish Sauce
Szczupak w Sosie Chrzanowym

3 lbs. pike
4 cups vegetable stock
Salt and pepper
Horseradish sauce

Clean fish thoroughly and cut into 3 inch pieces. Pour cold stock over fish and simmer slowly for about half hour until tender. While cooking, add 1 tablespoon of cold water to the fish three times. Remove fish carefully to platter and cover with horseradish sauce.

Baked Pike
Sandacz Pieczony

1 pike — salt — onion
½ cup melted butter
1 cup cream
1 cup white wine
Juice of 1 lemon

Salt fish, cover with onion slices and let stand at least one hour. Place in roasting pan and cover with cream, wine and lemon juice. Baste frequently. Bake at 350° for 30 to 45 minutes.

Trout or Pike Au Gratin
Pstrąg lub Szczupak Au Gratin

3 lbs. trout or pike
½ cup butter
½ cup bread crumbs
1 cup chopped mushrooms
1 small onion, chopped
1 cup grated Parmesan cheese
½ cup fish stock or water

Brush the grill with butter and sprinkle with bread crumbs. On this place the whole fish. Sprinkle generously with bread crumbs, the mushrooms and onion browned in butter, and the grated cheese. Dot generously with pieces of butter. Add stock. Bake in 350° oven for 45 minutes.

Creamed Shrimp with Rice
Potrawka z Krewetkow

3 cups cooked rice	1 cup milk
2 cups cooked shrimp	1 t lemon juice
2 T butter	Salt and pepper
2 T flour	Chopped parsley

Melt butter, blend in flour and cook until mixture bubbles. Add milk gradually, stirring constantly until smooth. Reduce heat and cook for three minutes. Add lemon juice and seasoning. Add shrimp. Mound hot rice on large platter, cover with the creamed mixture. Garnish with parsley.

Creamed Fish
Ryby Duszone w Śmietanie

Fish, cut in pieces	½ cup cream
2 large onions, grated	Salt and pepper
¼ cup butter	Lemon juice

Rub pieces of fish with grated onion and saute in melted butter. Add cream and seasonings and cook 5 minutes. Serve with a sprinkle of lemon juice and garnish with lemon slices.

Fish in Aspic
Ryba w Galarecie

3 lbs. pike
4 cups vegetable stock
4 peppercorns
3 bay leaves
6 capers or cooked mushrooms
1 T gelatine
2 T water
1 egg white

Clean fish. Remove head and thoroughly clean it. Cook head and spices in vegetable stock for half hour. Strain. Place whole fish in pan. Cover with the strained stock and simmer for half hour until tender. Remove fish, cook stock. To clarify stock, add slightly beaten egg white and bring to boiling point, stirring lightly. Strain through napkin twice. Dissolve gelatin in water, add to stock. Pour over the cooled fish. Garnish with capers, carrot rings, hard-cooked eggs and lemon slices.

Jellied Fish

1 carp (about 4 lbs.)
2 large onions, sliced
2 qts. water
salt
2 T sugar
½ t each of salt and gr. pepper.

Clean carp and slice in ½ in. pieces. Salt and let stand about 1 hr. In the meantime simmer onions for 20 min. add seasonings. Place the sliced fish in a pot and simmer for 10 to 20 min. over low heat. Put the fish in a large container where liquid covers the fish. When cooled put in refrigerator to jell.

SAUCE

Fluffy Horseradish Sauce
Chrzan z Bitą Smietaną

1 cup horseradish
1 cup whipped cream
Dash of ground pepper

Fold horseradish into whipped cream, add pepper.

Horseradish Sauce

½ cup grated horseradish	
1 cup sour cream	1½ t salt
1 T flour	2 T lemon juice or vinegar
1 T butter	1 t sugar

Melt butter in double boiler. Add horseradish, sour cream and flour and stir well to avoid lumps. Bring to boiling point and cook until thick. Add vinegar or lemon juice, salt and sugar. Serve hot or cold.

SALAD

Herring Salad

Toss together gently 4 cups firmly cooked potatoes, diced, and 1½ cups chopped pickled or smoked herring. Add 1 tablespoon each of minced onion and chopped dill and ⅔ cup French dressing. Chill the salad for at least 1 hour. Add 1 hard-boiled egg, diced, toss the salad gently, garnish it with minced parsley. Serve it with pickled beets.

Sauerkraut, Apple, Carrot Salad
Kiszona Kapusta z Jabłkami z Marchwią

2 cups sauerkraut	½ t salt
1 large apple, peeled and diced	3 T vegetable oil
2 carrots, grated	1 t caraway seed
1 T sugar	

Rinse and squeeze sauerkraut, chop fine. Add apple and carrots, mix seasoning, sugar caraway seed and oil with fork and stir into the salad. Chill.

VEGETABLES

Mushrooms in Butter

Grzyby w Maśle

1 lb. mushrooms	2 T buttered crumbs
3 T butter	1 t parsley, chopped
1 T onion, chopped	Salt and pepper

Fry onion in butter. Slice mushrooms and add to onion. Add seasonings and simmer slowly for 20 minutes. When mushroom liquid disappears, add crumbs, mix well and serve hot.

Creamed Mushrooms

Grzyby Duszone

1 lb. mushrooms
1 medium onion, chopped
3 T butter
1 T flour or bread crumbs
1 cup sweet cream
Salt and pepper

Chop mushooms. Cover with boiling water. Saute onion in butter. Strain mushrooms and add to onion. Season and cook for 30 minutes. Blend flour with cream, add to mushrooms and simmer for 10 minutes.

Buckwheat Groats

Kasza gryczana

1 cup groats or kasha
1 egg
1 teas. salt
8 T butter or ¼ stick
2-3 cups boiling water or chicken bouillon
4 cubes of bouillon
1 cup chopped onions
½ lb. fresh mushrooms, green pepper opt.

Cook onions and mushrooms in butter, combine egg, wheat or kasha and salt and add to onions. Pour liquid and bring to boil. Cover casserole and bake in 350° oven till water is absorbed. Serve as vegetable, in soups or with gravy.

Sauerkraut with Whole Dried Peas

Groch z Kapustą

1 qt. sauerkraut
½ cup dry mushrooms, chopped
1 onion sauteed in margarine
1 cup whole dried peas
Salt and pepper

Wash peas and soak in water overnight. Cook in same water, and add more if you have to, until tender, about one hour. Rinse sauerkraut. Wash and chop mushrooms. Cover sauerkraut and mushrooms with water, add salt and cook for one hour. Add peas, put into buttered covered baking dish and bake for half hour at 325°. Smelts or anchovies are sometimes added to this dish for *Wilia* supper.

If you decide to serve sauerkraut and peas on days other than fast days, cook sauerkraut and peas in the same way. When sauerkraut and peas are tender, thicken with a sauce made as follows:

½ lb. salt pork or bacon, chopped
1 onion, chopped fine
2 T flour
1 cup sauerkraut liquid

Fry onion with salt pork or bacon, until lightly browned. Blend in flour and add liquid. Stir until smooth and mix with sauerkraut and peas.

Baked Sauerkraut and Mushrooms

Kapusta z grzybami

1 qt. sauerkraut rinsed, and squeezed
1 ounce dried mushrooms soaked for 2 hrs. in ½ cup water
1 large onion, diced
1 tart apple, diced
½ teaspoon caraway seed (opt.)
2 T shortening
2 T instant flour
Some brown sugar to taste
Salt

Cook sauerkraut with mushrooms and water till tender, remove mushrooms and cut into strips. Brown onion in shortening, add flour and liquid from sauerkraut. Add diced apple, caraway seed, brown sugar and salt to sauerkraut and bake in buttered dish for one hour at 325°.

Red Cabbage

Czerwona kapusta

1 small onion, chopped
2 T bacon drippings or margarine
1 medium head red cabbage, shredded
2 apples, sliced
1 t sugar
2 T lemon juice
Salt and pepper
1 t caraway seed, opt.

Saute onion in drippings, add cabbage and apples, cover. Cook slowly for 15 minutes. Add lemon juice and sugar. Salt and pepper. Toss lightly.

Beets in Orange Sauce

Buraki

2 cans sliced beets	½ t salt
2 T butter or margarine	½ cup orange juice
1 T flour	1 T lemon juice
¼ cup water	½ t grated orange peel
1 T corn syrup	

Melt butter add flour and blend. Add rest of ingredients and cook till thick — over low heat. Add beets and heat for few minutes.

Harvard Beets

1 can beets (whole)
½ can of orange juice (6 oz. can)
½ cup sugar
½ t salt
½ cup vinegar
2 T butter
1 T cornstarch

Mix sugar, cornstarch and salt. Add to boiling juice and vinegar. Cook 5 minutes stirring constantly. Add butter and pour over beets and let stand awhile. Heat and serve.

Pickled Beets
Ćwikła

10 medium-sized beets
3 T grated horseradish
¼ t caraway seed
1 T sugar
1½ cup cider vinegar
½ cup water
1 T salt

Cook beets until tender. Slip off skins by holding under cold running water. Cut into thin slices. In glass or earthenware bowl, arrange layers of beets and sprinkle with horseradish and caraway seed. Boil the vinegar, salt, sugar and water and pour over beets. Let stand 24 hours.

Green Beans
Groch Szparagowy

1 small onion
½ lb. mushrooms
1 lb. string beans
Butter
Salt and pepper
Sour cream

Cook beans that have been juliened in small amount of water till tender. Saute the mushrooms in butter with small onion chopped fine. Add little salt and pepper and when ready to serve pour ½ cup sour cream over the beans.

Cauliflower
Kalafior

1 cauliflower, 2 to 3 lbs.
1 T vinegar
3 T butter
½ cup bread crumbs
2 hard-cooked eggs
1 t parsley
Salt
Dash of nutmeg

Soak cauliflower, head down, in cold water with vinegar for about half hour to draw out any insects. Drain well before cooking. Place in boiling water and cook for 5 minutes. Drain. Cover with fresh boiling water and cook about 25 minutes until tender. Salt during cooking. Do not over-cook. When done, lift out carefully and cover with bread crumbs browned in the melted butter. Chop eggs and sprinkle over cauliflower with parsley and nutmeg.

DESSERTS

Poppy Seed Coffee Cake
Strucel z makiem

1 cup milk
¼ cup lukewarm water
2 yeast cakes
¼ cup butter
½ cup sugar
1 t salt
4 egg yolks
4 cups flour
1 t vanilla
½ t almond

Scald milk and cool until lukewarm. Beat egg yolks with salt until thick. Cream butter and sugar. Add flavoring and egg yolks. Dissolve yeast in lukewarm water and add. Add sifted flour alternately with cooled milk, beginning and ending with flour. Knead until dough leaves the fingers. Cover with damp cloth and let rise in warm place until double in bulk. Punch down and let rise again until doubled. On floured board divide dough in two. Roll each half into rectangular shape to thickness of finger. Spread with poppy seed filling. Roll up tightly beginning with wide side. Seal edges by pinching together. Place in two greased pans about 13 x 4½ x 2½. Cover and let rise until dough fills pan. Bake 45 minutes in 350° oven.

Poppy Seed Filling

2 cups ground poppy seed
1½ cups milk
1 cup sugar or ¾ c honey
2 eggs
1 t vanilla
½ t almond
½ c golden raisins

Scald milk and add poppy seed. Cook until milk is absorbed, stirring constantly (about 5 min.). Add sugar and cook a little longer. Beat eggs slightly. Stir a little of the hot poppy seed mixture into the eggs. Then add to poppy seed, stir until thick but do not boil. Remove from heat and as it is cooling add flavoring. Use when cold.

* *Canned poppy seed filling can be used.*

Fillings for Coffee Cakes
Mixed Filling

1½ lbs. ground poppy seed
1 cup honey
3 cups thin cream
1 cup sugar
½ cup chopped raisins
¼ cup butter
1½ cups walnuts, ground

Mix ingredients in large iron skillet. Place over a low fire, stirring constantly until thick, for about 30 minutes. This burns easily. Cool before spreading on dough. This is enough to spread about one-quarter inch thick.

Nut Meat Filling

1 lb. mixed nut meats, chopped
½ cup butter
1 egg
1 cup sugar
1 lemon rind, grated
Cinnamon or vanilla
¼ cup cream

Melt butter, add beaten egg. Brush dough with butter and egg mixture. Spread with chopped nut meats. Cover with sugar, lemon rind, cinnamon and cream.

Walnut Filling

2 cups ground walnuts
½ cup butter
1 cup sugar
½ cup milk
2 egg yolks

Mix ingredients and cook for 5 minutes. Cool and spread on dough.

Christmas "Kutia"
Kutia Wigilijna

1 cup wheat
2 cups water
1 cup honey
2 cups water
1 cup poppy seed
1 cup gr. almonds or walnuts

Soak wheat for six hours. Cook in water until tender. Cook honey with water. Cool and serve with wheat. This dish is traditionally served in the southeastern provinces of Poland with other foods on Christmas Eve. Stir this mixture of wheat and water during cooking to prevent sticking. Grind the poppyseed or can of Solo poppy seed may be substituted. Cook honey and water to boiling and add this syrup to poppy seed and wheat mixture. Add ground nuts and place in refrigerator serve cold.

Dried Fruit or Prune Compote

1 lb. mixed dried fruit or prunes (tenderized prunes)
2 cups water
1½ cup sugar
Grated rind and juice of 1 lemon
1 inch stick cinnamon or 6 whole cloves
Brandy, opt.

All fruit in compote should be rinsed then soaked in 2 cups of water for several hours or overnite. Drain the liquid, add the sugar and heat till sugar is dissolved. Pour over the fruit and add lemon juice, rind, cinn. stick and brandy. Refrigerate.

Nut Pudding

6 eggs separated
½ cup sugar
1½ cups walnuts or almonds
Lemon peel and orange peel
Bread crumbs, butter and flour for mold

Cream egg yolks with sugar add lemon and orange peel. If almonds are used scald peel and chop. Fold in stiffly-beaten egg whites and mix with egg yolks and ground walnuts. Pour into buttered mold lined with bread crumbs and steam for 45 minutes. May be served with wine or vanilla sauce or whipped cream.

Cottage Cheese Cake
Serowiec

8 large graham crackers
1 T sugar
⅓ cup melted butter
¼ t cinnamon

Roll graham crackers fine. Mix with other ingredients and press firmly into the sides and bottom of an 8 x 11 inch cake pan. Keep 2 tablespoons of crumbs to sprinkle over top of cake.

Cheese Filling

1 lb. dry cottage cheese	1 cup heavy cream
4 eggs	Juice of 1 lemon
1 cup sugar	Grated rind of 1 lemon
½ t salt	1 T Cream of Wheat
¼ cup flour	¼ c golden raisins
½ t vanilla	

Press cheese through sieve. Add salt to eggs and beat thoroughly. Add sugar, flavoring and cream. Carefully fold in the cheese and flour. Mix well. Pour on graham cracker crumbs in pan. Sprinkle remaining crumbs on top. Bake 1 hour in 250° oven. At end of hour, turn off heat and leave the cake in oven for another hour. For a large cake double or triple the recipe.

Cream Cheese Cake
Serowiec

Crust:
1 cup sifted enriched flour
¼ cup sugar
1 t grated lemon peel
½ cup butter or margarine
1 slightly beaten egg yolk
¼ t vanilla

Combine flour, sugar, and lemon peel. Cut in butter till mixture is crumbly. Add egg yolk and vanilla. Blend thoroughly. Pat ⅓ of dough on bottom of 9-inch spring-form pan (sides removed). Bake in hot oven (400°) about 6 minutes, or till golden; cool. Butter sides of pan and attach to the bottom. Pat remaining dough evenly on sides to a height of 2 inches.

Cheese Filling:

5 8-ounce packages cream cheese
1¾ cups sugar — ¼ t vanilla
3 T enriched flour — 5 eggs
¾ t grated lemon peel — 2 egg yolks
¼ t salt — ¼ cup heavy cream

Stir cream cheese to soften; beat until fluffy. Combine sugar, flour, peel, salt, and vanilla; gradually blend into cheese. Add eggs and yolks, one at a time, beating well after each addition. Stir in cream. Turn into pastry-lined pan. Bake in extremely hot oven (500°) 12 minutes. Do not open oven door. Reduce oven temperature to very low (200) degrees. Bake cake one hour longer. Remove from oven. Cool on wire rack away from draft. Cake will shrink slightly as it cools. When cool, loosen cake from pan with spatula. Remove side of pan and chill cake.

Serve with frozen strawberries that have been thawed, or crushed pineapple.

Other Variations

Cheesecake with Sour Cream Topping

In a bowl mix together 1½ cups graham cracker crumbs, 5 tbs. melted butter, and 1 tbs. sugar. Press the mixture into a baking dish about 9 x 13 by 1¾ inches.

Put 3-8 oz. packages cream cheese, softened to room temperature, in a bowl and with an electric mixer or a wooden spoon beat in 5 eggs, one at a time. Slowly stir in 1 cup sugar and 1½ tsp. vanilla. Pour the cheese mixture over the crumb mixture and bake the cake in a slow oven (300°) F for 1 hour. Combine 3 cups sour cream with ½ cup sugar and 1½ tsp. vanilla, spread the topping over the cheese mixture, and let the cake stand for 3 minutes. Raise the oven temperature to a moderate (350° F.) and bake the cake for 5 minutes. Chill the cake for several hours.

Walnut Torte
Tort Orzechowy

12 eggs, separated
1 cup sugar
6 T flour
½ lb. walnuts, ground fine

Beat egg yolks until thick and lemon-colored. Add sugar gradually. Add the walnuts and flour and mix thoroughly. Fold in stiffly beaten egg whites. Bake in three layer cake pans for 30 to 35 minutes in 350° oven.

Filling

½ lb. walnuts, ground fine
1 cup powdered sugar
½ cup sweet cream

Mix well and spread between layers of cake.

Frosting

1 egg yolk
1 heaping T butter
3 T brandy
Powdered sugar to thicken

Mix and spread on top and sides of cake.

Chopins
Sandwich cookies with jam

1 c. soft butter
½ c. sugar
2 c. flour
1 c. finely chopped walnuts
Jam

Blend the butter, sugar, flour and nuts. Roll on lightly floured cloth-covered board to about a ¼ in. thickness. Have rolling pin covered with a baby stocking. Cut circles using the doughnut hole cutter. Bake on ungreased cookie sheets for about 10 min. in a moderate oven (350) degrees. Remove from cookie sheets. Cool. Frost or make into sandwiches.

Polish Tea Cakes
Ciastka z Konserwą

½ cup butter
½ cup sugar
1 egg yolk, slightly beaten
1 cup flour
½ t salt
½ t vanilla
½ cup chopped nuts
½ cup fruit preserves

Cream butter and sugar until light. Add egg yolk, mix well. Add flour sifted with salt. Mix. Roll dough in small balls, dip in unbeaten egg white and roll in finely chopped nuts. Place on buttered baking sheet and press down center of each with thimble. Bake in 325° oven for 5 minutes. Remove and press down again with thimble and return to oven for about 10 to 15 minutes. Remove from oven and fill identation with preserves while still warm.

Mazurek

1½ c. sugar — 1 c. chopped nuts
2 c. flour — Juice of 1 orange
¼ t salt — and 1 lemon
½ c. soft butter — Candied cherries
3 eggs — Pineapple in 3 colors
3 T heavy cream — Citron and orange peel
1¼ c. golden raisins — 1 jigger of rum
1 lb. pitted dates, cut up

Mix 1 c. sugar, flour and salt, cut in butter. Add 1 egg and the cream. Mix until well blended. Spread in a 15 x 10 x 1 pan. Bake in (350 degree) oven 20 min. Mix remaining eggs, ½ c. sugar, raisins, nuts and fruit. Spread on pastry. Bake 20 min. longer. Cut into bars. Decorate. Makes 4 doz.

Naleśniki

2 eggs, separated
1 cup flour
1 cup milk
¼ cup water
2 T butter and cube of pork fat to grease pan

¼ t salt, rounded
1 t sugar
1 t melted butter

Mix ingredients as above, except egg whites beat until stiff and fold in last.

Fillings:

Cheese

Spread thin on pancake, fold either into narrow roll or in 4 making a triangle. Fry in butter until lightly browned

1 large Philadelphia cream cheese
2 T sugar
Pineapple juice or vanilla for flavor

Fruits

Use any thick cooked preserves. Roll the cakes, sprinkle with red wine and powdered sugar and bake in 350° oven for 10 minutes.

Naleśniki

3 eggs
3 t flour
2 T sugar

½ cup milk
¼ t salt

Beat eggs well, then carefully add flour to avoid lumps. Add milk and salt.

Use olive oil or unsalted butter in frying pan. They burn quickly in salted butter. Some cooks prefer to use a piece of salt pork on end of fork for greasing frying pan. When pan is hot, pour in a small amount of batter, only enough to make a paper thin pancake. When medium brown turn over and remove from pan. Spread with good cherry or strawberry jam. Roll and dust lightly with powdered sugar and serve warm as a dessert. By tilting the hot frying pan in all directions, the batter will spread quickly. To assure tenderness the pancake should not be turned. This is a secret of fine *nalesniki*.

LIQUEUR

Hot Vodka with Honey
Krupnik

1 cup honey
1 cup water
Cloves, a few
2-inch piece vanilla
Bean or 1 t vanilla

Dash of cinnamon or
    stick cinnamon
¼ t fresh ground nutmeg
Lemon rind
2 cups of vodka or pure alcohol

Bring honey and water, combined with vanilla, spices and lemon rind to boil. Allow to boil again, remove from heat, cover and set aside for at least 20 minutes to steep. Add Vodka or alcohol; heat and serve piping hot.

A CHRISTMAS PLAY
JASELKA
— based on —
POLISH NATIVITY PLAYS
in
THREE ACTS
With Songs, Carols and Piano Accompaniment

CAST

CAROLERS— adults and children in Polish regional costumes

LEADER OF CAROLERS

SHEPHERDS (Appear in Zakopane costumes)

    BARTOSZ, the baca, the old leader of the shepherds

JÓZIK, Shepherd	ANTEK, Shepherd
WOJTEK, Shepherd	WALEK, Shepherd
FRANEK, Shepherd	KUBA, Shepherd
JASIEK, Shepherd	

    GRZESZ, young small shepherd boy

    KAZIK, another small shepherd boy

    ANGEL, messenger from Heaven

HEROD, King of the Jews

PAGE, HEROD'S page

CENTURION, captain of the palace guards

BALTHASAR, King of the Orient

CASPAR, King of the Orient

MELCHIOR, King of the Orient

RABBI I, from the Temple of Solomon

RABBI II, from the Temple of Solomon

KWINTUS, General of the Roman army

ARCHANGEL MICHAEL

BORUTA, Polish devil of the *Łeczycki Bogs*[*], has horns, a tail, dark garment

KUSY, a comical dwarf devil, has horns, tail and is clothed in some animal fur

GUARDS of the court

PEOPLE of the court

TWO KRAKOW LADS, wearing Krakow costumes

KRAKOWIAN and KRAKOWIANKA, in Krakow costumes

KUJAWIAN and KUJAWIANKA, in Kujawy costume

PRINCE, in semi-royal costume

PRINCESS, in semi-royal costume

MARCINOWA, fat Polish vender (woman)

ICEK, a Jewish vender (man)

MARY, mother of the newborn Babe

JOSEPH, MARY's spouse

PIAST, one of the rulers of Ancient Poland and attendants (PIAST wears homespun robe)

* Pronounced — Win chēet-skēe

55

JASELKA*

PROLOGUE

(It is dusk, a street scene in a Polish village. CAROL-ERS, adults and children appear in Polish regional costumes, and sing under lighted window of a cottage. One of them carries a huge lighted star on a pole.)

CAROLERS: (sing) TODAY IN BETHLEHEM,†
Dzisiai W Betleiem
GLORIA, GLORIA IN EXCELSIS DEO ‡

LEADING CAROLER: (Steps forward and recites prologue)
Praised be the Lord Jesus Christ!

> We bring to you this day gentle people,
> A traditional Jasełko, famous and old.
> Strange scenes will appear before you
> Therefore, incline your ears as the drama unfolds,
> And give attention to the story told.

> You will hear about the garden of Eden
> Adam's sin and Eve's part in it,
> As both ate of the fruit forbidden;
> And how this thoughtless act provoked God's wrath,
> And closed to man the gates of heaven.

> You will see King Herod in anger;
> You will fret o'er the Christ Child's danger,
> But you really need not bother,
> Since this is a concern of God, the Father.
> Praise be to Him forever and ever.

> On the hay you will see tiny Jesus,
> Beside Him, kneeling, Mother Mary and old Joseph;
> Sleepy shepherds bearing their gifts,
> And the Kings from the East with their offerings,
> Will come to the stable gates.

> Now that I have told everything
> From the beginning to the end,
> Accurately and well, not losing the thread,
> I can tell you gentle people, the stage is set,
> The curtain opens, and we begin our performance.

> Humbly I take leave of you.
> Praised be the Lord Jesus Christ.

---

* *Pronounced yah-sĕl'kah*
† *Music p. 72*
‡ *Music p. 73*

ACT I

*(The stage represents a pasture land with a small hill, including some foliage. There is a bonfire at the center of the stage with the SHEPHERDS, JASIEK, FRANEK, JÓZIK** beside it. JASIEK is stooping to adjust the fire, sits near it, deep in thought. FRANEK is stretched out in sleeping position. JÓZIK sits on a hillside, watching his sheep, while whittling on his new flute.)*

JÓZIK: (sings) HEY, HEY, MY LAMBKINS *

> Hey, hey my lambkins precious
> Oxen and sheep, hear this —
> Graze well upon this pasture
> Stay together, near.

> Hey, hey, while fresh food you take
> My flute of wood I'll make;
> Hey, I will play it for you
> While you graze in view.

> Hey, on the hillside yonder
> Grass there is much greener
> Hey, I know you would go there
> If I was not here.

BARTOSZ: (*off stage calls out as from a distance*) *He-lo, Bysiu,*† *He-lo!*

JASIEK: Old BARTOSZ is on his way.

WOJTEK: (*sings off stage*) I'LL TAKE MY VIOLIN ‡
WEZME JA SE SKRZYPKI

---

 * *Music p. 71*
** *Pronounced — yu' zēēk, with "z" like in azure*
 † *Pronounced — bēē' shōō*
 ‡ *Music p. 74*

56

I'll make a violin of the whitest linden,
Then by stream of flowing water,
Play the music I love,
Sing the songs I treasure,
Till the setting of the bright sun:
When I play melodies,
Hey, upon my violin,
O'er the running waters, hey,
They'll float o'er the cool mist,
Spreading and swelling,
And my voice on fresh dew,
Will ever travel with the wind.

FRANEK: (*stretching and yawning*) Really all day a person works, chasing the sheep, calling the dogs, and when he wishes to sleep, he has to listen to this. (*pointing to direction of singing*)

JÓZIK: O, stop your grumbling! I like to hear WOJTEK sing and when I sing I am happy! Now I will sing you a song you might really enjoy. (*walks toward FRANEK*)

FRANEK: Spare me please. I've heard them all.

JASIEK: I will accompany you on my fujarka*

JÓZIK (*sings*) IN THE VILLAGE†

In the village tavern tall,
Danced the brigands, large and small;
Ordered music, loud and gay,
Folks to watch their feet at play. Hu, Ha! (*dances*)
I will dance no more today;
Hurt my leg along the way;
Crooked legs won't dance, you know;
If I jump, they'll bend and go! Hu, Ha!
Nor can I sing more right now
For I really don't know how;
All the notes have left me too,
Through the big hole in my shoe. Hu, Ha!

BARTOSZ: (*calls off stage from a distance*) He-lo, By-siu, he-lo! Hej, SHEPHERDS! Are you watching? Stay awake. There are wolves about. He-lo! He-lo!

FRANEK: (*rising quickly to answer BARTOSZ's call*) Yes, yes! We are all awake!

JASIEK: (*sings*) Now it's my turn to sing. Listen to this. FRANEK LOOKED OUT‡

FRANEK: Remind me to give you sixty crow eggs, and something that will not be in a sack, a good whack on your precious back! Really, SHEPHERDS, I would like a little nap. (*Lies down beside the fire again*) Please be quiet!

JÓZIK: Pardon me, but where and when may I come for the feast of the scrambled eggs?

FRANEK: Anytime, when JASIEK catches enough mosquitos and renders their fat, so that he will have plenty for the frying.

JASIEK: I'll catch the mosquitos. JÓZIK will render the fat if FRANEK eats the eggs. Is it a bargain?

* Foo yar' kah — hand-made wooden fife or blow pipe.
† Music p. 75
‡ Music p. 76

JÓZIK

FRANEK: O, please be quiet and lie down beside me. We all need a rest. (JASIEK *and* JÓZIK *come closer to* FRANEK, *taking comfortable relaxing positions.* FRANEK *looks up at the sky.* SHEPHERDS *are quiet for a few moments*) All those bright stars up there! They really bother me.

JASIEK: But why should they? I like to watch them. Then the night seems only half as long.

FRANEK: Those mysterious stars seem to shine right through my eyelids when I close them.

JÓZIK: That is strange. They never bother me. . . . You know FRANEK, some people say strange signs are appearing in the sky.

FRANEK: Where? Among all those stars? Why?

JÓZIK: Who knows? Some people say the signs predict a terrible war. Others, that they foretell the coming of a Messiah, a man from heaven, the Son of God.

JASIEK: Oh, if he came, O my dear God, I would look for Him to the ends of the earth. I would truly and . . .

JÓZIK: (*interrupting*) What do you think, foolish one, that you could talk to Him as to one of us? Even to an earthly king, no one here would dare speak face to face. What then, to a divine messenger, a Son of God!

WOJTEK: (*enters singing*)

MAZURKA* – MAZUR

A good shepherd boy am I,
Living like a king.
I awaken in the evening
To watch sheep and sing.
Hu ha! dana da!
Dana mine, O dana,
Watch and sing;
Hu ha! dana da
Dana mine, O dana, Hu ha!

* Music p. 77

57

FRANEK: He has come! And he will be sounding off all night. Not one of us will get any sleep.

JÓZIK: Never mind! You are always grumpy, attacking like a thorn on a bush. WOJTEK's song reminds me of one my father used to sing. These were the words:

I'm a happy shepherd, though my life is simple,
Happier than princes' with their gold and title.
While I lay beneath the sky, sleeping, dreaming
They sleep on soft beds and drink with their fancy
    eating.
Indulgence brings woe on the morrow
And their great joys may bring them sorrow.
While a shepherd, though a poor lad
Is never ever ever sad!

Remember that FRANEK

WOJTEK: (sings) SONG* — KRAKOWIACZEK

FRANEK: Have you gone crazy singing this time of the night. A person can't even close his eyelids.

JASIEK: (sings) LITTLE FRANEK.†

BARTOSZ: (calling from off stage) He-lo, Bysiu! He-lo!

JÓZIK: (looking to side of stage, from where the voice is coming) Old BARTOSZ is coming. He will have some news for us. (SHEPHERDS sit up.)

BARTOSZ: (enters with shepherds, ANTEK, WALEK, KUBA, KAZIK and GRZESZ. BARTOSZ carries a shepherd's crook) I am glad you are all alert. (Looks up at the sky and says slowly) I cannot recall ever seeing such a pretty sight as lay before my eyes this beautiful night. The shimmering stars appear so near and bright, though the day is almost here. (Looking at the shepherds) Have you noticed the dark birds, the magpies, the wagtails, finches and sparrows, who are poor like we, chattering in their nests so happily? Something unusual is about to happen. I can feel it.

JASIEK: What could happen?

BARTOSZ: Who can tell what God's intentions are? Many people talk about the Messiah, a messenger of God, who will save mankind.

JASIEK: Dear BARTOSZ. We shepherds seldom hear about God. Tell us more. Where will He come from? What will he bring us? From what will he save us?

BARTOSZ: (slowly) What I can I will tell. When God created the earth and Adam and Eve, there was no death, illness or jealousy, only love and happiness. Adam and Eve lived in a paradise, a beautiful big land filled with lush vegetation and many interesting animals. Adam and Eve had freedom and could do whatever they wished on one condition: they must not eat the fruit of the apple tree. The devil who was always against God, and wanting to make trouble for Him, heard about this, so he quickly changed himself into a snake, one of the favorite animals of Eve. In this disguise, he flattered her and coaxed Eve to pick an apple from the forbidden tree. She ate some of it, gave it to Adam, and he also ate of the apple. This was an act of disobedience and God was greatly offended. It was then, He banished Adam and Eve from paradise forever. Henceforth they would know poverty, hate, jealousy, illness and death. But God was merciful. He did not send them out into the great darkness. God gave them the sun, the great, beautiful, light- and heat-giving sun.

JÓZIK: And now the sun is ours and belongs to the earth. But continue good BARTOSZ, we want to hear more.

BARTOSZ: (Speaks slowly, distinctly) Afterwards God said to Adam and Eve that since it was a woman who was responsible for the original sin, it would be another woman who would redeem man from it. She will be a virgin, chosen by God to become the mother of His divine Son. He, it is said, will be the Savior of mankind. This dear SHEPHERDS, is as I understand it. Many people are waiting for the Messiah, some over four thousand years. Let us pray He will come soon.

BARTOSZ and SHEPHERDS: (bow heads, take off hats) Dear God, send the Messiah, we pray!

BARTOSZ: The cattle are quiet and resting now. We also could relax. Our watch will come soon enough. (SHEPHERDS take comfortable sleeping positions)

JÓZIK: (confidentially) JASIEK, did I tell you . . .

FRANEK: (interrupting) There it goes again! —Jabber, jabber, jabber! How can anyone sleep?

BARTOSZ: Quiet please, everybody! (SHEPHERDS are quiet, lights are dimmed. After a few minutes CAROLERS sing off stage, softly at first, then louder)

CAROLERS: (sing) LORD DESCENDS FROM HEAVEN* — PAN Z NIEBA I Z LONA

JASIEK: (suddenly awakening) What was that? I heard some singing. (listens again) Was I dreaming? (returns to sleep)

CAROLERS: (sing off stage) GLORIA, GLORIA IN EXCELSIS DEO†

JASIEK: (Awakens at end of singing more startled than previously) As I live I heard some singing. (Looks about him) Where did it come from? Could it be the wind breathing through the branches. (Suddenly a bright yellow light appears. JASIEK is frightened) A fire! Something is burning! It's a walking flame! O my God, save us! SHEPHERDS, wake up! Wake up! (Runs to arouse them)

FRANEK: What is it? What is the matter?

JASIEK: A fire! Look, it's coming nearer!

JÓZIK: O great God! Our huts are burning!

* Music p. 78
† Music p. 79

* Music p. 80
† Music p. 73

FRANEK: The flames seem farther away. They could be over Bethlehem.

JASIEK: (*Guards his eyes to protect them from the blinding light*) Yes, yes, the brilliance is there.

JOZIK: (*runs to rouse* BARTOSZ) Wake up dear BARTOSZ! Wake up! Tell us what to do! (*CAROLERS softly hum Gloria etc.*)

BARTOSZ: (*Rubs his eyes, gets up, talks slowly, is frightened*) What is all this commotion? What is that great light? O my God, the sky is opening! An army flies from heaven — I hear music. — The army sings while it is burning the earth with its long rays. — The flames are spreading and appear to be coming closer — O my God, what is happening?

BARTOSZ: (*sings*) BROTHERS, LOOK THERE YONDER* — BRACIA PATRZCIE JENO

JASIEK: O my dear God, I am frightened. Let us dig a ditch and crawl into it, or run away!

JÓZIK: It is the end of the world! The end of all of us!

BARTOSZ: (*Sings to* SHEPHERDS *who are still sleeping*)

HEY, BROTHERS ARE YOU SLEEPING†
HEJ! BRACIA, CZY WY ŚPICIE*

1. Hey brothers are you sleeping?
    Shepherds are you watching?
    Events never heard of
    Now seem to be occurring.
    O God. Dear God!
    What is this mysterious happening?
    Bright the night! It is not the day.
    Bright the night! It is not the day.

SHEPHERDS: (*sing*)

2. We shepherds are watching
    To us it is fright'ning,
    Seeing this great miracle.
    O God! Dear God!
    O, what is really happ'ning?
    Hearts beat with great consternation,
    Hearts beat with our great consternation.

BARTOSZ: (*sings*)

3. O look! the great sky opens
    See the countless army!
    It is an army of celestial soldiers.
    O God, our frightened hearts
    Beat with great consternation
    O God, our frightened hearts beat
    With consternation.

JÓZIK: BARTOSZ please! We must do something!

JASIEK: Yes, yes, what will we do?

BARTOSZ: (*slowly, distinctly, loudly*) Calm yourselves SHEPHERDS! It will be all right. The army you see in the great light, are not soldiers as we thought, but heavenly angels. See their hair is golden and they wear silver gowns. Do not worry, I beg of you! We will wait here. They have seen us. At this very moment, one of

* Music p. 81
† Music p. 82

BARTOSZ

the heavenly creatures is flying toward us. Quickly, let us kneel! We will wait to hear what is demanded of us. (*As* SHEPHERDS *listen quietly, they are startled by the increasing brightness on stage, and huddle closer to* BARTOSZ *as they kneel.*) (*Suddenly an* ANGEL, *holding a green branch appears in the yellow light*) (*The* SHEPHERDS *remove their hats and bow*)

CAROLERS: (*off stage, sing*) GLORIA, GLORIA IN EXCELSIS DEO*

ANGEL: (*Dressed in long gown of white soft material, trimmed in silver or gold, wears wings and a shining tiara or star on her head, sings*):

4. Shepherds, be not frightened.
    I bring you joy this day,
    For the Christ Child is born,
    The Christ Child is born!
    To Bethlehem you must go
    There you'll find the Infant
    Born of Virgin Mary,
    The Blessed, precious Infant.

* Music p. 73

59

BARTOSZ: (sings to SHEPHERDS still sleeping) WAKE UP, SHEPHERDS*

ANGEL: Do not be afraid. Go follow the star! You will find Him in a lowly manger. Hasten to welcome this blessed Child.

ANGEL: (sings) CHRIST, THE KING, IS BORN† — GDY SIE CHRYSTUS RODZI

ANGEL: (blesses the SHEPHERDS) Peace to you and to all men of good will! (ANGEL disappears, SHEPHERDS slowly stand up, amazed, looking at each other, as the bright light disappears)

JASIEK: (sings) COME, SHEPHERDS, TO THE STABLE‡ — DO SZOPY, HEJ PASTERZE

FRANEK: I can't believe it! Was it a dream? Some kind of an apparition?

BARTOSZ: (happily excited, talks very slowly, distinctly) No my friends! It was not a dream! He is here! The great Messiah has come! Thanks be to God, my old eyes will still be able to gaze upon Him. It is a miracle. Hurry, SHEPHERDS! Get ready, all of you. We will do as the Angel commands. We will follow the star! We will go to greet Him! This happening is too wonderful to be true.

JASIEK: Please, dear BARTOSZ, could I stop on the way to fetch a gift for the Infant.

BARTOSZ: Indeed, and each of us will give what he can to this Holy Child.

JÓZIK: I'll give Him my little white lamb.

JASIEK: I'll give my chicken which lays an egg each morning.

FRANEK: I will bring the softest down to make a pillow for His head.

WOJTEK: I will give my proudest possession, my violin.

ANTEK: I'll bring cheese as white as snow.

WALEK: I'll bring butter made of sweet cream.

KUBA: I'll give Him my warm coat (kozuszek).

---

* Music p. 87
† Music p. 86
‡ Music p. 88

STASIEK: I'll give Him my fife (fujarka).

BARTOSZ: I will bring the finest homespun cloth for His swaddling.

KAZIK: (to GRZESZ, the other small SHEPHERD) What can we give? We are children and have nothing.

GRZESZ: We could give Him some raisins or almonds.

KAZIK: I will give him my pigeon.

BARTOSZ: Now that the matter of presents is settled, we will be on our way. Let us hope God will protect our sheep until we return. The town of Bethlehem is not far away. (SHEPHERDS bustle about, pick up clothing, put out the fire).

WOJTEK: (sings) HASTEN YONDER*—POJDZMY WSZYSCY DO STAJENKI

BARTOSZ: (sings) HURRY DEAR SHEPHERDS†

SHEPHERDS: (sing)

As you say! No delay!
Singing all the way.
Singing lullabies for the Blessed One,
Baby Jesus
Singing SHEPHERD songs
Happy SHEPHERD songs,
All the way for Baby Jesus.

BARTOSZ: (sings)

Born to us so very lowly
Glory be to Him on high!

SHEPHERDS: (sing)

We'll sing lullabies
For the Holy Child
We'll sing all of the way
For Jesus.
We'll sing SHEPHERD songs
Happy SHEPHERD songs
Singing all the way
For Jesus

(SHEPHERDS leave stage singing last stanza ever softer gradually as if going off to a distance).

Curtain — End of Act I

---

* Music p. 89
† Music p. 90

ACT II

Scene: (In HEROD's palace. Walls are hung with oriental tapestries. Drapes hang over doorways and windows. KING HEROD sits on a throne under a baldachin, in kingly raiment. At each side of him stands a Roman guard. At his feet is the PAGE with a huge fan made of feathers.)

HEROD: Well, here I am sitting on the throne, a great man among men. I am a King. I wear the crowns torn off the heads of many rulers, because my sword and word conquers all. I fear no one or the laws of any country. Indeed, I am an absolute monarch. I am King HEROD.

CENTURION: (enters) Greetings your majesty. (bows to king)

HEROD: Speak, CENTURION! What is it? What brings you here?

CENTURION: O mighty King, an important delegation is arriving.

HEROD: I am expecting no one at this time. Who are they? From where do they come?

CENTURION: Your majesty, they appear to be strangers to this country. Already they are nearing the gates. (Trumpet is heard backstage announcing the Kings' presence)

HEROD: Go quickly, CENTURION! Before they enter the courtyard, ascertain if they are friends or foes. (HEROD leaves the throne, walks to the window to

60

look down into the courtyard, then returns to the throne. CENTURION *returns, stands before* HEROD) Well, what did they say? What is their mission? Who are they?

CENTURION: They are three Kings from the East who wish to pay you respect, your majesty.

HEROD: Indeed! Kings from the East . . . They could be difficult. However kings are kings and equals. We cannot turn them away. (*to* CENTURION) Bid them welcome! (CENTURION *bows and exists.*)

CAROLERS: (*Sing off-stage, softly at first*)
GOD IS BORN* — BOG SIE RODZI

(*As the singing progresses the* THREE KINGS *enter followed by their* PAGES, *carrying their royal robes and gifts. All bow to* KING HEROD. *He smiles in approval, as he directs them to their places.* KINGS *sit,* PAGES *attired in their monarch's colors, stand beside them.* KINGS *wear crowns, gold sandals, colorful clothes under their luxurious robes trimmed in gold or silver. One king is dark-skinned, one has long curly hair, and one wears a rolled turban on his head*)

CASPAR: Honorable KING HEROD, the whole of the East through our lips pays homage to you, since it is your country in which God has chosen to perform one of his greatest miracles. A new King is born!

HEROD: (*confused*) A king? Here in my kingdom? What is the meaning of this? It does not make sense to me.

BALTHASAR: Great prophets, Sire, have told of his coming. He will bring a message of peace and joy. He will be the great One, who can turn the darkest day toward the sun.

HEROD: Who is he? Where does he come from?

CASPAR: It is written in the early scriptures, your majesty, that a Messiah will come to establish a new covenant. We believe He has come!

HEROD: Where is he? Where can I find him?

* *Music p. 92*

MELCHIOR: He is but an infant and has no strength, yet He is the exalted One, who has come to live among us. We have traveled far to pay Him homage.

HEROD: I, too must do so. (*turning to* PAGE) Go, my faithful servant to bring the RABBIS from the temple of Solomon with their big important books of scriptures. The great prophets have been writing for many years about past, present and future events. If this new king is expected, the information will be there. (*exit* PAGE, HEROD *speaks to himself*) The child, a king? Dethrone me? Never! I'll see to that!

CASPAR: (*puzzled, slowly*) What is it KING HEROD? A cloud has come over your countenance. Are you not pleased?

HEROD: But of course, I'm pleased. Naturally the news surprised me, and I am a little distressed. I should have known about it before your arrival. A new king is born! Is it not good news for all of us? (*Enter* RABBIS I *and* II, *bow and stand before* KING HEROD) (PAGE *takes his place near* HEROD)

RABBIS FIRST and SECOND: (*bow*) Greetings, honorable king.

HEROD: Learned RABBIS, you are of course familiar with the talk about the Messiah, the King of Kings, who is expected to come upon this earth?

FIRST RABBI: From these holy books, O KING, we shall read the predictions they contain concerning this matter.

HEROD: Read then! Read at once! We are waiting.

FIRST RABBI: (*reading from book*) A maiden will give birth to a son and will name him Emmanuel.

SECOND RABBI: (*reading from book*) He, who will be sent to us will be awaited by all nations.

FIRST RABBI: (*reading from book*) The kings of the Orient, THREE WISE MEN from the East, will bow before Him bearing precious gifts.

SECOND RABBI: (reading from book) And you Bethlehem, land of Judea, are by no means least among the princes of Judah, since from you shall come a ruler who is to shepherd my people Israel.

FIRST RABBI: So it is in Bethlehem of Judea, Sire, where the king of the Jews will be born.

SECOND RABBI: These are the writings of the prophets and scholars. Are you satisfied, O honorable King?

HEROD: Yes indeed. You may go now. (RABBIS bow and exit. HEROD turns to Kings and says) Honorable Monarchs, I should like to know where this child can be found, so that I, too can pay Him proper respect.

BALTHASAR: You are welcome to come with us KING HEROD. It will be our pleasure.

HEROD: Thank you! No! I would rather, worthy sovereigns, that you return here after your visit to tell me about it. Then I will make the necessary preparations to go to Him.

CASPAR: (signals departure to other kings) As you wish, honorable King. We leave you now to continue our journey. Our respects, Sire, and good day. (Each king bows in turn and leaves with his servants, as CAROLERS sing off stage)

CAROLERS: (sing) THREE GOOD WISE MEN* — MĘDRCY ŚWIATA MONARCHOWIE

HEROD: (to himself, after the singing) What shall I do now? . . . Something must be done! (turns to PAGE) Go quickly my faithful servant to notify KWINTUS, the general of our army to come to me at once. (exit PAGE) (HEROD paces the floor nervously) My blood is curdling! . . . My arteries are boiling over! . . . The world is turning! . . . He shall not take away my throne! . . . I am still the King! (walks back and forth) He must not live! (paces more) I have a plan! . . . I know what I must do . . . (KWINTUS enters, bows to king. PAGE enters, bows to king and takes his place near HEROD)

KWINTUS: You sent for me, Sire?

HEROD: Yes, KWINTUS. I want you to know about the distressing news brought to me by the three Wise Men from the East. They say a new king is born in Judea, a Messiah. The two RABBIS from the temple of Solomon, reading from the scriptures, agree with them. I am worried! . . . Something must be done! . . . It could mean trouble in our kindgdom. . . .

KWINTUS: I do not understand this. Surely everyone knows you are the King. Who is he, the one who is supposed to take your place?

HEROD: He is an infant now, but who knows what could happen later!

KWINTUS: Surely a smail child is no great threat!

* Music p. 93

HEROD: The bad seed must be weeded out while there is still time. Since we do not know which child it is, KWINTUS, the young male children of all Judea will have to be sacrificed, from the rich man's castle to the poor man's hut. I have given this serious thought. It needs to be done, and soon. This is an order for you and your army. You will go at once. There is a vast territory to be covered.

KWINTUS: But your majesty. . . .

HEROD: My command will stand as given! Go now, KWINTUS! There must be no hesitation, no mercy shown or heads will fall. Be on your way!

KWINTUS: But sire, do I understand that I am to take my noble warriors on a mass murder mission to kill infant sons? Never! Never!

HEROD: Silence! You heard my orders. Do you know what it means to disobey them?

KWINTUS: My King, I am a Roman, an enemy of the Jews. I have no fear of some unknown God. In brave deeds, I am not lacking and have more than one scar to show for them. I will fight for a righteous cause, protect my King and go to war with the fiercest enemy, even at the cost of my life, but I will not kill innocent children. I am a soldier with a soldier's honor.

HEROD: Enough! Enough, I say. How dare you speak to me in this manner and disobey my order?

KWINTUS: My King, I am a human being.

HEROD: Silence! I will not tolerate this talk any longer. You deserve no mercy. (to guards) Take him away! Off with his head! (guards advance, take him away) (HEROD turns to PAGE) You have heard the command given to the Roman?

PAGE: (quickly kneeling) You know I did, O Honorable King.

HEROD: Hasten then to HEBLON! He is now in charge of the army. Repeat my orders and tell him to proceed at once. (PAGE bows and exits, HEROD speaks to himself) Soon my worry will be over. It will drown in a sea of blood. Nothing must deter my decision. (after a pause, pacing nervously, then stops) I hear the weeping of a hundred thousand Jewish mothers and cries of anguish from their little sons. It will be worth all this wretchedness, however, if the child who is the source of my misery perishes with them. I trust it will be so. It must be! (walks nervously deep in thought. CAROLERS sing softly off stage) SHEPHERDS HEARD THE ANGELS SAY* — ANIOŁ PASTERZOM MÓWIŁ

HEROD: (looks about, as in a daze) What do I hear? Someone is singing. Who can it be? . . . My thoughts are torturing me . . . (listens again. Brightness appears on stage with the ARCHANGEL MICHAEL who holds a sword. HEROD is frightened, backs away)

* Music p. 94

62

ARCHANGEL MICHAEL: (*Appears as a young prince.*) KING HEROD!

HEROD: Who are you? What do you want? Am I dreaming or is this some strange hallucination?

ARCHANGEL MICHAEL: KING HEROD, you are not dreaming. You are a tyrant and a cruel king, full of false pride and madness. Your murders will come to an end this very day.

HEROD: (*angry*) Who are you to speak to me with such authority?

ARCHANGEL MICHAEL: I am the ARCHANGEL MICHAEL, a messenger of Him on high who has looked upon your long list of crimes, including the terrible murders of the Innocents. You shall pay the penalty.

HEROD: (*frightened*) Mercy I beg. Mercy! Mercy! To eternity I'll be grateful. I promise to make amends for all the wrongs I have committed. Mercy please!

ARCHANGEL MICHAEL: Sorry, your time has run out! (*Slowly touches HEROD with his sword and the king falls dead*) God's will be done! (ARCHANGEL MICHAEL *and blue bright light disappears. Suddenly a bright redness comes over the stage and with it the devil BORUTA, wearing a black cloak with red trim, and holding a pitchfork in his right hand. He laughs loudly.*)

BORUTA: Ha, ha, another corpse, another stiff for my playmates in hell. Good! Good! Who is the lucky creature? (*Looks closer, laughs loudly.*) I can't believe it! KING HEROD himself! Ha, ha! The killer of the Innocents. The scoundrel! The rat! The most despicable of murderers! Pfu! (*spits on him*) I would not touch him, even if I didn't have a corpse in a hundred years. I'm a Polish devil and I have some honor. (*looks at HEROD again*) The rotter, pfu, pfu! (*Shakes his head, walks away, and gives a weird wild loud call*) Br r r! (*The little comical dwarf devil runs in, somersaulting and making tricks*) KUSY come here! Do you see that ugly corpse? (KUSY *nods affirmatively, smiling, acting silly*) You may have him! Take him away!

KUSY: Tee hee! I may have him. (*hippity hops about HEROD's corpse*) Tee hee! Thank you very much master BORUTA. (*bows to him*) We little devils will have a ball. Tee hee! He is ours! (*Jumps over him, examines him from every direction and laughs foolishly.*)

BORUTA: Take him away KUSY! Out of my sight at once! Do you hear? (BORUTA *rushes off stage. KUSY puts chains on to HEROD and drags him off to side of stage.*) (*Red light dims out.*)

CURTAIN — END ACT II

Interlude

(*Street scene as in prologue.* CAROLERS *enter singing joyously carrying the big star.*)

CAROLERS: (*sing*)
TRIUMPHANT, HEAVENLY EXALTATION — TRYUMFY KRÓLA NIEBIESKIEGO

ACT III

Scene: (*It is dusk. In the background is the town of Bethlehem. The stable, with straw roof and closed door, occupies the rear center of stage, but is not seen by audience. There is foliage at both sides of stable and in front. Enter JÓZIK, JASIEK, FRANEK AND WOJTEK, each carrying his gift for the Christ Child*)

JASIEK: (*looking about*) The bright star has led us here. The stable cannot be far away. Let us wait here for the other SHEPHERDS, who will come with their gifts.

JÓZIK: Other people may come as we did, following the star. Some may come from far away lands.

KRAKOW COUPLE: (*Enter wearing their national costume, carrying a fruit basket with fruit. They sing*):
HIGH ON HILLS O'ER WAWEL — NA WAWELSKIEJ GÓRZE

KRAKOWIANKA: Fruit we bring from our land for the precious Infant.

KUJAWIAN COUPLE: (*Enter wearing their regional costume. They carry golden wheat and sing*) FROM KRUSZWICA* — OD KRUSZWICY

(*Enter* PRINCE *being chased by* PRINCESS. *The* PRINCESS (*sings*) PRINCESS SONG†

> Why do you persist
> In this long journey, dearest one?
> My new shoes are wearing badly
> This is no great fun!
> See my apron, vest and ribbon
> Looking very sad!
> You can go where peppers grow, love,
> I am really mad.

---

* Pronounced Vah-vel — Castle of ancient Kings in Krakow

* Music p. 98
† Music p. 101

PRINCE: (*Singing*) PRINCE SONG*

> This is surely no great worry
> Over clothes, my love,
> I would not make that much fuss
> Were I to lose my house.
> Do you think you would be frightful
> Without them, my love?
> Yes and no, it could be so,
> But it is you I love.

KRAKÓW LADS: (*Enter wearing regional costumes. They sing and dance*) KRAKÓW LADS† — KRAKOWIACY

JASIEK: Greetings, friends! We are shepherds following yonder star directed by an angel to see the newborn Babe.

KUJAWIAN: (KUJAWIANKA *stands beside him*) We came from the province of Poznan.

KRAKOWIAN: (KRAKOWIANKA *stands beside him*) We come from Krakow.

PRINCE: (*with* PRINCESS *beside him*) And we, from Warsaw.

KUJAWIAN: This is the Holy Night, the night of Gody‡ In Poland, as you perhaps know, it was called the Miracle Night or Night of Enchantment. Strange things can happen.

PRINCE: It is the night, some people say, when dumb animals can speak with human voices to praise God. It is a night of mystery. Look at the heavens. See the big bright star. We, too, have followed it here. This is a night to be gay. Come my PRINCESS, let us dance the Polonez. Please come join us! (*Couples and* KRAKÓW LADS *join the dance.* SHEPHERDS *applaud.*)

KRAKOWIAN: We will dance a Mazur. Please join us! *Kujawian couple, prince and princess join the dance, at conclusion of which, the* SHEPHERDS *applaud.*)

KUJAWIAN: It is our pleasure to dance for you the Kujawiak.† Please dance with us! (*Kraków couple and prince and princess join the dancing. At conclusion of dance* SHEPHERDS *applaud.*)

KRAKÓW LADS: It is up to us to do the Krakowiak.° (*ALL dance, including* SHEPHERDS.)

MARCINOWA: (*Enters at end of dancing with broom in hand, talking loudly, running between the actors, looking about*) You bums! You infidels! Where are you hiding? (*looks for them*) Come out! Return the apples to me at once, do you hear, or I'll report you to the constable. (*Looks about frantically*) They are not here? Where can they be? (*Notices the gathering and is suddenly surprised*) Are my eyes deceiving me?

---

* *Music p. 101 (same melody as Princess Song).*
† *Music p. 97*
‡ *Gody p. 27*
° *Music p. 104*

MARCINOWA

Where did you all come from? Pardon my intrusion. (*Holds hands on hips, sizing up the crowd. Nods her head from side to side, and smiling, says*)

> Welcome, welcome all gathered here
> I am Pani MARCINOWA,
> I sit near the Panna Marya Church,
> Selling produce at the Little Market Square.
> I sell groats, pearl barley, flour, figs, oranges,
> Apples, rolls, makagigi,* caraway seed and toys.
> In this manner quietly, peacefully
> Thank God I make my living.
> But today, I listen, what commotion, what talk!
> God is born — an infant. — a new King . . .
> Everyone who can, carries a present for Him,
> And who am I, not any worse than some,
> So I try to make a reasonable selection;
> Something special for this wondrous Child.
>
> When all at once, these rascals, God forgive them,
> Come in hurriedly and steal my pretty red apples.
> Then they run as fast as their legs can go, and
> I after them! The infidels! And here I am!
> But where are they? O dear, I must leave
> This distinguished company to retrieve the apples
> Or get the payment. Oh, those rascals!
> I have enough troubles without them!

(*Leaves with a lot of bluster and commotion, drops broom, bumps into* ICEK†, *Jewish vender with pushcart, and says loudly*) Sorry but why don't you look where you are going. (*exits*)

ICEK: (*enters, bows, tips his cap*) Greetings, greetings. So much conversation! What about, may I inquire? Something exciting, I like to think. Then maybe you will bargain with me. I buy and sell. I have eggs, cheese, herring, bread with sesame seed, Polish rye,

---

* *Confection — pronounced — mah-kah-gee'-gee.*
† *Pronounced — eet'-sĕck.*

pickles and sauerkraut, or maybe you look for lodging. With this head (*points to it*) I can do anything. (SHEPHERDS *are seen whispering together. They come toward him*)

JASIEK: But what if we ask something difficult?

ICEK: I can handle anything in the world.

WOJTEK: Anything we ask?

ICEK: (*suspecting some trickery*) But I must know what you want, Ay vay!

SHEPHERDS: (*sing*) SHEPHERD'S SONG TO ICEK*

> ICEK, ICEK, Christ in Bethlehem is born.
> Greet Him with a song this happy morn,
> As befits a royal son.
> **Laj-li-la Ploy!
> As befits the Lord's Son.

ICEK: (*sings*) ICEK'S SONG

> My ancient God I praise and love
> As I was taught to do.
> Ay vay, as I was taught to do.
> Your little one, I do not know
> And do not understand.
> Ay vay, vay. Do not understand.

SHEPHERDS: (*sing*) SHEPHERD'S SONG TO ICEK

> ICEK, ICEK, in the town of Bethlehem
> He lies in a lowly manger.
> He is king the angels say.
> Laj-li-la Ploy,
> Greet him with a song today.

ICEK: (*sings*) ICEK'S SONG TO SHEPHERDS

> You talk foolish! You have not won!
> A king humbly born!
> Ay vay! A king was humbly born.
> Royalty in a poor stable . . .
> You go to the devil!
> Ay vay, vay! You go to the devil!

(ICEK *walks off stage, motioning disgust with right hand*).

JASIEK: Don't go away angry. Your boast was premature, ICEK! Think twice before you speak next time. Ay vay!

WOJTEK: Poor ICEK, he made no bargain here, ay vay!

FRANEK: Do not worry about him. People say he is very rich. Who knows? (*shrugs his shoulders*)

(*Sudden noise in the background, bustle, thunder, after thunder*)

PRINCESS: (*frightened to the* PRINCE *and gathering*) Do you hear it? The thunder?

JÓZIK: Thunder, but look the sky is clear and full of shining stars. It is not going to rain! (*more thunder*)

* Music p.105
** Pronounced — Lie-lee-lah Ploy

KUJAWIAN: (*excited with the discovery*) Look! Look! There! (*All gather about him to look to where he is pointing*)

> Over the gates of Łeczycy* palace
> Above the ground, under the clouds,
> Over the fields and woods,
> A strange rider streaks across the skies.

PRINCE:

> Fire spurts from the nostrils of his steed,
> Flames mount with every stride,
> As he speeds in flashes of lightning
> Over the huge sea of stars.

KRAKOWIAN:

> Do you see the long trail
> Of black night birds following?
> Can you hear their chorus shrill?
> They are the frightful bats
> Cruising on quiet wing,
> As the lost flames scatter
> And their lights dim.

PRINCE: I see the trail. I know the rider well. I have heard about him often enough. He is the master of the Łeczycki** Bogs, the old Polish devil BORUTA. He is rushing to us with every breath.

PRINCESS: (*worried, frightened*) But what could he want from us? (*More thunder, lightning and BOOM, final blast, BORUTA surrounded by red light, appears in cloak, both hands on hips, takes smart stance, bows and smiles.*)

BORUTA: Hail, hail, one and all!

> This is quite a gathering, heh! heh!
> What puzzles me — it happened so peacefully,
> But I can wait, heh! heh! I can wait.
> Often, even with two people some quarrel will ensue,
> Grow bigger and worse with anger, even a curse,
> That is what I like, heh! heh! Trouble!
> I detest boresome agreement. Tell me, please,
> Why are you waiting here?
> Do you expect a miracle? heh! heh! heh!
> You are out of your minds —
> A King born in a stable, heh! heh!
> Who ever heard of such nonsense
> A Savior of mankind, heh! heh!

KUJAWIAN: (*stomping his foot in anger*)

> Silence, BORUTA! You are an evil spirit,
> Sowing discord, doubt and hate,
> You have come to us too late, and now
> You are worried lest the Child born this night
> Will crush your evil might.
> In that you are right. Very, very right! (*walks toward BORUTA*) Come with us this day. This is not a whim! In the name of God, (KUJAWIAN *makes the sign of the cross over the devil*) We will take you to Him. (*The devil puts his hands on his ears, runs off the stage screaming*)

* Pronounced — Win chee-tsee
** Pronounced — Win cheet-skee

BORUTA: No! No! Never, never. (*Red light slowly disappears*)

FRANEK: Now that the devil, BORUTA is gone . . .

WOJTEK: (*interrupting*) O look! The bright star is quite near. Come everyone! Let us follow it. We'll find the Blessed Infant.

PRINCE: We are coming!

KRAKOWIANKA: Let us hurry!

JASIEK: The ANGEL said, "Follow the bright star to Bethlehem."

KUJAWIAN: Everyone is coming (*all actors exit quickly. Stage is darkened for a moment. Foliage may be rearranged. Slowly the bright light appears over the stable. The door is opened. Mary and Joseph are kneeling beside the Infant at the manger. Mary wears a light blue gown and light veil over her head. Joseph has a beard and wears a brown cloak.*)

CAROLERS: (*sing off stage*) GLORIA, GLORIA, IN EXCELSIS DEO* (*BARTOSZ enters with all of his SHEPHERDS*)

BARTOSZ: (*sings*) SHEPHERDS GREETING†

SHEPHERDS: (*sing*) O POOR LOWLY MANGER*— ACH UBOGI W ZLOBIE

BARTOSZ: (*speaks*)

Accept dear Child, these humble gifts
Which we SHEPHERDS have brought.
We do not have much
But give with all our hearts. (*As JOSEPH accepts gift, BARTOSZ stands up to take his place to the side of stage, as the other SHEPHERDS, each in turn, present their gifts, and join him.*)

WOJTEK: (*sings*) IN THE STILL OF THE NIGHT†— W SROD NOCNEJ CISZY

CAROLERS: (*enter with star and sing*) QUICKLY ON TO BETHLEHEM‡ — PRZYBIEZELI DO BETLE-JEM

CAROLERS: (*Sing to SHEPHERDS*) SHEPHERDS DEAR° — PASTERZE MILI

SHEPHERDS: (*sing responses as indicated by song content.*)

(*Enter the THREE KINGS, with their attendants and PAGES, to present their gifts. The THREE KINGS kneel together before manger.*)

BALTHASAR:

Dear Child, we come from the East
Where the sun rises first,
To pay You great homage.
We welcome You to earth
And bring our offerings.

* *Music p. 73*
† *Music p. 106*
* *Music p. 107*
† *Music p. 110*
‡ *Music p. 109*
° *Music p. 108*

CASPAR: (*rises to present gift*) I bring gold, my choicest possession, to the Blessed Child who will become the greatest of men.

MELCHIOR: (*rises to present gift*) I bring precious myrrh with the hope that all nations can live in peace.

BALTHAZAR: (*rises to present gift*) I bring frankincense, fragrant as the spring flowers, that it may bind with love all the people of the world.

THREE KINGS: (*sing*) WE THREE KINGS* *MEDRCY SWIATA*

We Three Kings have journeyed far
To find the blessed Infant
From the East, we followed the star,
Guiding us to Jesus.
Though He has no royal raiment
Nor a crown to wear,
We are dust in His great presence.
He's King everywhere.

(*THREE KINGS exit with their attendants.*)

PIAST: (*Enters from opposite side of stage with his attendants, followed by the couples and the KRAKOW LADS*)

PRINCE: (*to SHEPHERDS and CAROLERS*) This is our ruler with his attendants. He is our great leader.

KRAKOWIAN: He is a quiet prophet and a wise counselor.

PRINCESS: He is loved by all his people.

PIAST:

Where my people go, so do I
There is no division among us;
In joy, worry, pain or toil
We share everything as one.

(*Piast kneels before manger. Couples and KRAKÓW LADS also kneel.*)

PIAST:

Blessed Infant, Precious Little Dove,
I too, PIAST of Poland, bring an offering.
I carry with pride not silver or gold,
But a loaf of bread made of native rye
And honey, culled in the month of July.
The honey came from the blossoms of the linden trees
That gently shade the roofs of our cottages.

Blessed Infant, Precious Little Dove
As we kneel before Thee, wondrous Child,
Bless our land and our people,
Bless the customs and traditions we cherish
And the beautiful language we possess.
These we promise to guard faithfully
And never, never let them perish.
This is our prayer, O Child of God
Blessed Infant, Precious Little Dove, Amen.

PIAST: (*sings*) PIAST SONG OF PRAISE†
(*Couples present gifts, while PIAST sings*)

* *Music p. 93*
† *Music p. 111*

66

CAROLERS: (*sing*) IN A MANGER* — W ŻŁOBIE LEZY

MARCINOWA:

> Pardon me everybody, I found the scoundrels!
> They have returned my apples. (*shows them and quickly kneels before manger*)
> Dear Child accept this humble gift,
> Which is really for your parents. Bless me,
> And protect me from those infidels!

(JOSEPH *accepts.* MARCINOWA *rises quickly, joins couples*)

CAROLERS: (*Sing, kneeling before manger, with their gift of song.*) CELESTIAL CHOIRS OF ANGELS† — ANIELSKI CHOR

JOSEPH: Dear kind friends, Mary and I are deeply grateful for your generosity and good will. The Child will sleep well tonight.

MARY: You were most kind.

JOSEPH: (*sings*) JESUS TINY BABY‡ — JEZUS MALUSIENKI

KAZIK AND GRZESZ: (*run to* JOSEPH) Please, may we sing Him a little song too?

---

* *Music p. 112*
† *Music p. 114*
‡ *Music p. 113*

JOSEPH: I think the BABY would like that (MARY *smiles, nodding affirmatively.*)

KAZIK AND GRZESZ: (*sing*) STRIPED DUCK* — KACZKA PSTRA

MARY: (*sings*) LULLABY SWEET JESUS† — LULLAJZE JEZUNIU

BARTOSZ: Having seen the Blessed Baby, having greeted Him with gifts and lullabies, we take leave of this wonder; say farewell to Him and his mother; also to Joseph. Now to our fields and sheep we'll go singing all the way.

SHEPHERDS: (*sing*) FAREWELL TO JEZUS.‡

> Singing lullabies
> Singing Shepherd songs
> Singing all of the way
> For Jesus
> We'll sing shepherd songs
> Happy shepherd songs
> All the way for Baby Jesus.

SHEPHERDS: (*repeat chorus as they exit.*)

CAROLERS and all: (*sing*) GLORIA, GLORIA IN EXCELSIS DEO‡

---

* *Music p. 115*
† *Music p. 118*
‡ *Music p. 111*

CURTAIN

67

Christmas Songs and Jaselka Music

1. Jaselka Prelude

(with recorder, violin or flute optional)

Larghetto

Original Composition by Rose Polski Anderson

Teneramente (recorder, violin or flute optional)

D. C. al Segno e poi la Coda

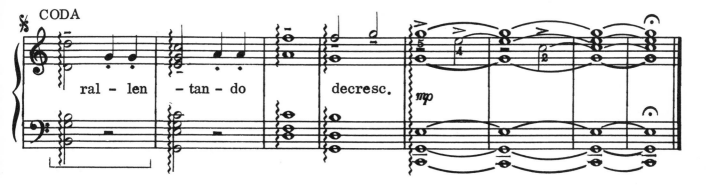

2. Hey, Hey, My Lambkins

From original Polish words-X. J. Labaj
English version-Josepha Contoski
Music Arr.-Stanislaw Niepielski

1. Hey, hey, my lamb-kins pre-cious, Ox-en and sheep, hear this_____
"Graze well up-on this pas-ture Stay to-geth-er near."

2. Hey, hey, while fresh food you take,
My flute of wood I'll make,
Hey, I will play it for you,
While you graze in view.

3. Hey, on the hillside yonder
Grass there is much greener,
Hey, I know you would go there
If I was not here.

71

3. Today in Bethlehem

Dzisiaj w Betlejem

English version–Cecily Kowalewska Helgesen
Music Arr. –Rose Polski Anderson

Largo—Introduction

Andantino

_ff_

In Beth - le-hem,
Dzi- siaj w Be-tle-jem,

In Beth - le-hem, Tidings ring Tri - um-phant! Sweet Vir-gin Mary,
dzi- siaj w Be-tle-jem, We so - ła No- wi - na! Że Pan-na czys-ta,

sweet Vir-gin Ma–ry, Bore the Ho- ly___ In - fant.
Że Pan- na czys-ta, po- ro- dzi- ła Sy- na.

Chorus

Born is our Savior, Born our re-deemer, An - gels are playing, Kings tribute paying,
Chrys- tus się ro-dzi, Nas os-wo- bo-dzi, A- nie- li gra-ją, Kró — le wi- ta-ją.

72

Shepherds all are singing, Sheep and oxen kneeling, Lo! what wonder! Each proclaiming.

Pas- te- rze śpie-wa--ją, By- dlę- ta klę- ka- ją, Cu- da, cu- da! O-gła- sza- ją.

2. CHORUS:
   Sweet Virgin Mary, sweet Virgin Mary
   O'er her Wee Babe bending,
   And kindly Joseph, and kindly Joseph
   Gently them attending.

2. CHOR:
   Marya Panna, Marya Panna,
   Dzieciątko piastuje,
   I Józef stary, i Józef stary,
   On Je Pielęgnuje.

4. Gloria, Gloria, in Excelsis Deo

Latin Doxology (Luke 2:14)　　　　Original Composition by Rose Polski Anderson

Glo - ri - a, Glo - ri - a, in ex - cel - sis De - o.

Glo - ri - a, Glo - ri - a, in ex - cel - sis De - o.

Glo - ri - a, Glo - ri - a, in ex - cel - sis De - o.

5. I'll Take My Violin

Melody and Polish words–W. S. Groele
English version–Josepha Contoski
Music Arr.–Rose Polski Anderson

I'll make a vi-o-lin of the whi-test Lin-den, Then by stream of flow-ing wa - ter, Play the music I love, Sing the songs I treasure, Till the setting of the bright sun. When I play me-lo-dies, Hey, up-on my vi-o-lin, O'er the running wa - ters, hey; They'll float o'er the cool mist Spread-ing and swelling And my voice on fresh dew Will ev-er tra - vel with the wind.

D. C. al Fine

6. In the Village

English version–Josepha Contoski
Music Arr.–Anda Kitschmann

With Vigor

1. In the vil-lage ta-vern tall, Danced the bri-gands, large and small,
Hań w Lip-tow-skiej piw-ni-cy Tań-co-wa-li zbój-ni-cy

Or-dered mu-sic loud and gay,___ Folks to watch their feet at play.
Ka-za-li se pi-knie grać i na nóż-ki spo-źe-rać.

Dance

Hu, Ha!

2. I will dance no more today,
Hurt my leg along the way,
Crooked legs won't dance you know
If I jump, they'll bend and go!
Hu, Ha!

3. Nor can I sing more right now,
For I really don't know how,
All the notes have left me too,
Through the big hole in my shoe.
Hu, Ha!

2. *Nie będę ja tańcował*
Bom sę nózki popsował
Bo ja krziwe nózki mom
Co wyskoce, to się gnom!

3. *Jakoź ja ci śpiewać mam*
Kiedy tego nie wiem sam
Uciekła mi ta nuta
Z dziwrawego haw buta.

75

7. Franek Looked Out *

English version–Josepha Contoski
Music Arr.–Adam Harasowski

Marciale

Poor Fra - nek looked out, looked from his shel - ter
To watch that his grey sheep would not scat - ter

mf While a mouse_____ big field mouse_____

Quickly ran in-to his shelter O, da - na! *f* Ate his food_____

Kieł - ba - sa,_____ Ate his cheese and good Kieł-ba-sa O, da - na!

*Music — Pognała Wółki Na Bukowine. — Treasured Polish Songs, p. 171.

8. Mazurka*

Polish Folk Melody
English version–Josepha Contoski
Music Arr.–Anda Kitschmann

Allegro

mf A_____ good shepherd boy am I_____ Liv-ing like a king._____

I_____ a-wak-en in the eve-ning watch the sheep and sing.

f Hu, Ha! da-na-da, Da-na-mine, O, da-na Watch and sing,

Hu, Ha! Da-na-da, Da-na-mine, O, da-na Hu! Ha!

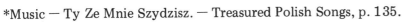

*Music — Ty Ze Mnie Szydzisz. — Treasured Polish Songs, p. 135.

9. A Krakow Lad
Krakowiaczek

English version–Josepha Contoski
Melody–Stanislaw Moniuszko
Music Arr.–Rose Polski Anderson

Allegretto

mf I'm____ a hap - py sing – er,_____ And____ it's right I

should be;_____ God____ has placed in my soul,_____

spe - cial pre - sents for me._____

piu mosso

I____ sing songs like
Songs____ of riv - ers

for - est birds, songs that have ma-ny pret - ty words,
lakes and woods, songs that_ I like ritard. most.

10. Little Franek *

Traditional Folk Melody
English version–Josepha Contoski
Music Arr.–Anda Kitschmann

Lit - tle Fra-nek wants to sleep_____

Let's make him a cra - dle deep_____

Place him in it gent - ly, Sing - ing ev - er soft - ly,

Sleep well, lit - tle Fra - nek, Sleep well, lit - tle Fra - nek, sleep.

*Quartet arr. - Od, Krakowa or Kupiłem se Pawich Piór — Treasured Polish Songs, p. 97.

11. Lord Descends from Heaven

Pan z Nieba i z Łona

2. Son of God, His Father, Light of God ever,
Born unto us lowly, as was His mother.
Thus paces follow, God's decrees holy,
That man repentent, his crown of glory,
May receive in heaven, dwelling there ever.

2. O Panie! Tyś z Ojca, Tyś światło z Boga
Ubogiś i Twoja Matka uboga,
Te czynią kroki Boskie wyroki
Aby stworzony człowiek korony
Dostąpił przez Ciebie i mieszkał w niebie.

12. Brothers, Look There Yonder

Bracia, Patrzcie Jeno

English version–Josepha Contoski
Music Arr. –Edmund Contoski

1. Broth-ers look there yon-der! Skies a-flame! O won-der!
Bra- cia, patrzcie je- no, Jak nie-bo go-re- je.

Ver-y strange the to-ken O'er the town Bethle-hem. We must leave huts,
Znać że coś dzi-wne-go w Be-tle-jem się dzie-je. Rzuć-my bu-dy,

sheep and ox-en,Lord over them will keep on watching While we go__ to Bethlehem.
war- ty sta-da, Nie-chaj nie-mi Pan Bóg wła-da, A----------- my----- do Be-tle- jem,

We go to Beth-le — hem, to Beth-le-hem.
a my do Be-tle- jem, do Be-tle-jem.

2. Brothers, see the great star,
    Spreading out its rays far.
    Surely, it is gracing
    God, in its swift racing.
    With bold steps we hasten to Him,
    Filled with joy, we'll bow before Him,
    Son of God in Bethlehem.
    God's Son in Bethlehem, in Bethlehem.

3. Little town Bethlehem,
    Brings to Juda great fame
    Everywhere remembered,
    By all countries honored.
    Let joy fill our hearts mankind,
    As we worship Him we find,
    In a manger, in Bethlehem,
    Manger in Bethlehem, in Bethlehem.

81

13. Hey, Brothers, Are You Sleeping

Hej! Bracia! Czy Wy Spicie

English version–Josepha Contoski
Arr. –J. Krogulski
Adapted by Rose Polski Anderson

BARTOSZ:

1. Hey, broth-ers, are you sleeping? Shep-herds, are you watching? E-vents nev -er heard of Now seem to be oc -cur-ring. O God! Dear God! What is this mys-te - ri -ous happ'ning? Bright the night! It is not day!__ Bright the night! It is not day!___

Hej! bra- cia czy wy spi- cie, czy wszyscy ba-czy- cie, dzi- wy nie-sły-cha- ne. dzi- wy nie-sły cha- ne. Oj trwo- ga dla Bo-ga co się dzie- je, Jas- no w noc-y Choć nie dnieje, jas- no w noc-y choć nie dnie-je.

SHEPHERDS:

p 2. We shepherds are watch-ing, To us it is fright-ning, see-ing
I my też pa-trzy-my. a- le się bo- i- my, Pa- trząc

this great miracle. O God! Dear God! O, what is
na te dziw- y. Trwo- ga, Trwo- ga, dla Bo- ga

real - ly happ ⌐ning? Hearts beat with great con - ster
co się dzie- je. Od stra- chu ser - ce tru

na — tion, Hearts beat with our great con - ster - na - tion.
chle- je ser- ce tru- chle- je, truch- le- je.

83

BARTOSZ:

3. O, look! The great sky opens! See the countless army! It is an ar-my of
Oj, nie- bo o-two-rzo- ne wojs-ko nie-zli- czo- ne, A- niel- skie wi- dzi- my,

ce - les-tial sol-diers.___ O, God! Our frightened hearts beat with great conster -
a- niel- skie wi- dzi- my. Oj! Trwa-go dla Bo- ga co → się

na - tion, O, God! Our frightened hearts beat with con - ster - na - tion.___
dzie- je, Od stra- chu ser - ce ser - ce truch- le- je.

Intrada   **ANGEL:**

a tempo   4. Shepherds, be not frightened I bring you joy
Hej! pa- ste- rze mi- li dzi- siaj o tej

84

this day,　　For the Christ Child is born!　　The Christ Child is born!＿
chwi- li.　　Chrys- tus się na-ro- dził!　　Chrys- tus się na-ro- dził!

To Beth - le - hem you must go,　There you'll find the In –fant,　Born of Vir – gin
Oj! do Be- tle- jem spiesz- cie tam dzie- cię znaj-dzie- cie　Tam dzie - cię znaj-

Ma – ry,　The Blessed pre-cious In –fant!　　*pp*　rall.　　*ppp*
dzie- cie tam dzie- cię　znaj - dzie- cie.

85

14. Christ, the King, is Born*

Gdy Sie Chrystus Rodzi

English version–Cecily Kowalewska Helgesen
Music Arr.–Adam Harasowski

Maestoso

1. Christ, the King, is born,_____ On an ear - ly morn,_____
   Gdy się Chry - stus ro - dzi, I na świat przy - cho - dzi,

Ra - diant glows the dark_ night, Skies a - flame with bright_ light,
Ciem - na noc w jas - no - ści pro - mie - ni - stej bro - dzi.

Allegro

All the an - gels are re - joic - ing Heavenly mu - sic, they are voic - ing,
A, - nio - ło - wie się ra - du - ją, Pod nie - bio - sy wy - śpie - wu - ją:

cresc.   rit.

Glo - ri - a, glo - ri - a, glo - ri - a, in ex - cel - sis De - o!
Glo - ri - a, glo - ri - a, glo - ri - a, in ex - cel - sis De - o!

2. Angels told the shepherds,
   Keeping watch o'er their herds,
   "Follow ye the bright star,
   Bethlehem is not far,
   /: For the Savior there is born,
   To the world this early morn,
   Gloria, gloria, gloria, in excelsis Deo!" :/

2. *Mówią do pasterzy, którzy*
   trzód swych strzegli,
   Aby do Betlejem czem prędzej
   pobiegli,
   /: *Bo się narodził Zbawiciel,*
   wszego świata Odkupiciel,
   Gloria, gloria, gloria, in excelsis Deo! :/

15. Wake Up, Shepherds

English version–Josepha Contoski
Music Arr.–Stanislaw Niepielski

Allegretto

Wake up, shep-herds, quick - ly,___ An-tek, Ku - ba___
Wake up, my dear broth - ers,___ God ful-filled our___

Grzesz!
wish!

Wake up, quick - ly for the An - gel

Brought from heav - en Mes-sage for us. The Mes-si - ah

has_____ come___ as it was fore - told.

Rallentando

16. Come, Shepherds, to the Stable

Do Szopy, Hej Pasterze

English version–Lucille Jasinski
Music Arr.–Rose Polski Anderson

1. Come, shepherds, to the sta – ble, be – hold this wondrous sight. See Je – sus
Do szo – py, hej pasterze, Do szo – py, bo tam cud. Syn Bo – ży,

in the manger In early morning light. An-gels sing very soft – ly, Shepherds play
w żłobie le – ży By zbaw – ić ludż – ki ród. Śpie – waj – cie a – nio – ło – wie, Pa – ste – rze

joyful-ly, Oh! Kings kneel, move with caution Lest he a – wakened be.
graj – cie mu. Kła – niaj – cie się Kró – lo – wie, Nie budz – cie Go ze snu.

2. Bend down and kneel before Him,
This Infant is our Lord.
He comes as our Redeemer,
Love, honored, and adored.   Chorus:

3. Beyond our understanding
Is your great blessed plan.
On hay among the cattle,
You take your humble stand.   Chorus:

4. Oh, Jesus, sweetest Infant
How could we not love Thee?
We give Thee our allegiance,
Our prayers, our destiny.   Chorus:

2. Padnijmy na kolana, to Dziecię to nasz Bóg
Witajmy Swego Pana, miłości złóż my dług.
Chór:

3. O Boże niepojęty, któż pojmie miłość Twą
Na sianie wśród bydlęty masz tron i służbę Swą.
Chór:

4. O Jezu mój najsłodszy, jakże nie kochać Cię
O Skarbie mój najdroższy, Tobie oddaję się.
Chór:

17. Hasten Yonder

Pójdźmy Wszyscy

English version–Cecily Kowalewska Helgesen
Music Arr.–Rose Polski Anderson

Allegretto

1. To the sta - ble, hast - en yon - der, To a - dore this
Pój - dzmy wszys - cy do sta - jen - ki, Do Je - zu - sa

Ho - ly Won - der, Babe of Heav - en, like no oth - er,
i Pa - nien - ki, Po - wi - taj - my Ma - leń - kie - go,

Vir - gin Ma - ry, sweet - est Moth - er, Babe of Heav - en,
I Ma - ry - ję, Mat - kę Je - go, Po - wi - taj - my

Ritardando e decrescendo

like no oth - er, Vir - gin Ma - ry sweet - est Moth - er.
Ma - leń - kie - go, I Ma - ry - ję Mat - kę Je - go.

2. Oh, Babe Jesus, we adore Thee,
   Twice your birth to us has brought Thee,
|: Once of God, through all the ages,
   Now of Mary, told by sages. :|

2. Witaj Jezu nam zjawiony,
   Witaj dwakroć narodzony,
|: Raz z ojca przed wieków wiekiem,
   A teraz z Matki człowiekiem. :|

89

18. Hurry, Dear Shepherds

Original Polish Words-X. J. Labaj
English version-Josepha Contoski
Music Arr.-Stanislaw Niepielski

BARTOSZ

mf Hur - ry, dear shepherds, with song we'll go, Hur - ry all,

heed the call. Come, shepherds, Come, brothers, Come to the man-ger.

SHEPHERDS

As you say! No de - lay! Sing - ing all the way,

Sing - ing lul - la-bies for the Bless-ed One, Ba - by Je - sus.

Sing - ing shepherd songs, Hap - py shepherd songs, All the way for

BARTOSZ

Ba - by Je - sus. Born to us so ver - y low - ly,

Glo - ry be to Him __ on High! We'll sing lul - la - bies

SHEPHERDS

for the Ho - ly Child. We'll sing all of the way for Je - sus.

We'll sing shepherd songs, Happy shepherd songs, Singing all the way for Je - sus.

91

19. God Is Born

Bóg Się Rodzi

Traditional Polish Air
English version–Cecily Kowalewska Helgesen
Music Arr. –Rose Polski Anderson

1. God is born on earth, powers tremble,__ Lord bereft of heav'nly splen-dor,
   Bóg się ro - dzi, moc tru - chle - je, Pan nie - bio - sów o - bna - żo - ny,

   Lustrous flames fade,__ fires dissem – ble,___ In–fin–ite un–end–ing Won – der!
   O - gień krze - pnie, blask ciem - nie - je, Ma gra - ni - ce Nie - skoń - czo - ne.

   Scorned yet clothed in radiant glo - ry, Mor - tal though He is Lord Je - sus,
   W sgar - dzo - ny, o - kry - ty chwa - łą, Śmier - tel - ny król nad wie - ka - mi;

   Thus the Word be – came the flesh_____ Dwell – ing without end a–mong us!
   A Sło - wo Cia - łem się sta - ło, I mie - szka - ło mię - dzy na - mi.

2. Why leave heaven for this bleak earth,
   Heaven bright in all its glory,
   To dwell humbly from day of birth,
   To fulfill the prophet's story.
   Lo, He suffered through our folly,
   Mortal, though He is Lord Jesus,
   Thus the Word became the Flesh
   Dwelling without end among us!

2. *Coż masz niebo nad ziemiany?*
   Bóg porzucił szczęście twoje,
   Wszedł między lud ukochany
   Dzieląc znim trudy i znoje:
   Nie mało cierpiał, nie mało,
   Żeśmy byli winni sami.
   A Słowo Ciałem się stało
   I mieszkało między nami!

20. Three Good Wise Men*

Mędrcy Świata

English version–Cecily Kowalewska Helgesen
Music Arr.–Adam Harasowski

1. Three good wise men, earth-ly monarchs, Whith – er are you search – ing?
   Medr – cy świa – ta, mo – nar – cho – wie, Gdzie spiesz – nie dą – ży – cie?

Will you tell us, Oh great pa-triarchs, Do you seek the In – fant?
Po – wiedz – cież nam, trzej Kró – lo – wie, Chce – cie wi – dzieć Dzie – cię?

In a man – ger, with-out a throne, No scep-tre does He hold,
O – no w żło – bie, nie ma tro – nu, ni ber – ła nie dzierż – y,

What is des-tined, has been long known, By all prophets fore – told.
A pro – ro – ctwo Je – go zgo – nu Już się w świe-cie sze – rzy.

2. Three good wise men, malice fearful   Yet the monarchs will not frighten,
   Persecutes the new King,   To Bethlehem hasten,
   Tidings dismal, tidings dreadful,   While the star proclaims the Savior,
   Herod is conspiring.   Life and Hope Redeemer!

*Treasured Polish Songs, p. 216.

21. Shepherds Heard the Angels Say

Aniól Pasterzom Mówil

English version–Cecily Kowalewska Helgesen
Music Arr. –Rose Polski Anderson

Andante—cantabile

1. Shepherds heard the an - gel say,_____ Christ is born to
   A - niól pa - ste - rzom mó - wil; Chry - stus się wam

you this day, Beth - le - hem____ is His low - ly place_ of__ birth,
na - ro - dził, w Be - tle - jem, nie bar - dzo pod - tem mie - ście,

Born so hum - bly to this earth, Lord___ of all cre - a - tion.
Na - ro - dził się w u - bó - stwie, Pan wsze - go stwo - rze - nia.

2. Thus the Lord through His great love,
Came from heaven, up above,
No great place, grand or costly had He here,
But a manger cold and drear,
Lord of all creation.

2. Jaki Pan chwały wielkiej
Uniżyt się z wysokiej:
Pałacu kosztownego, żadnego,
Niemiat z budowanego,
Pan wszego stworzenia.

94

22. Triumphant Heavenly Exaltation

Tryumfy Króla Niebieskiego

z Krakowa
English version–Josepha Contoski
Music Arr. –Edmund Contoski

Maestoso

1. Tri - um-phant heav'nly ex-al - ta - tion, De-scend-ing angels' sal-u - ta - tion
Try - um - fy Król - la Nie-bies-kie- go, z stą — pi - ły z nie-ba wy-so-kie- go

Wak - ens___ shep-herds fast___ a - sleep, Hum - ble___ shep-herds,
Po - bu - dzi - ły pa - ste - rzów, Do - by — tku swe-

and___ their_ sheep, With gay song, joy - ous song, glo - rious song.
go stró - żów, Śpie - wa-niem, śpie - wa - niem, śpie - wa - niem.

2. O glory to Lord God on highest,
    On earth peace to men, even lowliest;
    Born this day is Christ Savior,
    Heavenly host, Redeemer,
    One of us, born on earth, on this day!

3. The frightened shepherds all arise!
    Whence comes this music from the skies?
    What strange things take place this night?
    Heaven glows with wondrous light!
    Ever bright, is one star, this great night.

2. Chwała bądź Bogu w wysokości,
    A ludziom pokój na nizkości;
    Narodził się Zbawiciel,
    Dusz ludzkich Odkupiciel . . .
    Na ziemi, na ziemi, na ziemi.

3. Pasterze w podziwieniu stają,
    Tryumfy przyczynę badają;
    Co się nowego dzieje
    Że tak światłość jaśnieje . . .
    Nie wiedzą, nie wiedzą, nie wiedzą.

23. High On Hills O'er Wawel

Na Wawelskiej Górze *

Allegretto

English version–Josepha Contoski

con anima

High on hills o'er Wa - wel** Ring the joy - ous church bells,___
Na Wa - wel - skiej gó - rze Dzwo - ni dzwon wy - so - ko;

As we sail ev - er a - long the Wis - la*** Riv - er.
Pój - dę ja se pój - dę Nad Wis - tę sze - ro - ką

Fine

From Ta - tra**** mountains, it takes us to the Bal - tic.
Pój - dę ja se pój - dę Nad Wis - tę sze - ro - ką

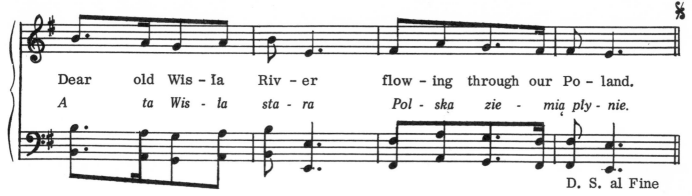

Dear old Wis - ła Riv - er flow - ing through our Po - land.
A ta Wis - ła sta - ra Pol - ska zie - mią pły - nie.

D. S. al Fine

*From *Jaselka-Walerja Szalay Groele*.

**Pronounced *Vah'věl* - ancient castle of Polish Kings in Poland.

***Pronounced *Vee'siwäh* - principal river of Poland.

****Pronounced *Tah'träh* - mountain range in Southern Poland.

24. Kraków Lads *

Krakowiacy

Polish folk melody
English version–Josepha Contoski
Music Arr. –Anda Kitschmann

Moderato

(Dance)

1. From Kraków we are two young lads

Peacock feathers on our hats; Heel plates on our red boots, dana, and a homespun sukmana.**

2. On days festive, with pride in chests,
   We wear our long blue vests,
   Stitched in gold and colored silk threads
   On back, front, and collar's edge. (dance)

3. Small rings jingle from our waistline
   Made of metal, they do shine!
   Striped pants and the long white coats
   Our costumes enhance - let's dance! (dance)

4. For the tiny blessed Baby
   We'll sing softly, dance sprightly
   For we are the Kraków young lads
   Peacock feathers on our hats. (dance)

*Wszystko Stare, *Co Do Czarta* - Treasured Polish Songs, p. 157

**sukmana - loose great coat.

25. From Kruszwica*

Od Kruszwicy

Tempo mazurka

English version–Josepha Contoski

We have tra-veled from Kruszwi – ca,** Hey, ha! Bring-ing gol – den
Od Krusz - wi -cy wę-dru -je - my Hej, ha! I psze - ni -czkę

wheat for Je - sus, Hey, ha! Grown on fer - tile na-tive mea –dows,___
przy-no -si - my, Hej, ha! Co ją ro-dzą na-sze ła - ny,

Hey, ha! By Ku-ja - wian*** hap - py farm-ers___ hey, ha!
Hej, ha! Nie-chaj ży - ją Ku - ja-wia-ny, hej, ha!

Far___ and___ wide___ Far___ as the eye can see, hey, ha!
Da - le -ko, sze-ro - ko Jak za-się-gnie o - ko czło - wie -ka,

98

Wave on wave, with-out end, Wheat greets the sun like a___ riv - er!

Chwie - je się Jo słon - ca pszen - ny łan bez koń - ca, Jak rze - ka.

*From *JASELKA* by W. S. Groele.
**Pronounced *Krū shvēē'tsah* — Territorial division in Poland
***Pronounced *Kū yâv'yan* — native of *Kujawy* region.

26 -1. Polonez

Dawne Czasy

K. Kurpinski

Moderato

26-2. Polonez

Pozegnanie Ojczyzny

M. Oginski

D. C. al Fine

27. Princess Song and The Prince Song*

Tempo Mazurka

English version–Josepha Contoski

Why do you per-sist in this long jour-ney, dear-est
I pó - kiż mie bę-dziesz ciąg - nął w tę strasz-ną dro-

one? My new shoes are wear-ing bad-ly. This is no great
gę Bu-ci-ska się roz-le-cia - ły, Da-lej nie mo-

fun! See my a-pron, vest and rib-bon, Look-ing ve-ry sad!
gę, Patrz, far-tu-chy, kre-zy, wstę-gi zmię-ły się do cna

You can go where pep-pers grow, love, I am real-ly mad!
U-cie-kaj - że, gdzie pieprz ro-śnie, Bom o-kru-tnie zła!

*PRINCESS SONG and PRINCE SONG (same melody) from *JASELKA* by W. S. Groele

101

28. Mazurka

Fr. Chopin, Op. 67, No. 3
(1835)

D. S. al Fine

29. Kujawiak *

Jan Różewicz

D. C. al Fine

*Another Kujawiak, Red Apple (Czerwone Jabluszko), is available in
Treasured Polish Songs, p. 149.

30. Krakowiak

Melodia Ludowa
Traditional Folk Melody
Music Arr. -K. Hofman

Giocoso

31. Shepherds' Song* and Icek's Song

Polish words and melody–Walerja Szalay Groele
English version–Josepha Contoski
Music Arr. –Rose Polski Anderson

SHEPHERDS' SONG

1. I - cek, I - cek, Christ in Beth-le-hem is born.
   Ży- dzie ży- dzie! Me-sy- jasz się ro- dzi,

Greet Him with a song this hap-py morn, As be - fits a
Więc Go to- bie, więc Go to- bie po- wi- tać się

roy - al son. Laj - li - lu ploy! As be-fits the Lord's Son.
go- dzi. Laj - li - lu ploy! Po- wi- tać się go- dzi.

ICEK'S SONG

1. My an-cient God I praise and love, as I was taught to do.
   Your lit - tle one I do not know and do not un - der - stand.
   Ja sta- re- go Pa- na Bo- ga jak na- le- zi u- miem.
   a- le te- go Ma- leń- kie- go je- szcze nie ro- zu- miem.

Ay, vay, vaj._____ Do not un-der - stand._____
Aj, waj, waj. Je- szcze nie ro- zu- miem.

*Other verses, *Jaselka*, p. 65
105

32. Shepherds' Greeting *

English version–Josepha Contoski
Music Arr. –Stanislaw Niepielski

Allegretto

We, poor shep- herds have___ come to Thee Sing-ing songs all

of the way, For the In - fant Ba - by Je - sus,

Whom we find up - on the hay. Now we shepherds kneel be-fore___ Thee,

Wor - ship, love and a - dore___ Thee, Grateful-ly we welcome Thee.

*W Złobie Łezy (above melody), p.112 (song no. 39)

33. Lowly Manger

Ach Ubogi Żłobie

English version–Josepha Contoski
Music Arr.–Rose Polski Anderson

Adagio

mp 1. Ah, poor low - ly man - ger, what do I be - hold here?
Ach, u- bo- gi żło- bie, cóż ja wi- dzę w to- bie?

Sight more precious than hath heaven In this ti – ny stran – ger. stran – ger.
Droż- szy wi- dok, niż ma nie- bo w ma-leń- kiej o- so- bie. so- bie.

2. Blessed Infant Saviour,
   Poor art Thou, Redeemer;
//: Choosing poverty among men
   Leaving heaven's splendor. ://

3. On our knees, we praise Thee,
   Bowing heads, adore Thee:
//: Thou art with the sheep and oxen
   When we come to greet Thee. ://

2. *Zbawicielu drogi,*
   Także to ubogi!
//: *Upuściłeś śliczne niebo,*
   Obrałeś barłogi. ://

3. *Przed Tobą padamy,*
   Czołem uderzamy,
//: *Witając Cię w tej stajence*
   Między bydlętami. ://

107

34. Shepherds Dear *

Pasterze Mili

English version–Cecily Kowalewska Helgesen
Music Arr. –Adam Harasowski

Moderato

CAROLERS:

Shepherds dear, oh pray, What saw you this day? Shepherds dear, oh
Pas-te - rze mi - li, Coś-cie wi - dzie - li? Pas - te - rze mi -

SHEPHERDS:

Piu mosso

pray, What saw you this day? We have seen the
li, Coś-cie wi - dzie - li? Wi - dzie - liś - my

In — fant Je — sus, Born to earth, from sin to free us,
ma - leń - kie - go Je - zu - sa na - ro - dzo - ne - go,

rall.

Son of God and man, Son of God and man.
Sy - na Bo - że - go, Sy - na Bo - że - go.

*Treasured Polish Songs, p. 222

108

CAROLERS: 2.

CAROLERS: 2.   Was His castle grand?
            What did He command?
            Was His castle grand?
            What did He command?

2.   *Co za pałac miał*
     Gdzie gospodą stał?
     Co za pałac miał
     Gdzie gospodą stał?

SHEPHERDS: |: He was born in an old stable,
            Roofless, cold, fit but for cattle,
            Such was His domain,
            Such was His domain. :|

|: *Szopa bydła przyzwoita,*
I to jeszcze żle pokryta,
Pałacem była,
Pałacem była. :|

35. Quickly on to Bethlehem

Przybieżeli do Betlejem

English version–Cecily Kowalewska Helgesen
Music Arr.–Rose Polski Anderson

Andantino

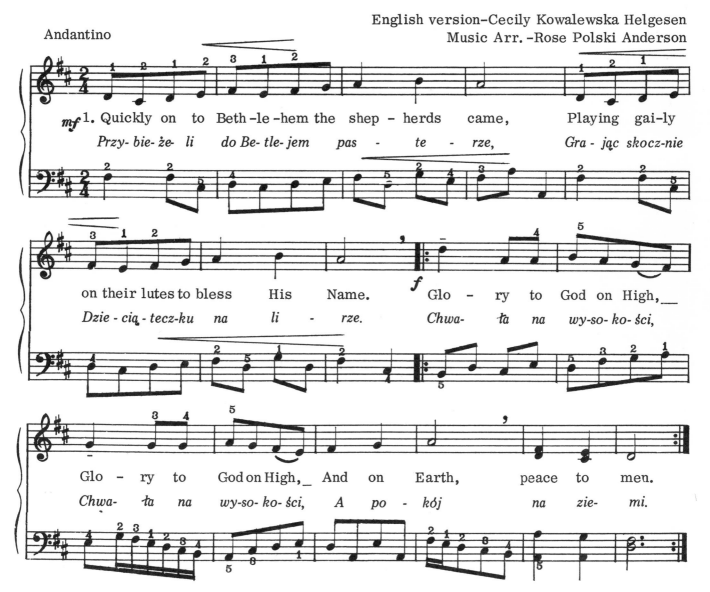

1. Quickly on to Beth-le-hem the shep-herds came, Playing gai-ly
Przy-bie-że-li do Be-tle-jem pas-te-rze, Gra-jąc skocz-nie

on their lutes to bless His Name. Glo-ry to God on High,__
Dzie-cią-tecz-ku na li-rze. Chwa-ła na wy-so-ko-ści,

Glo-ry to God on High,__ And on Earth, peace to men.
Chwa-ła na wy-so-ko-ści, A po-kój na zie-mi.

2.   Giving their respects in all humility,
     To the Infant Jesus from hearts lovingly,
|: Glory to God on High,
     Glory to God on High,
     And on earth, peace to men. :|

2.   *Oddawali swe ukłony w pokorze,*
     Tobie z serca ochotnego, o Boże!
|: *Chwała na wysokości,*
     Chwała na wysokości,
     A pokój na ziemi. :|

36. In the Still of the Night *

Wsrod Nocnej Ciszy

Old Christmas Carol
English version-Edmund Lukaszewski
Music Arr. -Adam Harasowski

1. An - gels from heav - en sang a thrill-ing psalm, Wak - ing the
   Wśród noc - nej ci - szy, Głos się roz - cho - dzi, Wstań - cie pas -

shep - herds from their drowsy calm. Rise ye shepherds, hur - ry on-ward,
te - rze, Bóg się wam ro - dzi. Czym prę - dzej się wy - bie - raj - cie,

Greet the new-born Son of Dav - id, King Em - man - u - el!
Do Be - tle - jem po - spie - szaj - cie, Przy - wi - tać Pa - na!

2. They found the Saviour with His Mother mild,
   Laid in the manger, Infant Jesus Child.
   |: Bow ye shepherds to the Christ King,
   Bring to Him your humble offering,
   King Emmanuel!

2. Poszli, znaleźli, Dzieciątko w żłobie,
   Z wszystkimi znaki danymi Sobie.
   |: Jako Bogu cześć Mu dali,
   A witając, zawołali
   Z wielkiej radości! :|

*Treasured Polish Songs, p. 214

37. Piast Song of Praise *

(A capella or with accompaniment)

Traditional Polish Air
Polish verse–X. J. Labaj
English version–Josepha Contoski

Solo

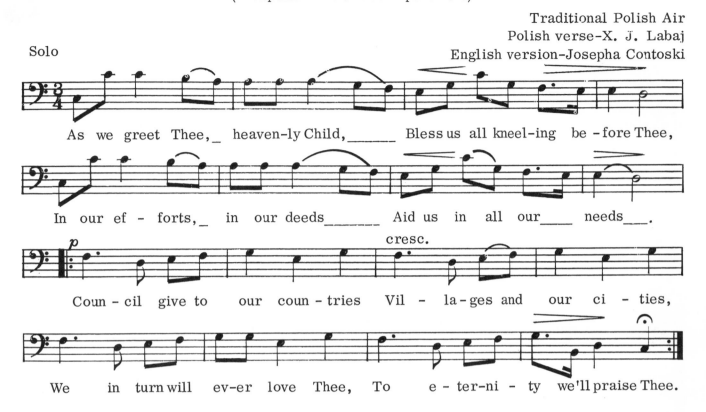

As we greet Thee,_ heaven-ly Child,_____ Bless us all kneel-ing be-fore Thee,

In our ef - forts,_ in our deeds_____ Aid us in all our____ needs___.

Coun - cil give to our coun - tries Vil - la - ges and our ci - ties,

We in turn will ev-er love Thee, To e - ter-ni - ty we'll praise Thee.

*See page 92 for accompaniment. Melody is the same as GOD IS BORN, *Bóg Sie Rodzi.*

38. Farewell to Jesus

English version–Josepha Contoski
Music Arr. -Stanislaw Niepielski

Andante
SHEPHERDS:

Sing-ing lul -la-bies, Singing shepherd songs, Singing all__ the way for Jesus;

We'll sing shepherd songs, Happy shepherd songs All the way for Ba-by Je-sus.

39. In a Manger *

W Żłobie Leży
Quartet

Peter Skarga (1536–1612)
English version–Zofia Kowalska McGinn
Music Arr. –Rose Polski Anderson

Moderato (Tempo Polonez)

1. In a man-ger sleeps the In - fant, Hasten all to find Him there. Lit-tle
W żło-bie le - ży! któż po - bie - ży Ko - lę - do - wać ma - łe - mu Je - zu-

Je - sus, to us heav'n sent, Blessings with us all to share.
so - wi Chry - stu - so - wi Dziś do nas ze - sła - ne - mu?

Hur-ry, shep – herds, kneel be-fore Him, Play sweet mu - sic like Se -
Pa - stu - szko - wie przy - by - waj - cie, Je - mu wdzię-cznie przy - gry -

1. ra – phim, Worship Him as Lord and King.
waj - cie, Ja - ko Pa - nu na - sze - mu,

2. Worship Him as ___ Lord and King.
Ja - ko Pa - nu na - sze - mu.

*From Treasured Polish Songs, p. 223.

112

2. We shall follow, singing our song,
   Bringing homage, gifts of prayer,
   Little Saviour, bless this large throng,
   Watch us with loving care.
   Hurry, children, see Him sleeping,
   Holy parents watch are keeping,
   So let us all adore Him.

2. *My zaś sami z piosneczkami*
   Za wami pospieszymy,
   A tak Tego Maleńkiego
   Niech wszyscy zobaczymy;
   Jak ubogo narodzony
   Płacze w stajni położony,
   Więc go dziś ucieszymy.

40. Jesus, Tiny Baby

Jezus Malusienki

English version–Josepha Contoski
Music Arr. –Edmund Contoski

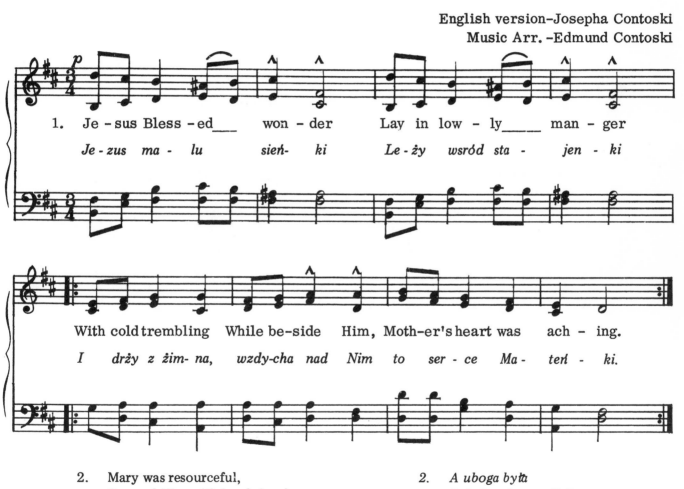

1. Je - sus Bless - ed___ won - der Lay in low - ly___ man - ger
   Je - zus ma - lu sień- ki Le - ży wśród sta - jen - ki

With cold trembling While be-side Him, Moth-er's heart was ach - ing.
I drży z żim- na, wzdy-cha nad Nim to ser - ce Ma - teń - ki.

2. Mary was resourceful,
   Covered Him with head shawl:
   //: Then with fresh hay
   Wrapped him gently,
   Kept Him warm on this day. ://

2. *A uboga była*
   Rąbek z głowy zdjęta,
   //: *W który Dziecię*
   Uwinąwszy,
   Siankiem Je okryła. ://

3. Jesus had no cradle.
   Nor a downy pillow;
   //: So in small crib,
   Mary placed Him
   On hay, soft and mellow. ://

3. *Nie ma kolebeczki*
   ani poduszeczki
   //: *We złobie mu*
   Położyła
   Sianka pod głoweczki. ://

113

41. Celestial Choirs

Anielski Chór

English version–Josepha Contoski
Music Arr.–Rose Polski Anderson

Moderato

1. Ce-lestial choir_ of an — gels pro-claim man's sal- va- tion,
A - niel -ski chór pa - ste - rzom o - gła-sza zba - wie -nie,

Announcing that__ the bless -ed word now has con-firm - a - tion; In
Zwias - tu - jąc im Bo - skie- go sło - wa wy - peł- nie --------- nie, Że

man - ger, of a vir - gin, was born the In - fant Sa - viour, To
w szo - pie zczy - stej Pan - ny nasz Zbaw - ca się na ro - dził, By

free_ the right-ful heirs_ of heav-en this day for-ev- er. -er.
nas dzie - dzi - ców nie-ba, zwięz-zów o - swo - bo - dził. by dził.

2.
In want and lonely stable, the Lord is born this day,
Through His great suff'ring, He prepares for us a glorious way;
As He now weeps in manger, upon the cross He will perish;
Through His great miracle of love, salvation we cherish.

2.
W niedoli i ubóstwie Pan nieba przychodzi,
On tem cierpieniem nędzy, wszystko, nam osłodzi.
Jak leżąc płacze w żłóbku, tak i na krzyzu skona,
Wielkim cudem miłości, odkupu dokona.

114

42. Striped Duck

Kaczka Pstra

English version–Lucille Jasinski
Music Arr.–Rose Polski Anderson

1. Stri - ped duck, on a rock With your ma - ny duck - lings sit - ting, Mak - ing mu - sic with your quack - ing, "Quack, quack, quack", ech - oes___ back.

Kacz - ka pstra dziatki ma sie - dzi so - bie na ka - mie - niu, Trzy - ma dut - ki na ra - mie - niu, "Kwa, kwa, kwa", pięk - nie gra.

2. Gosling small, turkey tall
Drumming rhythms they are pounding,
Grateful maidens praise their cackling,
"Ge, ge, ge," with much glee.

3. Yellow bird, golden bird,
From your throat you warble music,
Sounding like played violin strings,
"Lir, lir, lir" they do sing.

4. Nightingale, your notes sail
Every one knows, no one else could
Sing as gently as your warbling,
"Tweet, tweet, tweet," sounds so sweet.

2. *Gęsiorek, jędorek,*
Na bębenku, wylulają
Pana wdzięcznie, wychwalają
"Gę, gę, gę!" gęgają.

3. *Cyzycek, scyglicek,*
Na gardłećkach, jak skrzypeczkach
Wygrywają, w jaseleczkach
"Lir, lir, lir," śpiewją.

4. *Słowiczek, muzyczek,*
Gdy się głosem, popisuje
Uciechę światu zwiastuje
"Ciech, ciech, ciech!" Zwiastuje.

43. Shines a Star for Little Jesus

Świeci Gwiazda Jezusowi

English version–Evelyn Cieslak Nahurski
Music Arr.–Rose Polski Anderson

Shines a star for lit - tle Je - sus In the sky,
Jo - seph with the Vir - gin Ma - ry Tends Him nigh,
Świeci gwiaz - da Je - zus - o - wi w ob - ło - ku,
Jó - zef z Pan - ną a - sys - tu - ją przy bo - ku,

in the sky.
tends Him nigh.
w ob - ło - ku,
przy bo - ku,

Raise your hearts in great ac -
Hej - że i - no dy - na,

cord, Born to us the In - fant Lord,
dy - na, Na - ro - dził się Bóg Dzie - ci - na,

In Beth - le - hem, in Beth - le - hem.
W Be - tle - hem, w Be - tle - jem.

44. From the Heavens, Little Angels

Przylecieli Aniółkowie

English version-Lucille Jasinski
Music Arr.-Rose Polski Anderson

Comodo—dolce—cantabile

From the heavens, lit–tle an – gels, Like the birds came wing – ing.
Przy – le – cie – li a – nioł – ko – wie, Jak pta – szę – ta z nie – ba,

To the ti – ny In–fant Je – sus, mer–ry tunes were sing – ing.
I śpie – wa – li dzie – ciątecz – ku, We – so – ło jak trze – ba

Lu – li, lu – li, dear–est Je – sus, All our songs are for you.
Hej – że, hej – że, Pa – nie Je – zu, Hej – że, hej – że, hoć, hoć!

There's no sleep–ing for the shep – herds as they sing the night through.
Śpie – wa – liś – my, bu – dzil – iś – my pas – tusz – ków ca – łą noc!

45. Lullaby, Sweet Jesus*

Lulajże, Jezuniu

English version–Evelyn Cieslak
Music Arr.–Rose Polski Anderson

Andantino

1. Lul - la - by, sweet Je - sus, pearl ve - ry pre - cious,
Lu - laj - że, Je - zu - niu, mo - ja pe - reł - ko,

Lul - la - by, sweet Je - sus, sleep now, Your cries hush.
Lu - laj - że, Je - zu - niu, me pie - ści - det - ko,

Lul - la - by, sweet Je - sus, lul - la - by Ba - by,
Lu - laj - że, Je - zu - niu, lu - la - jże, lu - laj,

Sleep In - fant
A Ty Go

be - lov - ed, Moth - er will lull Thee. Moth - er will lull Thee.
Ma - tu - chno w pła - czu u - tu - laj. w pła - czu u - tu - laj.

2.   Close now Your wee eyelids, blinking
        with soft tears,
    Still Your wee lips trembling, for slumber
        time nears.
    Lullaby, sweet Jesus, lullaby, baby,
    Sleep Infant beloved, Mother will lull Thee.

2.   *Zamknijże znużone płaczem powieczki,*
    Utulże zemdlone lkaniem usteczki. Lulajże ...
    Lulajże piekniuchny nasz Aniołeczku,
    Lulajże wdziecznuchny świata Kwiateczku Lulajże ...
    Lulajże Różyczko najozdobniejsza,
    Lulajże Lilijko najprzyjemniejsza. Lulajże ...

46. *Joyful Tidings*

Wesołą Nowinę

English version-Lucille Jasinski
Music Arr.-Stanislaw Siedlewski

Har - ken to joy-ful tid - ings Oh shep-herds, list - en.
We - so - łą no - wi - nę bra - cia słu - chaj - cie,

Let us this heav'nly In - fant A - dore and greet Him.
Nie - bie - ską Dzie - ci - nę ze - mną wi - taj - cie.

Where is this blessed stran - ger Born in___ a___ low-ly man - ger?
Jak mi - ła, ta no - wi - na Mów, gdzie jest ta dzie - ci - na?

Hast - en this ho - ly night,___ to the won - drous sight!
Byś - my tam po - bie - że - li I uj - rze - li!

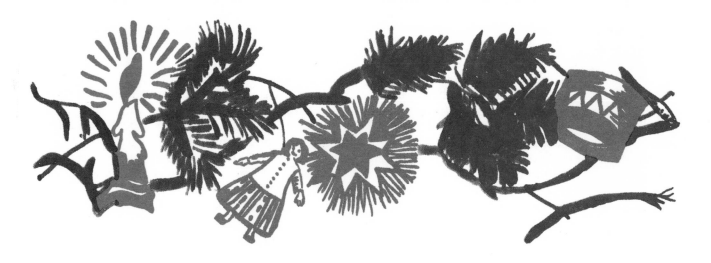

POLISH CHRISTMAS TREE ORNAMENTS

and made Christmas tree toys have been an important part of a traditional Polish Christmas for many reasons. Not only does the effort yield colorful and useful decorations, but the individual finds hidden talents brought out by each creation. It is easy to decorate a tree with manufactured ornaments, but they will never be as meaningful or creative as those homemade. Besides, the commercial Christmas tree ornaments are expensive, and seem to have a duplicate uniformity which is not as pleasing.

Folk art is an affinity for anything beautiful, since folk art is the most natural outlet of expression. Therefore, folk art has no bounds; it comes from the heart and individual talent of the maker, and thus, no decoration can ever be the same. It preserves history by displaying the works of the people of the times, and it never seems to go out of style.

Toy-making is a folk art. Because of the peasants' poverty, anything available is used in their creations — odd scraps, leftover material, etc. Folk art produces ingenuity; ingenuity to produce a thing of beauty from the materials at hand. Each member of the family contributes to decorating the tree, members of all ages and artistic talents. No matter how crude the ornament may be, each member of the family is represented by hanging his creation on the Christmas tree.

Christmas ornaments made by hand have many advantages. First of all there is very little investment of money. If there is a regular gathering of scraps, such as colorful paper from gift wrappings, tin foil, or art supplies, interesting material such as brocades,

laces, braids, and ribbons or broken beads of various hues, shapes and sizes, there can be a never ending chain of ideas that can evolve. Folk art exercises your ingenuity to produce a thing of beauty from the materials on hand. It is also a pleasant pastime for both adults and children that both can enjoy, while enjoying each other. It can be an easy task and each finished toy teaches many new skills. Dexterity in using scissors, expression in painting, patience in pasting, all come into use. It teaches the simplest forms of manipulation while working in a variety of materials.

Ornaments can be made with good individual results. There is no need for special artistic talent, but for people excelling in painting a limitless field of decoration can be created.

For those with only natural talent, exactness, patience and the will to accomplish are the prime requisites. To have difficulty with the first piece of work is to be expected, but it is also true that each succeeding toy will be better than the last. Mastery comes with practice.

Reading instructions for making ornaments, preparation and information about materials are important before one begins to work. This will make it easier for you to avoid unforeseen difficulty and to maintain your enthusiasm.

The tools you use are simple; small and large scissors, a ruler, clippers, a compass and tweezers. Another handy tool is a sharp knife, a razor blade or a pen knife. Pencils, water colors, crayons, paste, colored paper, tin foil, straw, beads, needles, thread, egg shells, and shells of nuts are also useful. Whatever one has on hand, improvise, create — and have fun!

121

DZIAD

During the holiday season, or during any other festive time, it is customary to decorate the walls and ceilings with the spider-like *pająk*. It can be made of *opłatek* (unleavened bread) paper, flowers, straw, beads or a combination of these materials. The design was part of an ancient ritual and when it was made of paper it was cut with sheep shears. Every region of Poland has its own characteristic *pająk*, but the best known of them all is called the *Dziad* (old man) or the Baba (old lady). Since they were made exactly alike, the name chosen was dependent upon the gender one wished to flatter. The *Dziad* is fashioned from a bunch of wheat tied at one end and opened up umbrella-fashion to allow the grain to form a fancy border. It is then hung over the table for the *Wilia*, or Christmas eve supper.

In other regions of Poland, it is customary to bring three sheaves of wheat into the home. One is placed on the table as a decoration, the second is put in a corner of the room and the third is hung from the ceiling. These are called St. Joseph, Angel Guardian and the *Dziad*. The *Dziad* is the most important of all the *pająk* ornaments because it has various uses, traditions and superstitions. The *Dziad* is not only used at Christmas, but also on New Years day when greetings for the coming year are extended to friends and neighbors. In carrying the *Dziad*, a stick is used to beat against it causing the grain to fall, while the verse "*Na szczęście, na zdrowie*" (for your good luck, for your good health) is repeated over and over. The Rumanians, Bulgarians, Slavs and Germans have a similar custom. However, they use sticks or tree branches and strike their friends and neighbors to make their greetings more meaningful. After the New Year, the *Dziady* are strewn in the fields where cabbage will be planted in the spring, in hope that the heads of the vegetable will resemble the *Dziady's* large umbrella appearance. Sometimes only the wheat of the Dziad is saved to be placed under the hoofs of a cow in the stable with the wish of successful and abundant delivery of calves.

The *Dziad* (m) or *Baba* (f) is always hung above the table. This is a Christmas custom which came much before any Christmas tree ornaments or Christmas decorations. The *Dziad* is such a characteristic tradition that the hanging of sheaves of wheat was not only done on the farm and in villages, but in the city homes and apartments as well. Because of the importance of the *Dziad* to the Polish Christmas, a variety of Christmas ornaments have evolved, the *pająks* of chandelier type, to the small ornaments found on the Christmas tree.

The New Years greetings given with the *Dziad* of long ago, prevail today in another manner. Since wheat is no longer readily available, nuts in the shell are substituted for the grain. As guests enter a home, the same greeting is chanted, "For your good luck, for your good health" as they scatter the mixed nuts. The nuts, as the wheat, signify bountiful harvest and many good wishes for health and wealth in the ensuing year.

OLD MAN-DZIAD

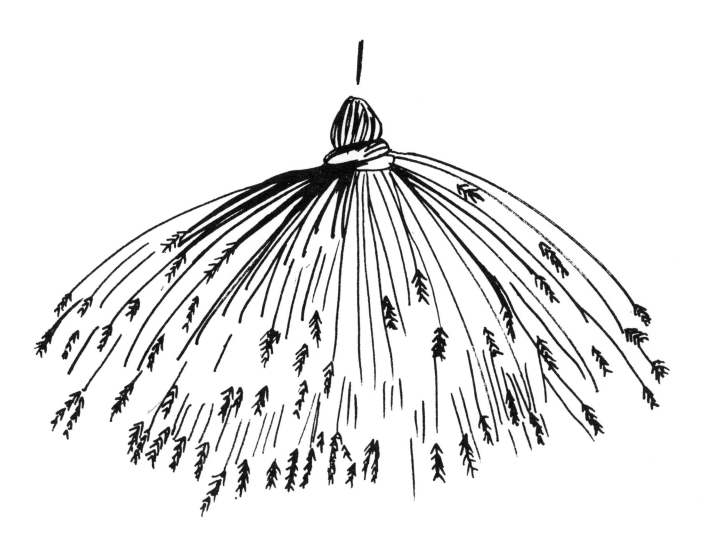

OLD LADY-BABA

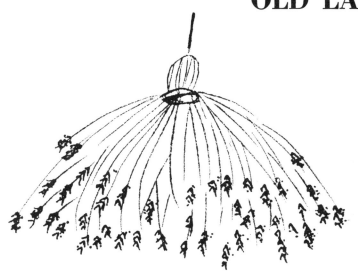

Soak a bunch of wheat for several hours in water so that it will be pliable and will not crack, or split when handled. Tie tightly at the end of the stalks with string. Place a large ball in the center, causing the bunch to flare out umbrella fashion. Allow it to dry completely before hanging so that it will retain the expanded shape.

CROSS–KRZYŻ

Materials needed:
  Wheat stalks
  Red yarn

   Take twenty stalks of wheat (or more) and divide into
four equal portions. Overlap straw at the center and weave
red yarn over and under to form another cross.

STAR-GWIAZDA

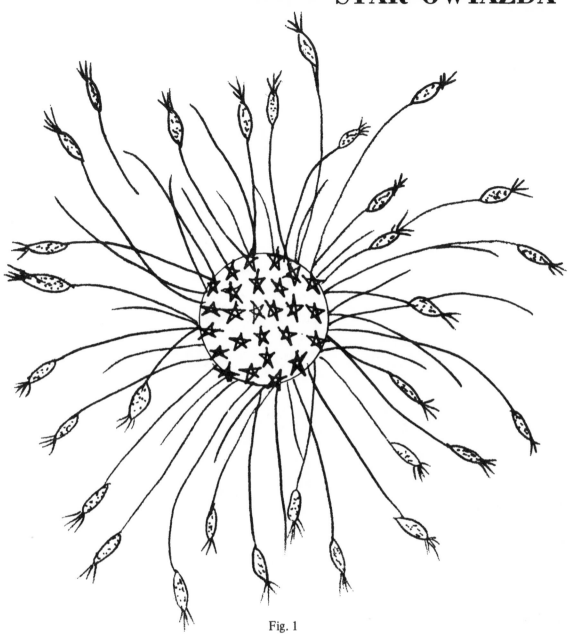

Fig. 1

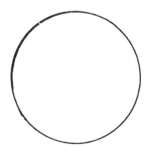

Fig. 2

Fig. 3

Insert uneven lengths of straw in a styrofoam ball that has been cut in half the size of #2. Cut #3 from colored paper and place over ball. Secure by pinning sequin stars through paper star and into styrofoam ball.

125

FLOWER–KWIAT

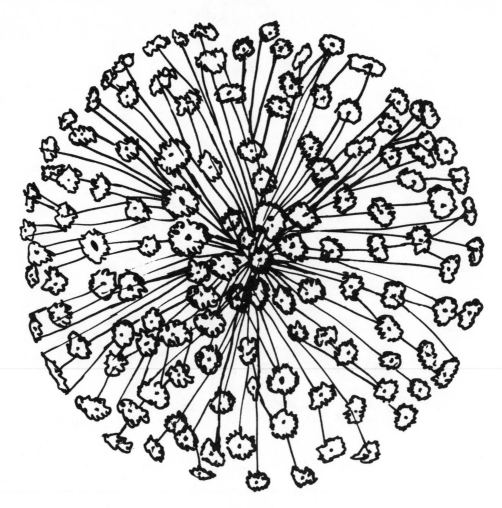

Fig. 3

Fig. 1

Fig. 2

Materials needed:
    Drinking straws
    Construction paper
    String
    Twistems

Take a full handful of straws. Tie tightly in the middle causing the straws to flare out to make a ball. Cut enough flowers as per pattern to be inserted in all the ends of the straws. Punch holes through #1 and use twistems the length of #2. Curl one end of twistems around a pencil point and insert through center of flower. Put paste on the other end of twistem before inserting the straw.

126

STRAW MOBILE — PAJĄK

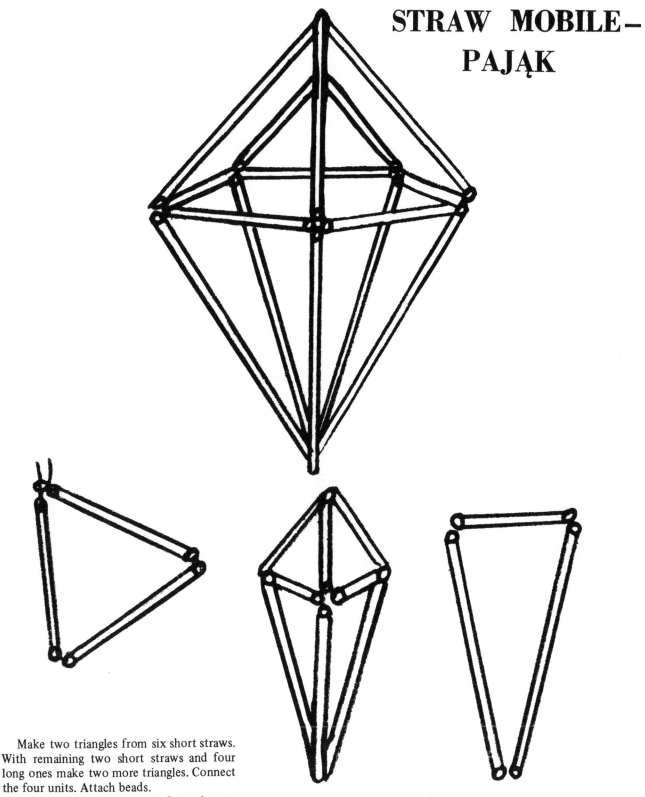

Make two triangles from six short straws. With remaining two short straws and four long ones make two more triangles. Connect the four units. Attach beads.

When this pajak is inverted, it changes from a chandelier to a bird cage. Add paper flowers at the top and protruding spokes and a large paper flower at the bottom. Add a golden bird as per pattern. Attach a feather for the tail and make a perch of straw that rest on the ribs of the cage.

Materials needed:
  Straw
  Needle and thread
  Beads
  Tissue paper
  Gold paper
  Feather

BIRD CAGE

Cut 12 circles from bright colored tissue
paper for each flower
Cut into middle to make fringe all around.

Fig. 4

Large flower

Small flower

Fig. 2

After circles are cut, string 12 circles together and flare out for a round flower.
Use large flower on top and bottom of cage and small flower for the sides.

128

MOBILE-RUCHOMY

Materials needed:
Thin paper
Scissors
Glue
Thread

Take two sheets of paper and fold in half. Copy only half of the design and cut through four sheets of paper to make the mobile. Dip a double length of thread in glue forming a loop at the top. Using the folded line as the axis of the ornament, place the thread between the two papers. After the glue dries, open up for a 4-sided effect.

LOVE BIRD MOBILE– RUCHOMY

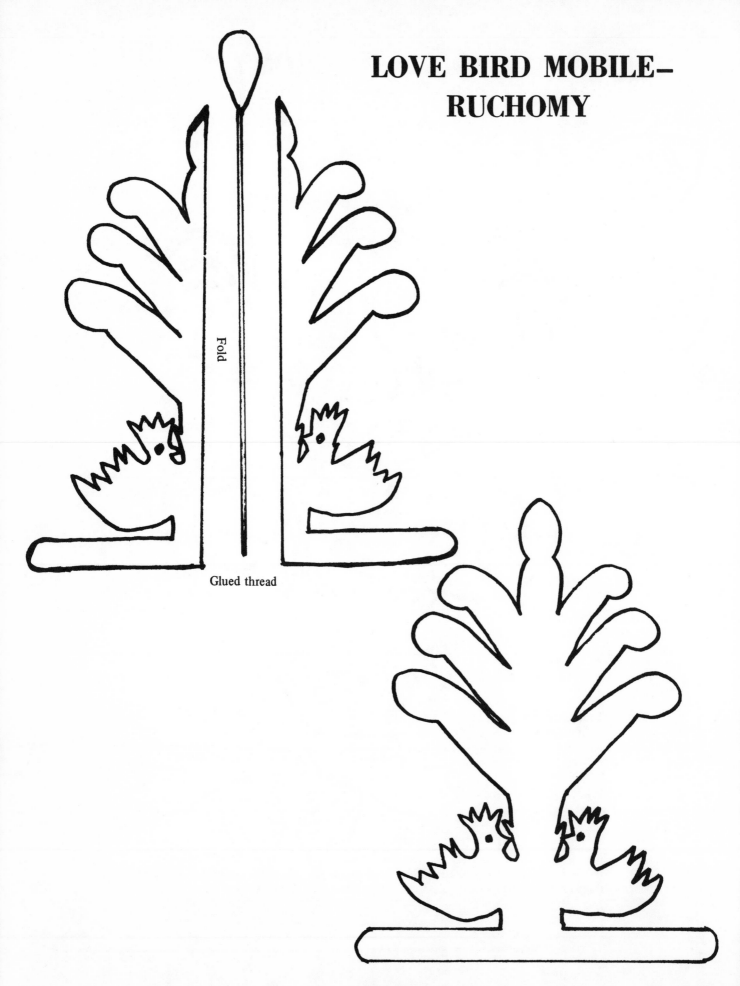

Fold

Glued thread

130

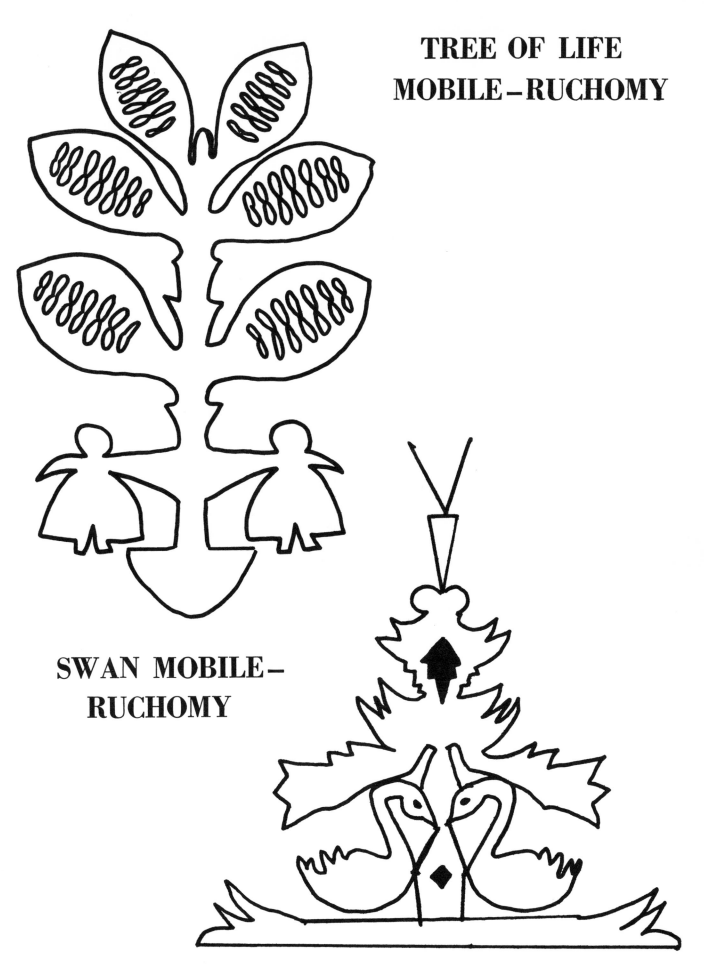

TREE OF LIFE
MOBILE–RUCHOMY

SWAN MOBILE–
RUCHOMY

131

CHICKEN MOBILE– RUCHOMY

SNOW FLAKE MOBILE— RUCHOMY

133

ROOSTER MOBILE—RUCHOMY

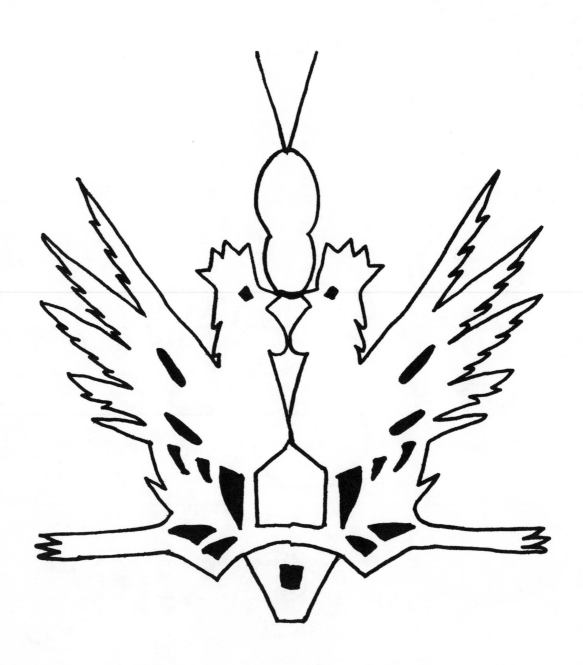

STAR AND POM POM PAJĄK

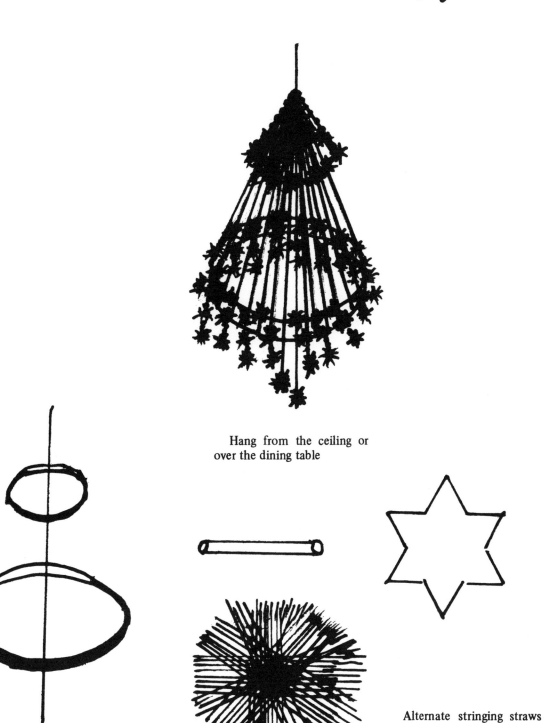

Hang from the ceiling or
over the dining table

Alternate stringing straws
and stars to form streamers
on which pom poms are
attached

Take the top and bottom rings of an old lamp shade or make a bottom ring out of a
coat hanger and the top ring from the plastic cover of a coffee can. Make thirty pompoms
from seven bright colors of yarn. Leave a long piece yarn on eight pompoms so that ten
christmas beads can be strung on them before they are tied equidistant on the large ring.
Cover both rings with fringed strips of green tissue paper.

135

POLISH ANGEL–ANIOŁ

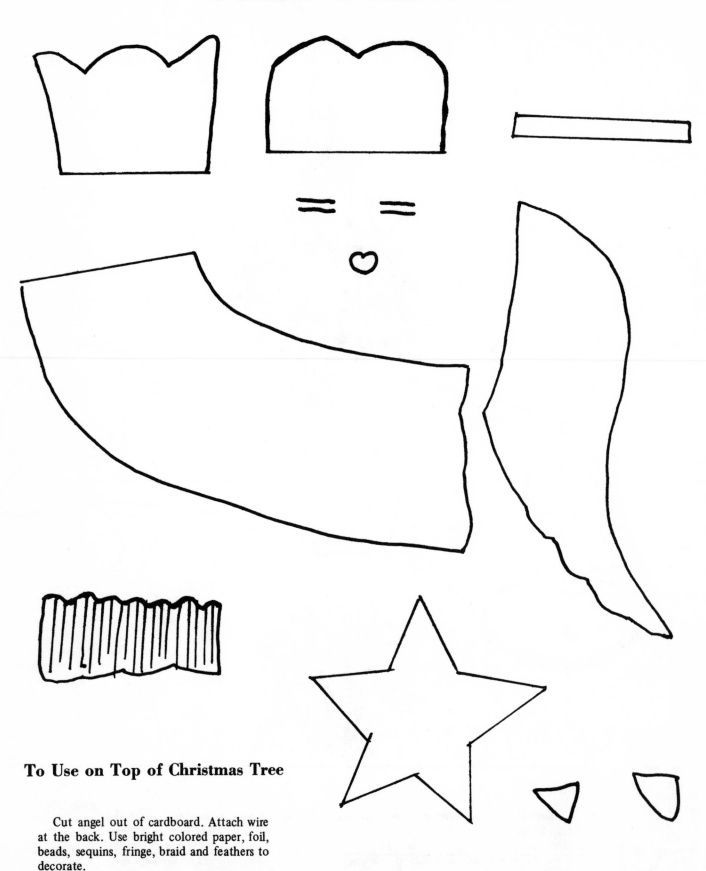

To Use on Top of Christmas Tree

Cut angel out of cardboard. Attach wire at the back. Use bright colored paper, foil, beads, sequins, fringe, braid and feathers to decorate.

POLISH ANGEL–ANIOŁ

ROOSTER–KOGUT

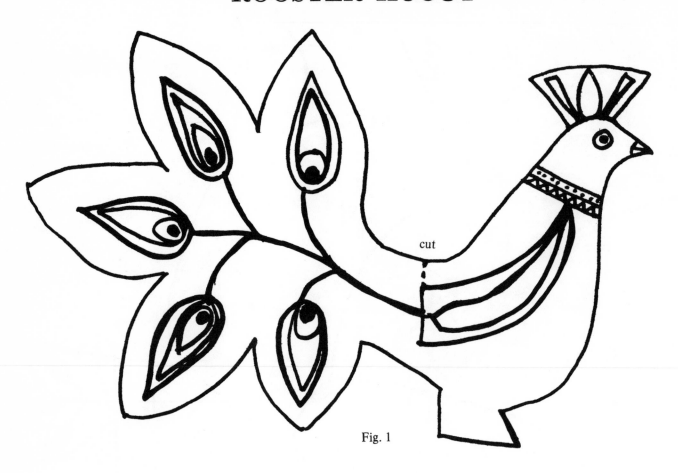

Fig. 1

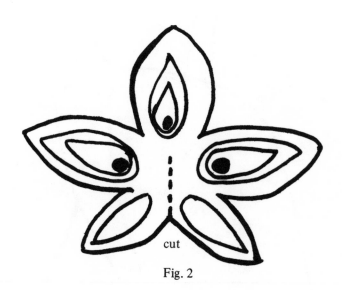

Fig. 2

Materials needed:
  Paper
  Glue
  Scissors
  Marking pencils

Cut out two of each pattern #1 and #2. Use marking pencils or bits of colored paper to make designs on the rooster. Paste together. Cut on dotted lines to insert wing.

ROOSTER–KOGUT

PITCHER–DZBANUSZEK

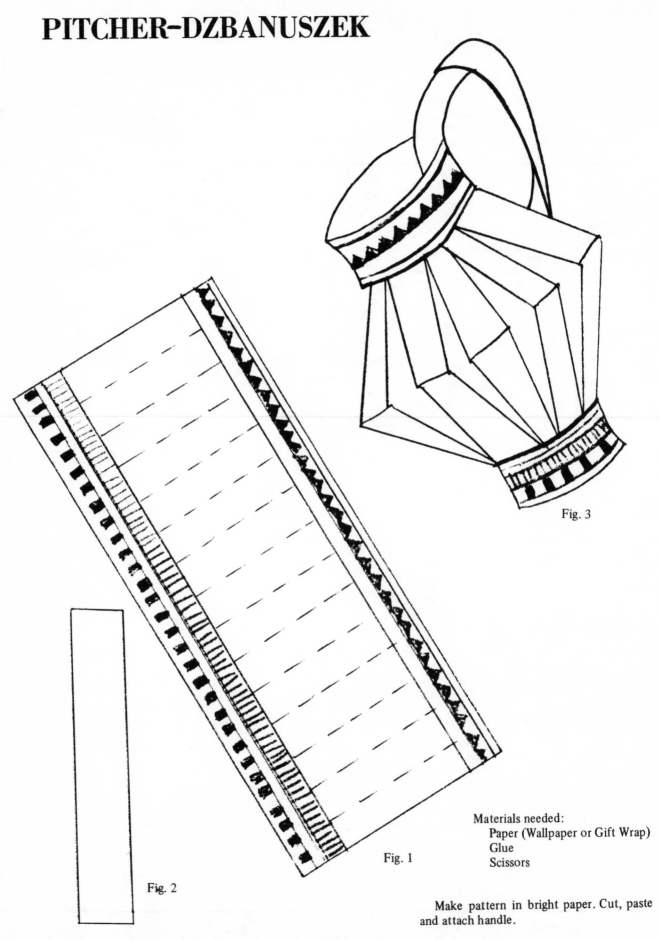

Fig. 3

Fig. 1

Fig. 2

Materials needed:
   Paper (Wallpaper or Gift Wrap)
   Glue
   Scissors

Make pattern in bright paper. Cut, paste and attach handle.

140

PITCHER-DZBANUSZEK

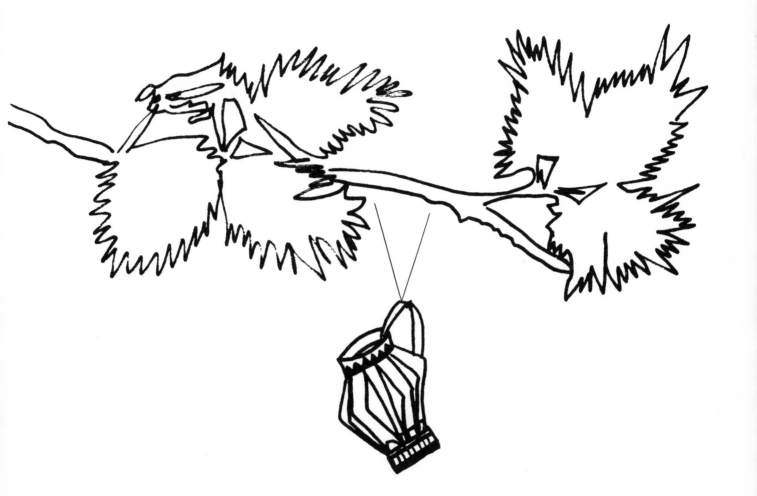

CUBE–SZEŚCION

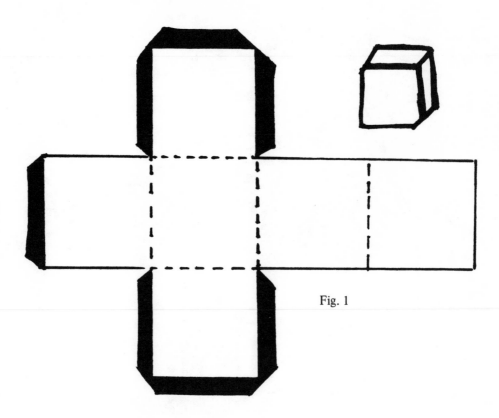

Fig. 1

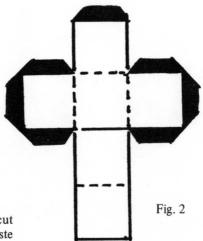

Fig. 2

From heavy paper cut one #1 and cut four #2. Fold on dotted lines and put paste on the black lines. Form one large box and four small ones. Attach the small cubes to the corners of the big cube by stringing a combination of beads and straw or beads and paper flowers.

CUBE–SZEŚCION

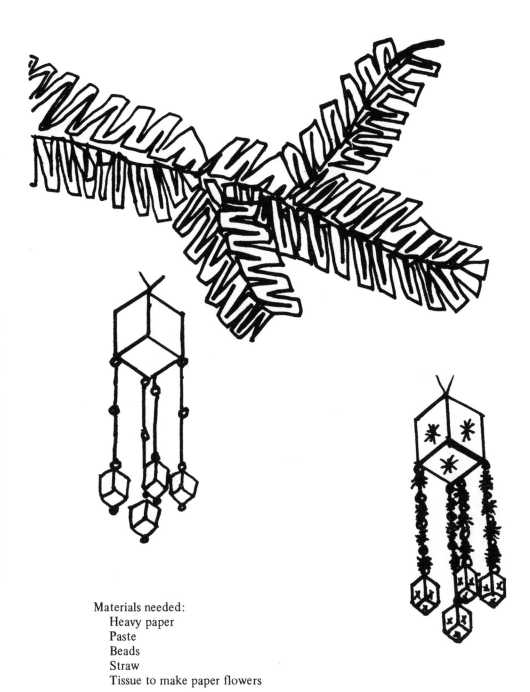

Materials needed:
   Heavy paper
   Paste
   Beads
   Straw
   Tissue to make paper flowers

To make paper flowers cut circles from tissue paper as per pattern. Use at least 8 to 12 circles and snip almost to the center. Separate papers and fluff out after stringing on the ornament.

SPIRAL CORK-SCREW—KORKOCIĄG

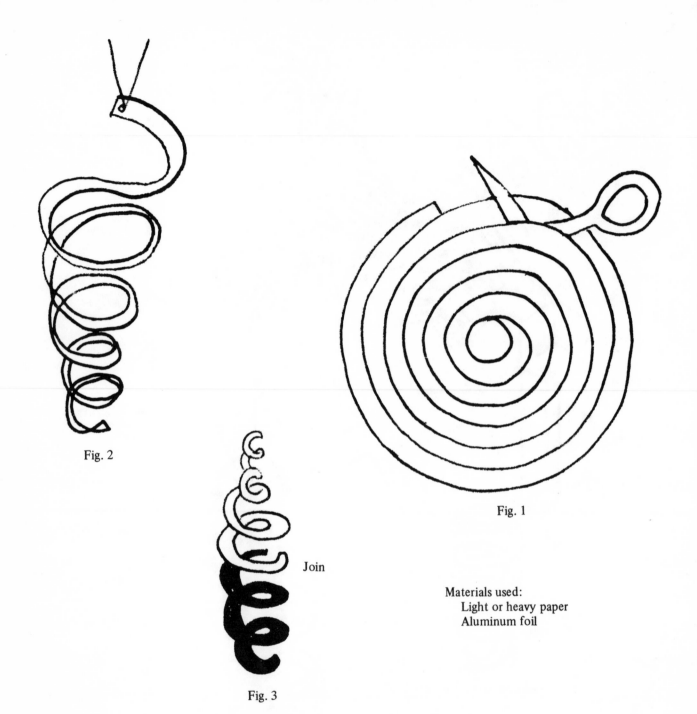

Fig. 2

Fig. 1

Join

Fig. 3

Materials used:
   Light or heavy paper
   Aluminum foil

Cut out a circle as in #1 and follow cutting lines until you reach the center. Hang by a thread. If a longer and a more complicated spiral is desired, cut two circles and join them at one end, as shown in figure #3.

SPIRAL CORK-SCREW–KORKOCIĄG

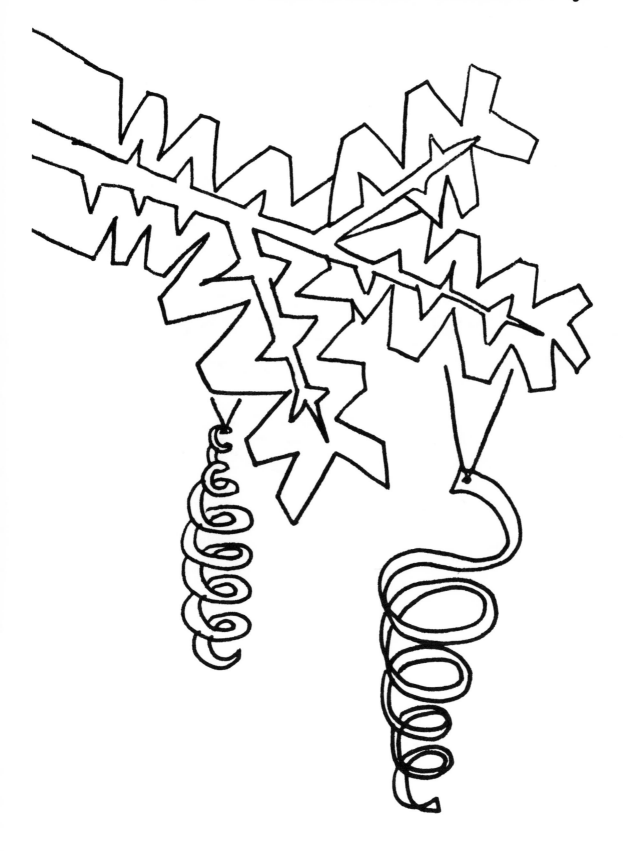

PIGEON-GOŁĄB

cut

Materials needed:
    Paper
    Paste
    Scissors
    Colored pencils

Make two patterns. Color the designs. Paste together. Cut on dotted lines. Curl tail feathers.

PIGEON-GOŁAB

STRAW MOBILE–RUCHOMY

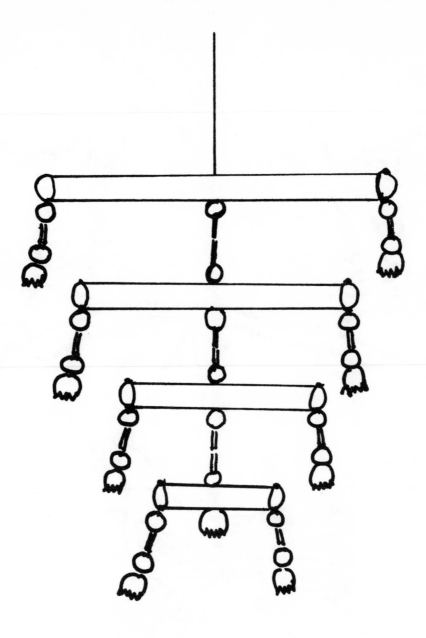

Materials needed:
   Drinking straws
   Foil
   Thread
   Beads

   Take four drinking straws of graduating lengths and wrap them in foil. String beads at the ends. Using the center of the straws as an axis, thread beads and straws. Form a loop for hanging.

148

STRAW MOBILE-RUCHOMY

PAJĄK OF STRAW

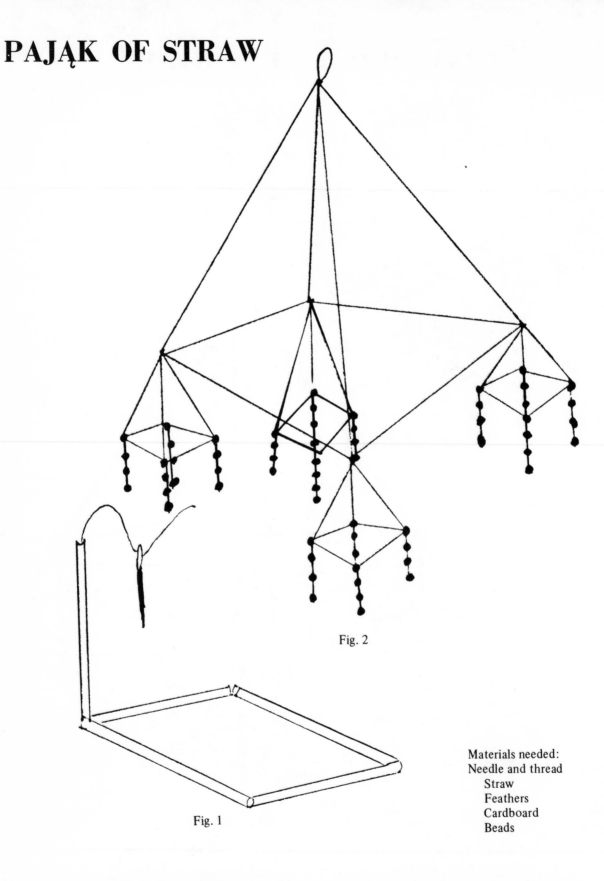

Fig. 2

Fig. 1

Materials needed:
Needle and thread
Straw
Feathers
Cardboard
Beads

Thread four small straws in a square. With the same thread attach the four long straws to form a cone. Fasten four more short straws to the four corners of the squares of paper. Attach these to the corners of the chandelier. String the beads to the squares of paper.

150

PĄJAK OF STRAW

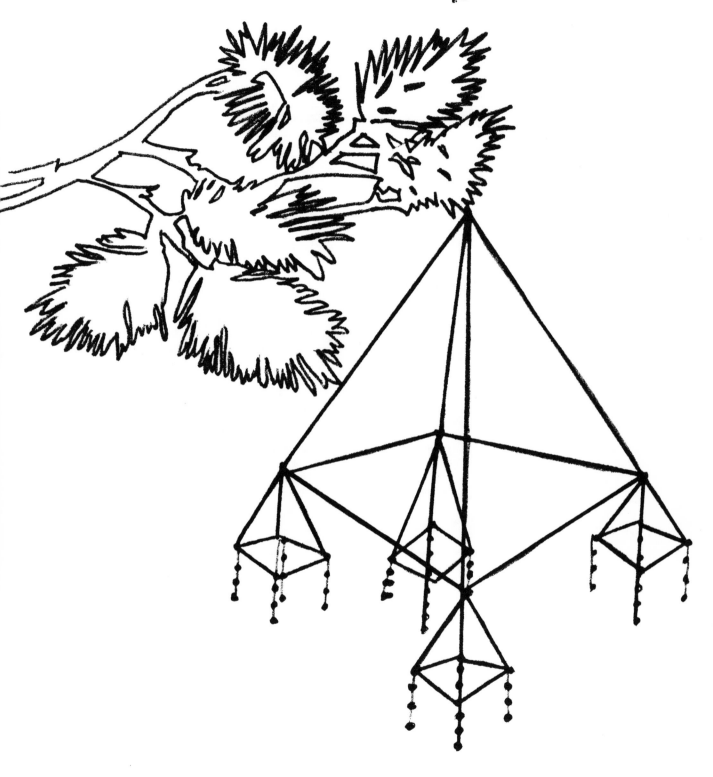

MILKWEED POD BIRD—PTASZEK

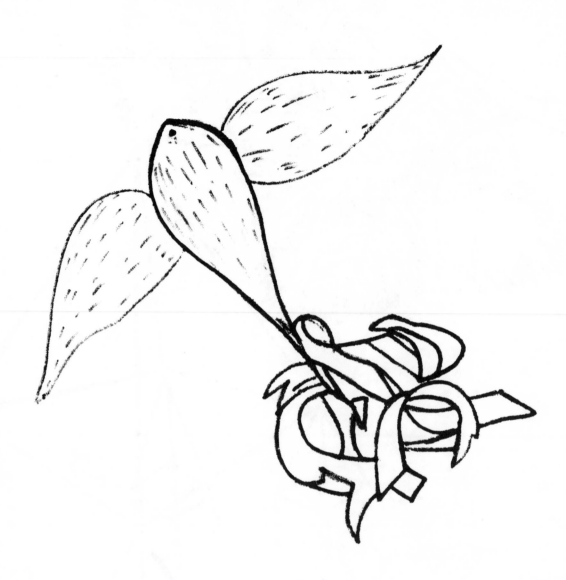

Milkweed pods are used for this bird. Take two pods, use one whole for the body and split the other in two for the wings.

Cut slit in the body sides, and glue the ends of the wing in the slit. Cut narrow strips of colored paper and curl. Tape together on the end of the bird body for a tail. Paint a bright yellow or gold. Make loop for hanging.

MILKWEED POD BIRD–PTASZEK

TRIANGLE MOBILE–RUCHOMY

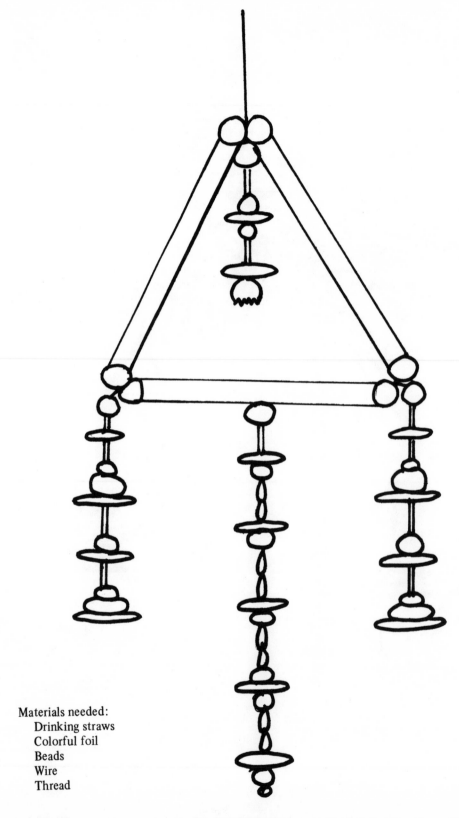

Materials needed:
  Drinking straws
  Colorful foil
  Beads
  Wire
  Thread

Take three drinking straws of equal length. Cover each with foil. String a piece of thin wire through each straw beginning and ending with a Christmas bead. There will be three straws and six beads. Twist wire and tie securely to form a triangle. Use beads or paper flowers for the corners.

154

TRIANGLE MOBILE-RUCHOMY

WORLD-ŚWIAT

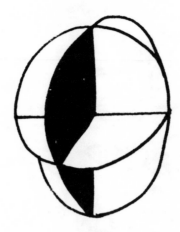

Fig. 4

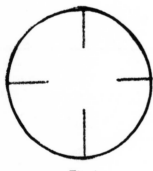

Fig. 1

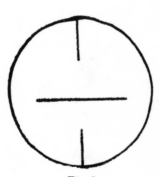

Fig. 2

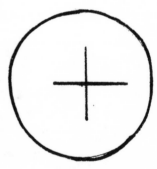

Fig. 3

Materials used:
    Construction paper
    Foil

    Cut three equal circles and cut indicated lines on each. Fold #1 in half and insert through center of #2. Open up #1. Fold #1 and #2 and insert through center of #3. Open and interlock into a ball as in #4.

WORLD-ŚWIAT

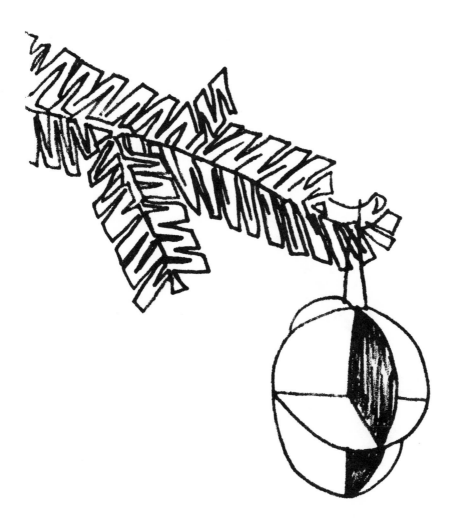

This pająk is called the world (świat) because of its many sections and its spherical shape. At one time it was made of the opłatek (thin Christmas wafer) but because of the difficulty of handling and obtaining this bread, it is now made of construction paper or foil cardboard. Size is determined by the circles. This is one of the easiest ways of making the świat.

The świat is so important that it has another name Wilyka. It is one of the central and most important ornaments on the tree. When it was made of the opłatek it demanded certain respect. The feeling was one of reverence and it could not be destroyed. After the tree was taken down, the świat was carefully hung from the ceiling. Delicate and light and suspended by a thread, it moved in the warm air and gave beauty and enjoyment to the household until the next year.

MUSHROOM-GRZYB

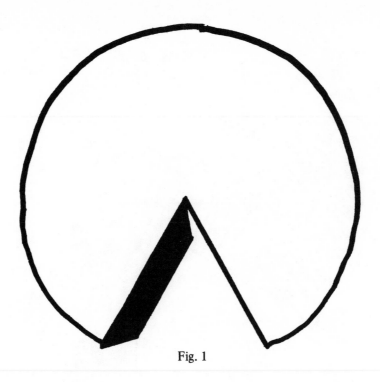

Fig. 1

Fig. 2

Materials needed:
    Red and white paper
    Paste
    Scissors
    Cotton
    Egg shell

Fig. 3

    Use red paper to cut out pattern #1. Decorate it with twenty white dots #3. Cut #2 from white paper and paste on indicated black line to form a tube. Fill the tube with cotton and allow a little to protrude at the top and bottom of the tube. Paste one end on the inside in the middle of #1. Or, use an empty egg shell to form the stem.

MUSHROOM–GRZYB

This is a very versatile ornament. It can be fashioned from threaded pieces of straw, squares of colored cardboard, or varying lengths of dyed feathers. The size can be determined by the cut dimensions of materials. Furthermore, it can be elaborated upon by adding more square units of straw, paper or feathers. Beads added to the four corners adds beauty to the pajak.

STAR CARRIERS–GWIAZDORZY

The star can be made from heavy colored cardboard paper with a stick attached. A more elaborate one can be made with two stars and a tin can inbetween to allow a flashlight or a candle to illuminate it.

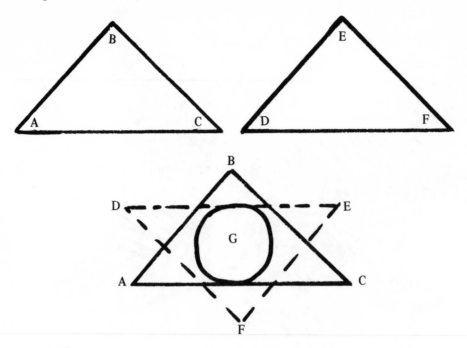

Simple Star

Cut two equilateral triangles and superimpose one on another, as in drawing, to make a six pointed star.

Cut circle as in figure G and cover with sheer paper so that a light can shine through.

Attach stick.

Elaborate star with light enclosed.

Cut front H and back I from a can that once contained ham.
Make a hole in the flat bottom of the can to accommodate a dowel.
Attach a flashlight or a candle to the flat part of the can. Fig. J.
Place two stars with circles cut out (fig. G) to either side of the can to make a lantern.
Use any adhesive that will hold it firmly.

160

STAR CARRIERS—GWIAZDORZY

On Christmas eve in Poland, the children carry a homemade lighted star on a pole and go from home to home singing Christmas carols. The carolers known as Gwiazdorzy (star carriers) convey the tradition of the star of Bethlehem symbolizing in their actions the same star that led the three kings to the manger and the Child Jesus. The custom of the star carried by the Gwiazdorzy is practiced, enjoyed and anticipated each Christmas season in Poland.

PEASANT ANGEL

Fig. 1

Fig. 2

Fig. 4

Fig. 3

Fig. 5

Fig. 6

Fig. 7

Fig. 8

PEASANT ANGEL

DIRECTIONS:

1. For body of angel, make a semi circle with 8"
    radius.

2. For the hem, cut a border from wallpaper,
    silver or gold paper, or paint a design on
    lightweight paper. (Fig. 2.)

3. For the arms, use a 4" radius to make circle. (Fig. 3). Divide circle into 4 or 5
    segments. Use two of these segments for shaping arms (Fig. 4).

4. For angel's cape, make a circle 4" in diameter. Shape it into a shallow cone (Fig. 5).

5. For the head use a wooden bead or Christmas ball (Fig. 6). Paint features. For hair use
    narrow strips of paper, curl ends and glue to head (Fig. 7).

6. For wings, make a circle 4" in diameter and cut in from any point on the circle toward
    the center (Fig. 8). Turn down flaps as shown (Fig. 8) and glue or staple in place.

7. Fasten arms to body of angel with glue.

8. Attach cape (Fig. 5) over arms, and insert head. Glue or staple wings to back of body
    and paper halo to back of head.

ROOSTER – KOGUT

Fig. 4

Fig. 6

Fig. 11

Fig. 5

Fig. 2

Fig. 3

Fig. 8

Fig. 9

Fig. 1

Fig. 7

Fig. 10

ROOSTER – KOGUT

NOTICE: Cut 'right' and 'left' of all pieces except tail, and when pasting one part on top of another, trim where necessary to make it look neat.

Fig. 1. - Tail, green, cut 1
Fig. 2. - Stripes, black, cut 2
Fig. 3. - Triangles at base for pasting onto egg
Fig. 4. - Head, orange, cut 2
Fig. 5. - Comb, red, cut 2
Fig. 6. - Wattel, red, cut 2
Fig. 7. - Beak, red, cut 2
Fig. 8. - Eyes, gold, cut 2 (larger circles)
           Eyes, black, cut 2 (smaller circle)
Fig. 9. - Wing, green, cut 2 (small size)
Fig.10. - Wing, orange, cut 4 (larger size)
Fig.11. - Legs, gold, cut 4

1. Paste stripes (Fig. 2) onto tail (Fig. 1). Glue together on center fold-line leaving triangles (Fig. 3) free for pasting onto egg. Spread the triangle part so it fits the egg firmly. Paste on to form tail.
2. Glue together 'right' and 'left' of head. Finish head by pasting on 'right' and 'left' of comb (Fig. 5), wattel (Fig. 6), and beak (Fig. 7) over corresponding part on both sides of head. Glue on eyes (Fig. 8), bigger circle first, with smaller circle over it. Attach head to egg at dash lines' - - - - '.
3. Glue small wing decoration (Fig.9) on top of each wing, as shown on pattern, pasting on dash lines of larger wing. Use one right and one left of the larger wing (Fig. 10). Finish wing by pasting corresponding parts on back of each wing, but glue only about 1/2 of the wing leaving remaining portion free to use for attaching to egg. Fold back the wing.
4. The legs (Fig. 11) are first glued right and left pieces to form legs. Attach to body of egg at dash line ' - - - ' indicated on top of leg.
5. Attach string for hanging on tree.

BIRD WITH CROWN-DOVE

Fig. 1

Fig. 1A

Fig. 2

Fig. 3

Fig. 4

BIRD WITH CROWN—DOVE

DIRECTIONS:

1. Use lightweight paper of any color for body (Fig. 1). Body strip (Fig. 2), wings (Fig. 3), can be made of a contrasting color. Whenever using paper that is colored on one side, be sure to cut a 'right' and 'left' and glue pieces together to make color uniform. The crown should be gold colored or other suitable contrast.

2. Trace body (Fig. 1). The tail is cut evenly at the back edge (Fig. 1 A). Pleat tail as shown in picture.

3. Trace and cut 2 body strips (Fig. 2), two wings (Fig. 3), and two crowns (Fig. 4).

4. Crease wings and body strips to appear pleated. The pleats are shown on pattern in dark color.

5. Glue pieces in place on both sides of the body as shown in pattern. Attach string with needle and thread for hanging on tree.

167

HANGING BASKET

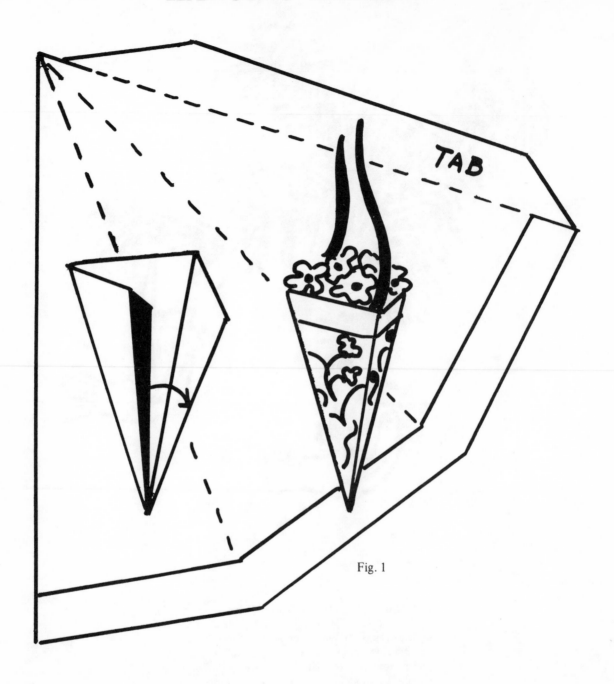

Fig. 1

Fig. 2

168

HANGING BASKET

Materials used:

1. Colored paper of firm quality. Metallic or decorative wrapping paper is also suitable.

2. Small amount of ribbon for making bows on handle of basket.

3. Flowers to fill basket. Use small sized artificial flowers of your choice.

DIRECTIONS:

1. Trace and cut pattern for body of basket from any colored paper. Fold on dotted lines. Glue tab under opposite edge.

2. Cut strip of same paper or contrasting color 1/2 inch wide and 6 inches long, and glue to inside of basket top at opposite sides to form handle. Attach bow on top of handle and fasten on string for hanging on tree.

3. Baskets may have designs painted on, or pasted on, or any other creative idea for decorating the outside. This is best done when basket is flat, before the tab is glued. Fill basket with flowers.

169

STAR WITH POMPOM

Fig. 7

Fig. 4

Fig. 5

Fig. 6

Fig. 1

Fig. 2

Fig. 3

STAR WITH POMPOM

DIRECTIONS:

1. Using colored paper cut 3 pieces of 2-1/2 inch squares. (Fig. 1). Each star is made of 3 pieces of decorative paper and a tissue pompom.

2. Fold the squares in half both ways. (Fig. 2).

3. Fold once more on the diagonal line (Fig. 3). Cut on dotted line as shown in pattern. You will have an 8-pointed star. (Fig. 4).

4. Using needle and thread, string 3 stars through center (Fig. 5) with colored side of paper on top. Next prepare the pompom.

5. Cut 10 pieces of white tissue paper 1-1/2 inches in diameter (Fig. 6), and thread onto top of star. Pull thread tight enough to make a pompom of the tissue. (Fig. 7). Using your fingers, ruffle the tissue to make it look curly. Leave enough of the string for hanging star on the tree.

CHRISTMAS TREE AND CHRISTMAS BELL

Fig. 2

Fig. 1

CHRISTMAS TREE AND CHRISTMAS BELL

Directions: BELL

1. Use craft paper or any suitable colored paper that has a little firmness. Decorative or metallic papers make good variations. Trace from pattern (Fig. 1), and cut three bells.

2. Staple together as indicated. Attach loop of colored thread for hanging on branch.

3. Spread sections by pinching together to form dimensional bell.

4. Bell can be decorated for greater variety.

Directions: TREE
1. The tree can be made of green craft paper. It can also be made of white paper and decorated (Fig. 2).

2. Cut three trees and assemble in the same manner as the bell.

PAPER BASKET

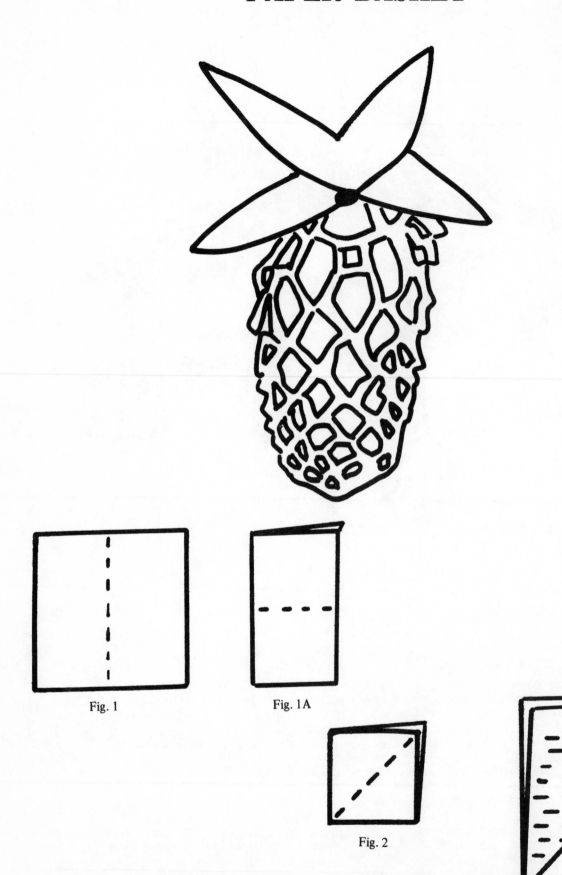

Fig. 1

Fig. 1A

Fig. 2

Fig. 2A

PAPER BASKET

DIRECTIONS:

1. Using white or colored tissue paper, or paper equally lightweight, cut 3 inch square of paper and fold in half (Fig. 1). Then fold in half again (Fig. 1A).

2. Fold the paper now to form a triangle (Fig. 2) and (Fig. 2A).

3. With scissors, cut in on the triangle almost to the edge, first on one side, then on the other, until you reach near the top. Leave a space uncut. See (Fig 2 A).

4. Open up the cut paper carefully to form a basket. Insert candy, nuts, or tiny Christmas balls, and tie firmly just below the top edge, with string long enough to use for hanging on the tree.

5. The basket will have an edge of the uncut paper at the top where you have tied it, to form a petal-like decoration. A narrow ribbon with bow is an attractive addition.

EGGSHELL PITCHERS

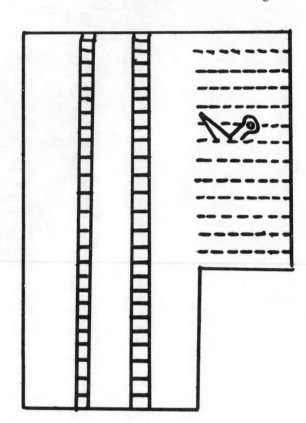

STEP 2: Roll and glue spout

STEP 4: Attach handle

STEP 3: Attach to eggshell

176

EGGSHELL PITCHERS

DIRECTIONS:

When making projects with blown eggs, paint the egg with clear drying glue after it is blown out. This strenghtens the shell and makes them easier to handle.

1. Use large white eggs. Punch hole in one end with pin. Make a very small circle of holes in the outer end and carefully remove this tiny circle of shell and skin. Shake or blow the egg into a cup. Wash out and allow to drain overnight.
2. Shells can be dyed, painted, or left white.
3. Use glue to attach a plastic white dressmaker ring to the shell to form a base.
4. Cut oblong of strong, brightly colored paper about 2 and 3/4 inches by 4 inches. Next, cut away - out of this oblong a rectangle 1 by 1 and 1/2 inches. See Step 2. Fringe the remaining 2 and 1/2 inches by 1 inch that is left on the oblong.
5. Roll oblong into cylinder and glue to form spout (Step 2), then glue fringe down on the eggshell (Step 3). Toothpick is handy for applying glue on fringe.
6. Cut strip of paper 5 inches by 1/4 inch for the spout handle. Glue to eggshell.
7. Decorate pitchers with Christman tape, decorative trim, sequins, or ribbon.

BIRD

Fig. 2

Fig. 1

DIRECTIONS:

1. Trace pattern of bird (Fig. 1) on colored paper. Cut 2 and paste together to make body of bird firm if using lightweight paper. Coated metallic wrapping paper is attractive but you must cut a 'right' and 'left' side and glue together to make body one color.

2. Cut 2 patterns of wings (Fig. 2). Wings may be same color as bird or a contrasting color.

3. Attach a wing to each side of body as shown in pattern.

4. Paint eyes on each side of head of the bird, and attach string with needle and thread for hanging on tree.

BIRD

NUT FAN

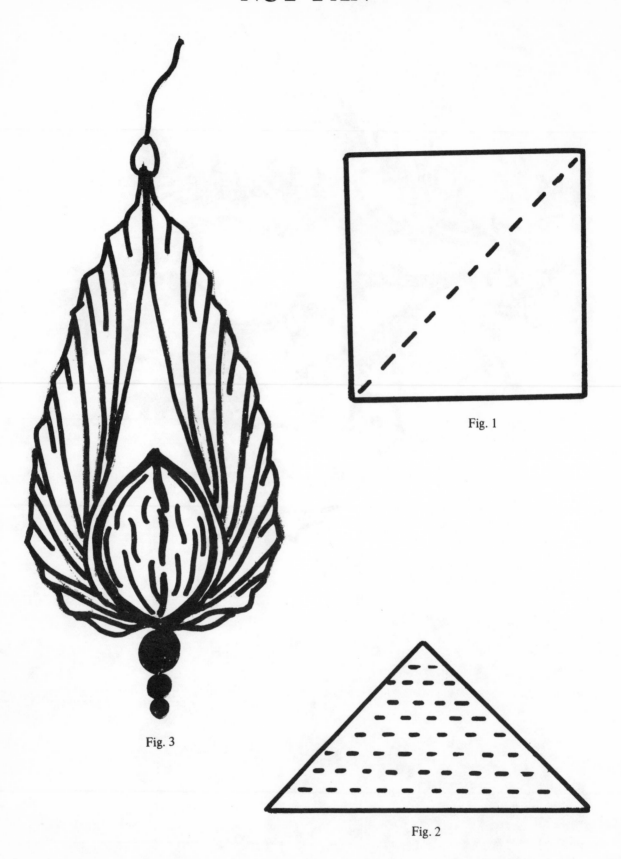

Fig. 1

Fig. 3

Fig. 2

NUT FAN

DIRECTIONS:

1. Using any kind of lightweight decorative paper, metallic or wrapping paper, cut a 7 inch square. Fold the sheet diagonally as shown in Fig. 1 to form triangle.

2. Lay triangle with longest side down, and pleat the doubled paper into narrow pleats, about ½ inch wide. Fig. 2.

3. Fold the pleated triangle and using needle and thread (about 12 inches long) stitch through the two points, knot, and leave enough string for hanging on tree. Fig. 3.

4. Take a gilded walnut, make a hole in one end big enough for a toothpick to enter. Glue tip of toothpick and insert into end of walnut. Now push the toothpick through the bottom of the pleated fan. Use pin to make hole for easier insertion. Variations can be created to decorate the fan.

5. Tiny beads can be glued to extended tip of toothpick (Fig. 3), or use a string filled with beads in center of fan instead of the walnut. If beads are used to replace nut, start with long thread, put several beads on it and push through from bottom working up — through the bottom of the fan; continue adding beads to string until enough to fill center, then put thread through top of fan points, knot, then leave long enough thread for hanging on tree.

STARS AND STRAWS–AND CHERRY CHAIN

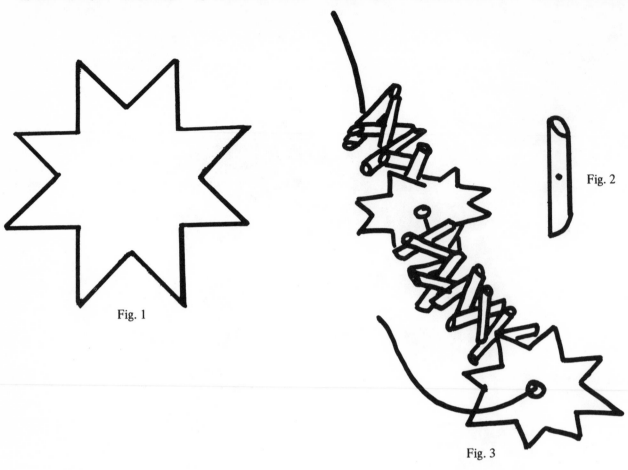

Fig. 1

Fig. 2

Fig. 3

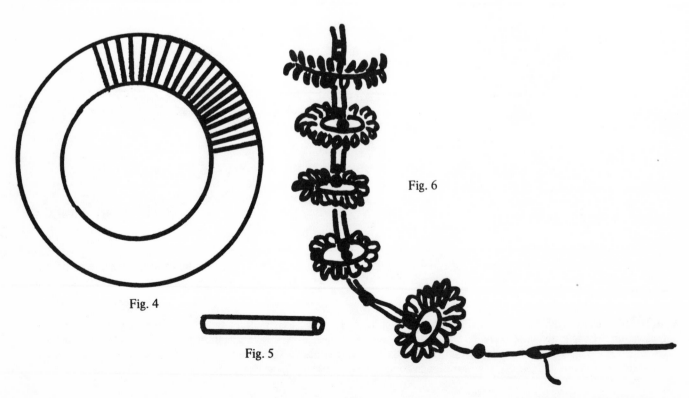

Fig. 4

Fig. 5

Fig. 6

STARS AND STRAWS—AND CHERRY CHAIN

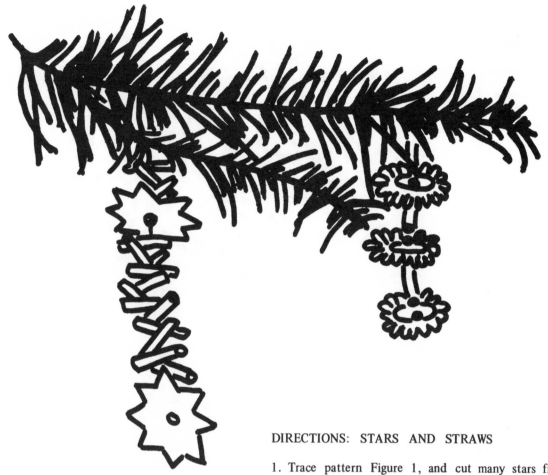

DIRECTIONS: STARS AND STRAWS

1. Trace pattern Figure 1, and cut many stars from colored construction paper, using as many colors as possible.

2. Cut drinking straws into 1½ inch segments, Fig. 2. Use either white or colored straws.

3. Using large-eyed needle and string, thread through the centers of the stars, then follow with 12 straw segments. Put needle through straws "crosswise" where indicated with dot in Fig. 2.

4. Repeat process, alternating colors of stars, until chain is the desired length.

DIRECTIONS: CHEERY CHAIN

1. On the top sheet of several layers of tissue paper, trace and cut many circles, 2-1/2 inches in diameter. Cut "in" toward center of circle as shown in Fig. 4.

2. Cut drinking straws into 1-1/4 inch segments, Fig. 5.

3. Put 2 tissue circles together and curl edges carefully. Sicssors pulled gently across the cut edge - outward from center curls the paper. String in this order:
   a) 2 circles, separated after curling and placed back to back in opposite direction, so the curls are facing up and down;
   b) beads;
   c) straws;
   d) bead, and repeat. Fig. 6.

TISSUE GARLAND – CIRCLE CHAIN

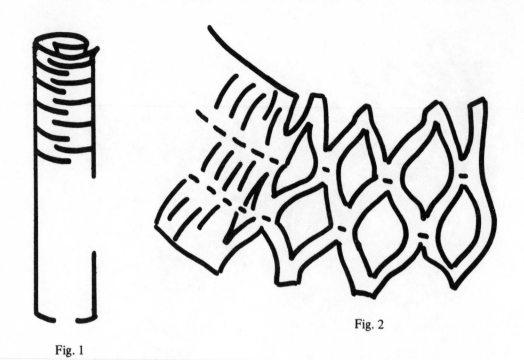

Fig. 1

Fig. 2

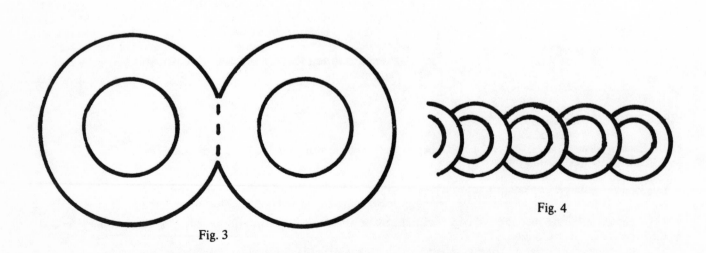

Fig. 3

Fig. 4

TISSUE GARLAND–CIRCLE CHAIN

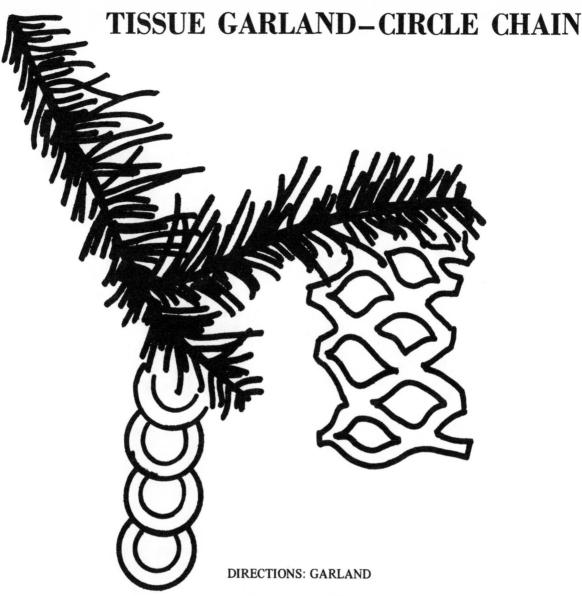

DIRECTIONS: GARLAND

1. Using a strip of white or colored tissue paper 3 inches wide and any desired length. Fold the paper vertically into thirds. Alternate cutting slits as in Fig. 1.

2. Open the folded tissue carefully and pull out to form a garland like Fig. 2. To make enough length for the tree in a continuous garland, glue together the segments (Fig. 2) until you have the desired length.

DIRECTIONS:CHAIN

1. With various colored construction paper cut out many Figure 3 patterns. Trace from pattern for convenient size. Bend each circle double on the dotted line to form one double circle that is open on all sides except on the fold.

2. Lace each circle, one through the other to form chain (Fig. 4). Hold double circle in your hand with the fold at the bottom, then insert next circle through center hole, pull towards top of circle keeping the 'open' end facing upward. Keep lacing one circle into the other until chain is desired length.

CHRISTMAS BALLS

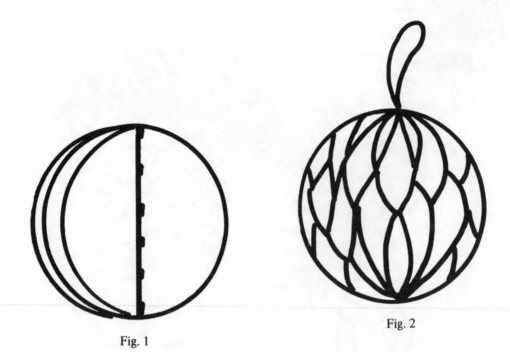

Fig. 1

Fig. 2

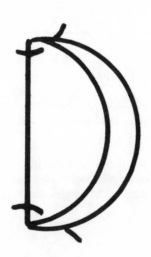

Fig. 3

Fig. 4

CHRISTMAS BALLS

DIRECTIONS:

1. These Christmas balls can be made in two different kinds of decorative ball, using the same basic pattern. Use lightweight paper, such as butcher paper, or coated metallic paper, or any decorative wrapping paper.

2. Cut 10 or 12 circles (Fig. 1), any size you prefer. The larger the circle, the bigger will be the ball. Circles about 6 inches in diameter are easiest to work with.

3. Crease the circles across center and staple or sew together. Then carefully spread out the folds.

4. Fasten alternate edges as shown in Fig. 2. Use glue, knot with one sewing stitch, or staple the folds together, creating a diamond-shaped design. Add string with needle and thread at top for hanging on tree.

5. Fig. 3 and 4 show the same circles strung on a thread through top and bottom. Spread the outer edges of the circle to form a round ball.

187

CHRISTMAS TREE

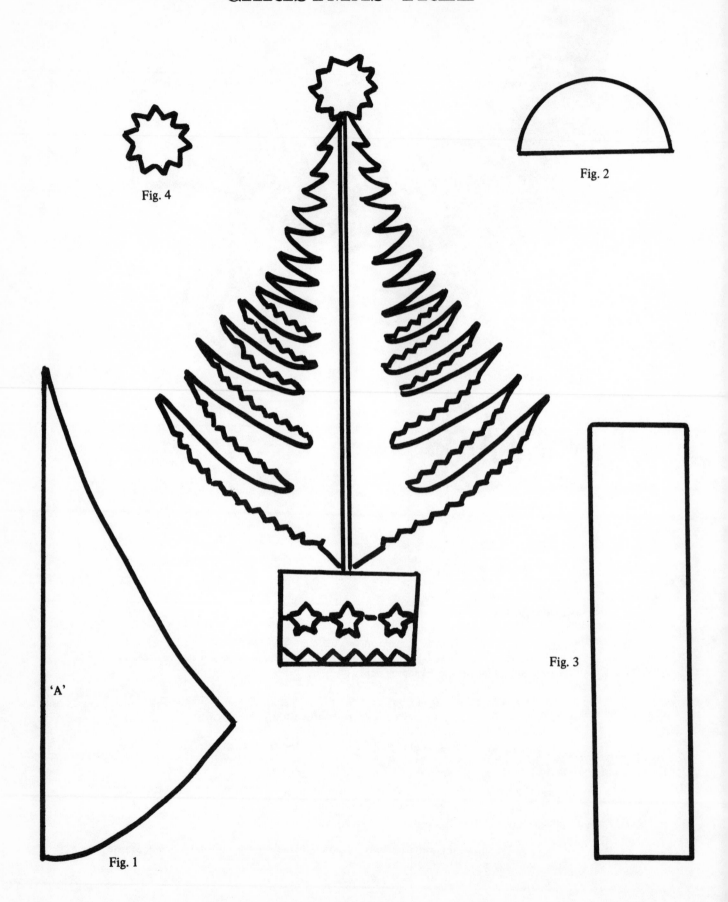

Fig. 4

Fig. 2

Fig. 3

'A'

Fig. 1

188

CHRISTMAS TREE

DIRECTIONS:

1. Use craft weight paper for tree, either one or two shades of green. Using one sheet of the construction paper, fold it and cut 2 pieces (Fig. 1) for the tree. The fold is on 'A' on the pattern.

2. Cut out and fringe branches. Staple or sew tree on center fold. A 6 inch straw can be glued on the fold to form the trunk of the tree. Spread the 4 sections to make a dimensional tree.

3. To form tree base, cut in two a styrofoam ball (Fig. 2), 1-1/2 inch in diameter. Insert the straw into the styrofoam ball, leaving a little on top of the tree for attaching the star.

4. Use colored strip of paper 1 inch by 4-1/2 inches long (Fig. 3) and decorate. See pattern. Wrap around styrofoam ball to make a pot for the tree. Glue edge.

5. Trace and cut 2 (Fig. 4) stars, of gold or silver paper. Before glueing the 2 sides of the star together, paste string into star for hanging on tree, and glue the star over the extended tip of straw. Tiny pieces of straw can be glued on edges of branches to look like candles, or decorate tree by adding sequins or colored balls painted on for design.

POLISH STAR OR PORCUPINE

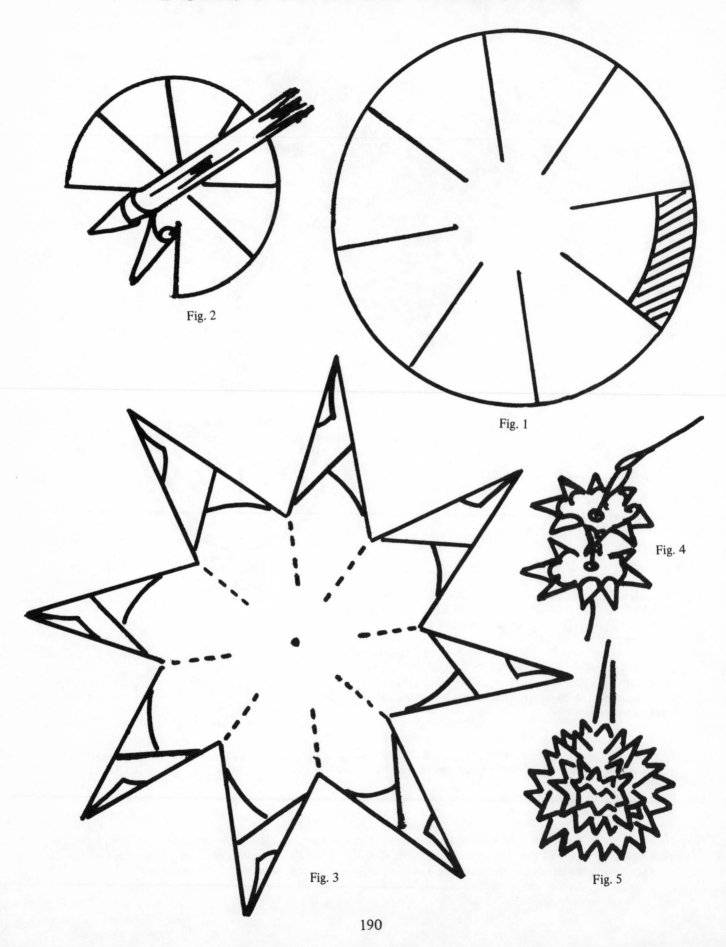

Fig. 2

Fig. 1

Fig. 3

Fig. 4

Fig. 5

190

POLISH STAR OR PORCUPINE

DIRECTIONS:

1. Star can be made any size and from any kind of paper. A white star is attractive but variations are unlimited. Stars made with gold or silver paper on the tips of points are very effective. This is achieved by pasting a 3/4 inch border on the original circle before the star is made up.

2. Make and cut 10 or 12 circles 4 inches in diameter. Fold each circle in half, then again in half twice more. Crease edges to make outline of 8 sections (Fig.1).

3. Cut circles on creased lines, starting from outer edge upto 1 inch of center.

4. Using sharpened pencil, with lead broken off, place pencil pointed toward outer edge (Fig. 2); roll around pencil and glue flaps. Points should appear sharp (Fig. 3).

5. Make 10 or 12 such circles, depending on thickness of paper; string them together tightly (Fig. 4). Use embroidery needle and strong sewing thread. Start with a tiny disk of cardboard to hold knot of thread, and when all circles are threaded, pull tightly; use another tiny disk and knot thread over the side of it leaving a 7 or 8 inch loop for hanging on tree. (Fig. 5).

DOUBLE STAR—EIGHT POINTS

Fig. 4

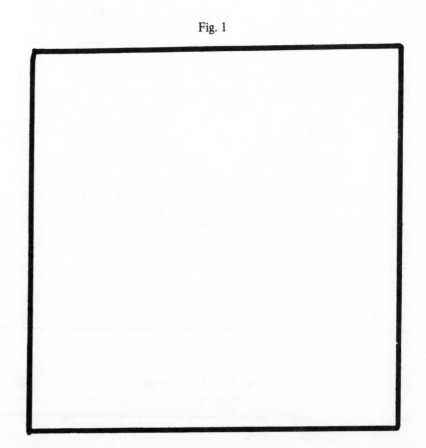

Fig. 5

Fig. 1

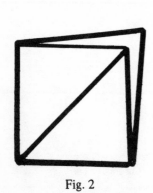

Fig. 2

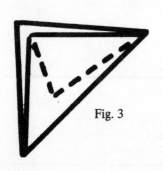

Fig. 3

DOUBLE STAR—EIGHT POINTS

DIRECTIONS:

1. Using white or colored paper cut 4 pieces of 4 inch squares Fig. 1

2. Fold the squares in half both ways. Fig. 2.

3. Fold once more on the diagonal line Fig. 3. Cut on dotted line as shown in pattern. The result will be an 8-pointed star Fig. 4.

4. Glue together 2 star patterns to form one star with two sides that are alike. Using needle and thread, start with bead and thread through center of 2 stars, and end with bead on the other side. Knot thread. Spread the star and adjust to give effect of 3 dimensions Fig. 5. Attach string to one of the points to hang on tree.

STARS AND CHAIN

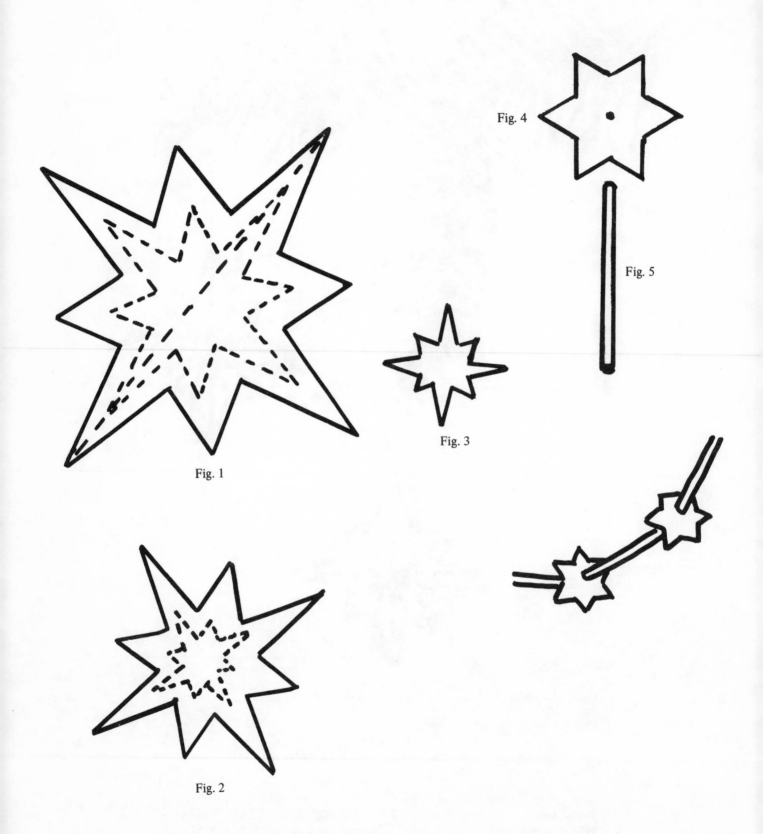

Fig. 1

Fig. 2

Fig. 3

Fig. 4

Fig. 5

STARS AND CHAIN

DIRECTIONS: STARS

1. Cut 5 stars, same as Fig. 1, out of gold, silver, green, red, or blue
   paper. Also, cut 5 each of the smaller sized stars, Fig. 2 and Fig. 3.

2. The smaller stars should be cut from contrasting colored papers,
   harmonizing with the large stars.

3. Paste stars Fig. 2 onto large star Fig. 1; then paste stars Fig. 3 onto
   Fig. 2. You will have 5 stars of 3 colors each.

4. Crease the star Fig. 1 diagonally on dash marks as shown in pattern.

5. Starting with 1/2 of the star, glue it to the adjoining half, and continue around until
   all 'halfs' are glued together to form a star.

6. With needle and thread insert a string through top point of star for hanging on tree.

DIRECTIONS: CHAIN

1. From a variety of colored papers, cut stars Fig. 4. Glue together stars so that each has
   two similiar sides.

2. Cut straws (soda straws) about 2 inches long segments Fig. 5. Using needle and strong
   thread, string the stars and straws alternately, until chain is length desired.

EGGSHELL FLOWERS AND MOUNTAINEER CUP
–'CZERPAK'

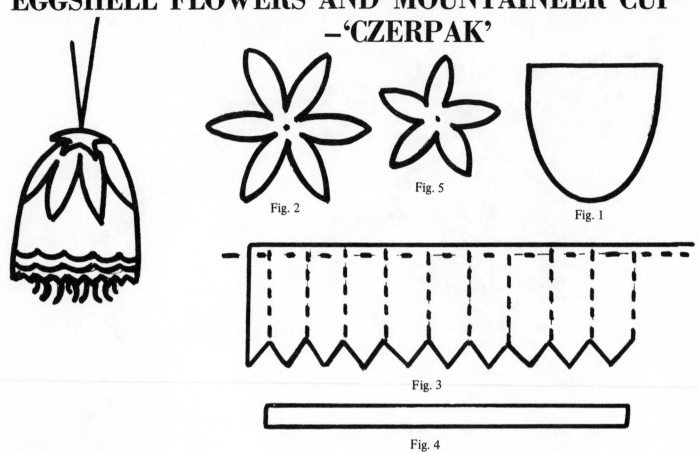

Fig. 2

Fig. 5

Fig. 1

Fig. 3

Fig. 4

CZERPAK

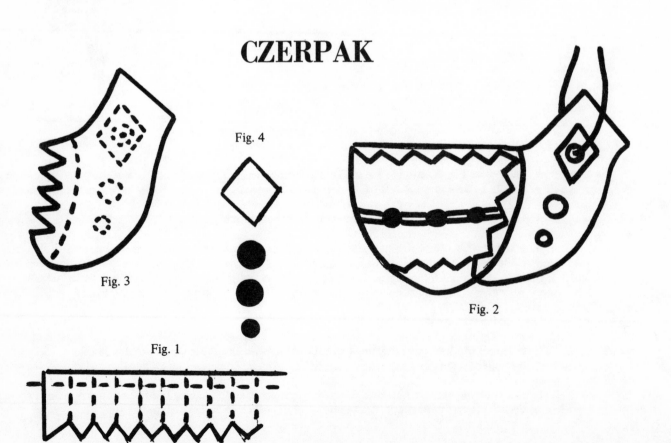

Fig. 4

Fig. 3

Fig. 2

Fig. 1

EGGSHELL FLOWERS AND MOUNTAINEER CUP
–'CZERPAK'

DIRECTIONS: FLOWER

1. Follow instructions for 'blowing eggs' on page for Eggshell Pitchers, and when egg is empty, carefully cut away or break away shell to form as even an edge as possible (Fig. 1). Glue very narrow strip of colored paper or fine rickrack onto edge.
2. Cut flower petal (Fig. 2) out of red tissue paper and glue on end of egg as shown. Cut strip of red tissue 5 inches long (Fig. 3), and cut into strip on dotted lines about 3/4 of the way to the straight edge. Using needle and thread, gather upper edge, and glue the tissue into the egg to form lining.
3. Using brown or black tissue paper, cut 5 strips (Fig. 4) about 5 inches long and 1/4 inch wide. With scissors curl the strips. Then thread them at one end to form a cluster. Now push the needle through the top of egg and through the green petal (Fig. 5) which is glued on top to finish the flower. Leave enough thread for hanging the eggshell flower on the tree.

DIRECTIONS: MOUNTAINEER CUP – CZERPAK

1. Follow directions for preparing egg as above. Cut 5 inch strips of decorative paper to glue on edge of egg (Fig. 1). Slit paper to make it curve easily. Decorate egg according to your own creative ideas. (Fig. 2).
2. Cut 2 pieces (Fig.3) of paper for handle. Use construction or firmer paper. Glue together leaving the triangles on edge free for glueing onto egg. Glue at dashline.
3. Fig. 4 are decoration dots for the handle. Cut 2 each and paste on each side of handle. Thread through handle as shown in Fig. 2 to hang on tree.

BIBLIOGRAPHY

A KOLEBKI PRZED OŁTARZEM NAD MOGIŁĄ,
H. Biegeleisen

A NEW LOOK AT CHRISTMAS DECORATIONS,
Sister M. Gratia Listaite and Norbert Hildebrand

A C P C C BULLETIN, Jan., Feb., March, 1967

ASHES, Stefan Zeromski

BETTER HOMES AND GARDENS, Dec. 1968

BLIŻEJ OJCZYZNY, Barbara Gorzechowska, Warsaw,
1959

BOŻE NARODZENIE W MĘDRZECHOWIE

CHŁOPY, Wladyslaw Reymont

CREATING WITH PAPER, Pauline Johnson, Seattle,
1958

DO BETLEJEM – JASEŁKA IN TWO ACTS, Printed in
Poznan

DZIEJE OBYCZAJÓW W DAWNEJ POLSCE,
Jan Bystron

ENCYKLOPEDIA STARODAWNA, A Bruckner

HEJ KOLENDA, KOLENDA, Piotr Greniuk,
Marian Mikuta, Lodz

HOLYDAY BOOK, Francis X. Weiser

JASEŁKA, Walerja Szalay-Groele

KANTYCZKI, ZBIÓR NAJPIĘKNIEJSZYCH KOLENDI
I PASTORAŁEK, Josef Cebulski, Krakow

LUD – Oskar Kolberg

LUD POLSKI, Zygmunt Gloger

LULAJŻE JEZUNIU, THREE ACTS, Eva Szelburg-
Ostrowska, Warsaw and Krakow

MADE IN POLAND, Louise Jarecka, N.Y.,
Alfred A. Knoff, 1949

MAZURKA, Frederick Chopin, Op. 67, No. 3

NASZA OJCZYZNA, Październik, 1965

NASZA SZOPKA, THREE ACTS, Hel Romer, Wilno

OZDOBY NA CHOINKĘ, Barbara Maslankiewicz,
Warsaw, 1957

PAN TADEUSZ, Adam Mickiewicz

PASTERKA, Stanislaw Siedlewski

PASTORAŁKI I KOLENDY Z MELODYJAMI,
Warsaw, 1843

PIĘKNE I WESOŁE JASELKA, W. Poturalski, Kraków

PIEŚNI KOSCIELNE Z MELODYAMI, Ks. J. Siedlecki

150 PIEŚNI I PIOSNEK, Jan Gall, Vol. I and II, Lwów

PO KOLENDZIE, Kazimierz Turzanski, Katowice

POLAND MAGAZINE

POLAND AND THE POLES, Boswell

POLISH BETHLEHEM, NATIVITY PLAY IN VERSE,
Lucyan Rydak, Viola Piszczek, Kraków, 1906

POLISH-ENGLISH DICTIONARY, Kosciuszko
Foundation

POLSKA I JEJ DOROBEK DZIEJOWY, edited by
Dr. Henry Paszkiewicz

POLSKE BOŻE NARODZENIE, Maria Ginalska,
London, 1961

POLSKI ŚPIEWNIK SZKOLNY, Piotr Maszynski, part 5

POLSKIE KOLENDY I PASTORAŁKI, Eva Grotnik,
Krakow

PRZYBIERZELI DO BETLEJEM, Janina Porazinska

ŚWIĄTECZNE ZWYCZAJE, Dr. Jan Jaworski, London

ŚPIEWNICZEK KOSCIELNY, J. Siedlicki, 1880

SKARBCZYK, Wladislaw Grot

SKARBCZYK, K. Hofman

SONGS, DANCE AND CUSTOMS OF PEASANT
POLAND, Sula Benet

SZEŚĆ KUJAWIAKOW, Jan Rożwicz

SZOPKA, Marja Konopnicka

SZTUKA LUDOWA, Irene Czarnecka, Warsaw, 1958

SZTUKA LUDOWA, Joseph Grabowski, Warsaw, 1955

THE DELUGE, Henryk Sienkiewicz

TIME LIFE BOOKS OF CHRISTMAS, Vol. I, II, III

TREASURED POLISH RECIPES FOR AMERICANS,
Polanie, Minneapolis, Minn.

TREASURED POLISH SONGS, Polanie, Minneapolis,
Minn.

WARMIO MOJA MIŁA, Marja Malewska

WESELE PIOSENKI, Anda Kitschmann

WESOŁE NOWINY GŁOSZĄ ANIELI, IN THREE
ACTS, Zenon Promieński, Krakow

WYCINANKI LUDOWA, Joseph Grabowski, Warsaw,
1955

ŻŁOBEK, X. J. Labaj and Stanisław Niepielski

Every so often the POLANIE CLUB of Minneapolis and St. Paul comes up with a new and treasured contribution to our knowledge of the traditions and customs of the Polish people. The work of many dedicated and loving hands, whatever this unique club brings forth is sure to have a deservedly warm reception, for they present in colorful yet authentic manner the ideas and beliefs we all are eager to know about one of the great peoples making up our composite American life. For years the POLANIE volume of "Treasured Polish Songs" has remained a family and library classic, as has their "Treasured Polish Recipes." This new collection, even more ambitious in scope and far more comprehensive will assuredly take its place beside the other two and occupy a position of honor, bringing joy to many throughout the years.

MARION MOORE COLEMAN